Provided
by

Measure B

which was approved by
the voters in
November, 1998

Celia

Celia MY LIFE

CELIA CRUZ
with Ana Cristina Reymundo

Foreword by *MAYA ANGELOU*

Translated from the Spanish by José Lucas Badué

rayo *An Imprint of* HarperCollins*Publishers*

Translation copyright ©2004 José Lucas Badué

HarperCollins books may be purchased for educational, business, or sales promotional use. For information, please write: Special Markets Department, HarperCollins Publishers Inc., 10 East 53rd Street, New York, NY 10022.

FIRST EDITION

Book design by Shubhani Sarkar.

Cover treatment co-designed by Carlos Rodriguez, REG/SI

Printed on acid-free paper

Library of Congress Cataloging-in-Publication Data is available upon request.

ISBN 0-06-072553-2

04 05 06 07 08 DIX/RRD 10 9 8 7 6 5 4 3 2 1

Un Son para *Celia*   A Song for *Celia*

Celia Cruz canta que canta,   Sing, Celia Cruz, sing.
y de su canto diré   Her voice is the
que el son, de Cuba se fue   Rhythm of Cuba
escondido en su garganta.   That she took with her when
                                       she fled.

Hay en su voz, una santa   Her voice is a natural song of
                                       praise

devoción por la palmera;   For the Royal Palm,
vibra en ella Cuba entera,   Her nation's collective voice
                                       resonates in her own,

y es tan cubano su acento   And her inflection is so
                                       distinctly Cuban

que su voz, al darse al viento,   That when it travels through
                                       the air

flota como una bandera.   It's akin to her nation's flag
                                       unfurled.

En su más leve gorjeo   The cry of the Cuban
                                       freedom fighter

hay el grito de un mambí,   Resonates in the tenor of her
                                       voice,

que unas veces es Martí,   Sometimes lyrically,
pero que siempre es Maceo.   But always commanding.

Su voz, ardiendo en deseo
por la Cuba soberana,

tan pronto es una campana,

como se torna en clarín

queriéndole poner fin
a la esclavitud cubana.

Canta, Celia Cruz, en tanto,
ya que no hay nada que vibre
y recuerde a Cuba libre
como el sabor de tu canto.

Tu canto, que sabe al llanto

de los hijos de tu tierra;

tu canto, donde se aferra
la libertad al decoro
y es como un himno sonoro

llamándonos a la guerra.

Dios puso en tu piel oscura

de reciedumbre mambisa

la claridad de tu risa

Her voice burns passionately
In defense of Cuban
  sovereignty.
At one moment it's a bell
  tolling for freedom
And suddenly it becomes a
  blaring trumpet
That calls for an end
To the bondage of her people.

Sing, Celia Cruz, sing,
Since the most spirited
Reminder of a free Cuba
Is the tenor of your song.

Your voice has the taste of the
  tears
Shed by your homeland's
  children.
Your voice is a blend
Of free will and decorum.
Your voice is a ringing
  melody
That calls us to join the
  struggle for freedom.

God added the beauty of your
  smile
And the rhythm of your
  body
To your black skin

y el ritmo de tu cintura.	That glows with the valor of a Cuban freedom fighter.
De canela y sabrosura	God anointed your African skin
ungió tu carne africana,	With cinnamon and spice.
y al viento de la mañana,	And watching you dance
quien te haya visto bailar	Is akin to seeing
habrá visto tremolar	A Cuban flag
una bandera cubana.	Fluttering in the morning breeze.
Muñequita de café,	You're a beautiful woman,
de caña, tabaco y ron,	Part coffee, part sugarcane, part tobacco, and part rum.
dame tu son, ese son	Give me your rhythm, the same rhythm
que sabe al Cucalambé.	Which is the poetic soul of our people.
Dame ese son que se fue	Let me feel that rhythm that fled
entre lágrimas y penas	With your voice
huyendo a manos ajenas	Amid tears and sorrow
en tu garganta sonora.	To distant lands.
dame tu son, que ya es hora	Let me feel your rhythm, since it's time for us
de ir a romper las cadenas.	To break free.

A Song
for Celia

vii

Dame el son. Dámelo ya.

Y al dármelo, negra linda,

dámelo como el que brinda
en cristal de bacará.

Que Cuba te premiará
con un manto de capuz,
y así que brille la luz
de la dignidad del hombre,

el son cambiará de nombre,

se llamará Celia Cruz.

Let me feel your rhythm. Let
me feel it now.

And when you finally let me
feel it,

You beautiful black woman,

We'll toast to it with Baccarat
crystal glasses.

Cuba will reward you.

It will cloak you with honor.

And when light finally shines

On the dignity of every
Cuban

The nation's rhythm will be
given a new name:

Celia Cruz.

Ernesto Montaner

NOVEMBER 1967

Contents

Foreword

THERE ARE CERTAIN ARTISTS WHO BELONG TO ALL THE people, everywhere, all the time. The list of singers, musicians, and poets must include the images in the Old Testament, Aesop the Storyteller, Omar Kayyam the Tent Maker, Shakespeare the Bard of Avon, Louis Armstrong the genius of New Orleans, Om Kalsoum the soul of Egypt, Frank Sinatra, Mahalia Jackson, Dizzy Gillespie, and Celia Cruz. The names could go on until there was no breath to announce them, however, the name of Celia Cruz would also figure among them as one of the artists who belonged to all people, all the time and everywhere.

In the early 1950s I first listened to a Celia Cruz record and although I spoke Spanish fairly well and loved her music, I could not translate it. I went on a search for everything about Celia Cruz and realized that if I was to become her devoted fan, I had to study Spanish more diligently. So I did.

I enlisted the help of my brother Bailey in New York to find every record and every magazine that mentioned Celia Cruz. Because I listened to her so carefully, my Spanish increased. When I worked with Tito Puente, Willie BoBo, and Mongo Santa Maria, I could hold my own on stage as well as in conversation with them.

When I had begun singing professionally, my repertoire contained Calypso songs and some Mexican Rancheras. I found a wonderful audience, not because I could sing well, but because my rhythms were fascinating, and those were rhythms I lifted whole and wholly from the records of Celia Cruz.

When she came to the United States and played in the theater on Upper Broadway in New York City, I went to see her every day. She exploded on the stage and was sensual and present. From her, I learned to bring everything I had onto the stage with me. And now, some 40 plus years later, without music and by simply reading poetry, I am able to hold audiences of thousands for an evening without losing their attention. Some of the power of performance I learned from Celia Cruz.

She sent me a note before she died telling me what a fan she was of my work. I never had a chance to tell her how much I thank her for her work and for her life.

I can now say to her family, her friends, and to all the world to which she belongs—thank you, Celia Cruz.

Maya Angelou

Prólogo

JUST LIKE BIRTH, LIFE'S LAST DAYS CAN OFTEN BE VERY dramatic and baffling. People recall the end not just out of a sense of chronology, but because it allows us to analyze all the miracles that unfolded throughout a whole lifetime. And this was most definitely the case when it came to Celia Cruz.

Celia was born in Cuba, a place where music is as important as the air we breathe, yet nothing in her background gave any indication of the heights she would reach. Nevertheless, in the warmth of her home in a corner of Havana of yesteryear, everything came together perfectly to shape her stellar destiny.

Her voice was her passport to the world, and with it, she embraced everyone with the warmth of her beloved native land. Nowadays, the mere mention of Cuba brings to mind the image of two individuals: one who will inevitably be condemned to the annals of infamy; and Celia Cruz, who will always sparkle in the constellation of superstars. There lies the difference between those who dedicate their lives to spreading love and those who turn it into a cheerless experience based on hatred and fear.

As Fate Would Have It

A few years before the radical revolution that installed the dictatorship still ruling Cuba and that has forced millions of its people into exile, we in Mexico were also going through our own "Cuban revolution," but ours was of a musical nature. The sensual trumpets, the evocative drums, and the unparalleled voice of Celia Cruz stirred the heart of any Mexican who had the privilege of hearing a recording of the Sonora Matancera and Celia Cruz.

For the privileged few in Mexico City, seeing the diva of Afro-Cuban rhythm perform in places like La Terraza Cassino, the Blanquita Theater, and Los Globos nightclub was a de rigueur pilgrimage. Every night, Celia Cruz and the Sonora Matancera served up a sensual banquet to Mexican audiences that included the likes of composer Agustín Lara and screen legend María Félix, just two of the names on the long and distinguished list of celebrities who frequented their performances.

I count myself among the lucky few who saw Celia perform live; however, in my case, I was something of a stowaway. In 1960, my mother worked in the coat check at Los Globos, and I used to hide under the rods where the fabulous furs and shawls of the elite clientele were hung. In the midst of French cologne and Cuban tobacco, I snoozed peacefully, lullabied by drums and Celia.

Years passed, and as fate would have it, our paths crossed forty-two years later in New York, when as a writer I interviewed the legendary performer. That day, the time for our appointment came and went, and the "Queen of Salsa" still didn't show up. Since Celia was known for being punctual, the twelve-member crew working on the interview, wardrobe, and photo op began to worry. We kept asking ourselves what could possibly have happened to her. Was her limousine stuck in one of New York's notorious traffic jams? Was she ill? Had she had an accident? Waiting for her to arrive, we paced in front of the windows at that small nightclub where we were to meet. Just when our concern was turning to panic, the diva finally arrived.

Pedro Knight, Celia's husband and inseparable companion, and her agent, Omer Pardillo, accompanied her. She apologized for being so late: "*Chica,* I'm so sorry for keeping you waiting. I know your time's as valuable as mine. My day's been just too busy, but I thought it was better to arrive late than not at all." Months would pass until I fully understood the depth of her gracious flair for downplaying the cruel realities of life. In fact, she was famous for her ability to spread beauty, joy, and love to everything she touched.

Celia was wearing a pair of black pants, a colorful blouse, and a simple black turban that complemented her impressive presence. Not only did she have a dynamic personality and a regal way about her, she was also a very gentle and kindhearted woman. She asked where she should change and we pointed to a small bathroom without air-conditioning. I'm sure she noticed my concern and embarrassment, since it wasn't an appropriate place for someone of her legendary caliber, but she said, "*Chica,* don't worry about it. What can you do?" She spoke so candidly that to my surprise, she instantly put me at ease. Her friend and stylist, Ruth Sánchez, got her clothes ready and did her makeup. In just a few minutes, Celia came out wearing a glistening sequined dress imprinted with all the colors of the rainbow, the moon, and even the sun. She wore a long blond wig, and her eyes sparkled beneath her exceptionally long eyelashes. Her two-and-a-half-inch nails and expressive hands topped off that unique and unmistakable Celia Cruz look, and that's how she appeared on the cover of the magazine I was interviewing her for.

Everyone who was there was stunned by her presence. A stereo played her Grammy Award–winning song "La Negra

Tiene Tumbao" at the back of the club. The dancers took their places, and Celia sang and danced for the cameras. Her stimulating personality electrified everything and everyone around her.

Yet the true dramatic moment took place behind a pair of curtains from where Omer called out to me. He told me Celia was ill, and he asked me to be considerate and patient with her. He explained they were late because that same day she had undergone a battery of tests, and at six in the morning the following day, Celia would be admitted to the hospital. In the same despondent way a son would speak of his mother, Omer spoke to me about Celia. I was brokenhearted. He asked me to pray for her, and more important, he asked me to be tactful about the situation. He also told me that Celia hadn't wanted to cancel the interview or the photo op, regardless of how she felt. While Omer spoke, I peeked through the heavy curtains and saw Celia sharing her joy with all the people surrounding her. It was six p.m. In only twelve hours, she would be fighting for her life in an operating room, although at that moment, and when the pictures were published four months later in January 2003, no one would have imagined that she was as ill as she was on the day of the shoot.

She didn't show us any gloom or fear. Without once losing her patience or her grace, Celia endured three costume changes, a four-hour-long photo shoot, a dinner, and an interview. There was a transcendent elegance to her decorum. I felt such reverence for her that I asked myself, How can she be acting this way, knowing she is ill? The answer had to be something more powerful than her well-developed sense of professionalism. The more I heard her speak, the more I understood. The answer lay deep in her heart, which gradually revealed itself like a blossoming flower as she told me about the story of her life.

We Mexicans are obsessed with fate, which is why we really

don't believe in coincidences. I don't think it was any accident that I began my life lullabied by that angel who was Celia Cruz. Nor do I think it was a twist of fate, either, that before bidding farewell to her earthly existence, she would give me the great privilege of participating in the writing of her memoirs. Only God knows why this all happened.

In the following pages, Celia relates her story in her own words. It's not only a narrative of a musical journey that flourished for more than half a century, nor is it just a chronological and autobiographical account of one of the most important figures in the world of music. In fact, it's actually more like an unsung bolero, the most important one she would ever record and the only one she would put on paper. In her own words, and in this book, Celia finally sings to all of us about the one thing she was ever reluctant to: herself.

Ana Cristina Reymundo
JANUARY 2004

Uno

MOTHER CUBA

Yo soy de Cuba la voz, yo soy de la Cuba de ayer.
I am Cuba's voice, and I come from Cuba of days gone by.

—Rudy Calzado. Celia Cruz, "Yo Soy la Voz."

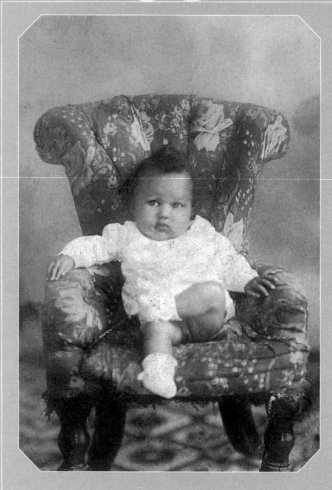

Celia in the house where she was born
and raised, 47 Serrano Street, in Havana's
Santos Suárez neighborhood.

I ALWAYS SAID I NEVER WANTED TO WRITE AN AUTO-
biography. I always dreamed to have a movie made about my
life, but I never imagined a book. Yet here we are. So what finally convinced me to write my story? I realized that when
I'm gone, there will be those who'll say, "Celia was like this,"
and others who'll dispute that and say, "No, she wasn't like
that at all, she was more like this. . . ."

Everyone is entitled to an opinion, but I decided to tell my
story in my own words, so no one could ever dispute the true
facts about my life. Who better to tell my story than the
woman who actually lived it, right?

This book is a collection of my own opinions, memories,
points of view, and feelings. Wherever my recollections may
differ with those of others, I just want to remind readers that
every individual sees things his or her own way. Interpretation
is a funny business. This book and these memories are all mine.

My name is Úrsula Hilaria Celia Caridad Cruz Alfonso. I
am the daughter of Catalina Alfonso, whom everyone knew as
"Ollita," and Simón Cruz. I was born in Havana, Cuba, in a
little house located at 47 Serrano Street, in the poorer section
of a working-class neighborhood of different races and eth-
nicities called Santos Suárez. Since Cuba has undergone terrible changes since I left, and I have never stepped foot on the
island since I became an exile, I don't know if the little house

I once lived in exists anymore, or if it does, it still looks anything like I remember it.

I'll never reveal the actual year I was born. By no means do I claim to be younger than I am, but I won't ever divulge my age. Whoever wishes to know how old I am will have to wait. I'm sure when the time comes, the funeral home will make that public. But I'll never tell. Everyone will simply have to keep on guessing.

My birth was marked with drama. It was a major event for my aunt Ana Alfonso. "Tía Ana," as everyone called her. Tía Ana and my mother shared a deep love for each other. When my mother was pregnant with me, Tía Ana's newborn daughter had just died. The death of her newborn daughter scarred her so deeply that she never had another child—of her own, anyway.

My mother, Ollita, was in Havana when Tía Ana's little girl died. Since Tía Ana lived some two hundred miles west, in the city of Pinar del Río, my mother—who was then pregnant with me—traveled all the way to Pinar del Río to console her. When Ollita finally arrived at Tía Ana and Uncle Panchito's house, she found her sister holding her dead daughter in her arms. Tía Ana was surrounded by other women, pleading dramatically with her to let her dead baby go. She refused. Ollita approached her sister and, after kissing her tenderly, calmed her down until Tía Ana finally agreed to let go of her daughter. My mother convinced Tía Ana to resign herself to fate.

Given that Tía Ana was heartbroken, my mother said to her, "Ana, when a child dies at birth, or if it's born dead, that means that its soul will return. You have to leave a mark on that little child so you'll recognize her when she's reborn. She's sure to come back to us." I don't think my mother realized how much to heart Tía Ana would take her words.

They prepared the dead baby girl for her wake and began to

pray. Apparently, Tía Ana wouldn't cry: she stared at the coffin in silence. Without saying a word, my mother told me that Tía Ana got up, walked toward her dead daughter, hunched over the casket, and began to whisper into her ear. My mother said that she whispered, "I know one day you'll come back, and I'll be waiting for you. I'm going to mark you so I can recognize you when you return to me." And with that, Tía Ana grabbed the dead baby's pinkie fingers and pulled them back so hard toward her thumbs that they broke. Everyone in the room gasped.

My mother, who was sitting close to the coffin, told me that she was so stunned by what her sister had done that she felt as though someone had punched her in the chest. She lost her breath and almost fainted the second she heard those fingers break. Later she told me that the instant those fingers were broken, she felt me jump inside her womb. The other ladies at the wake ran toward my mother, giving her water and calming her by fanning her face with fans made of straw. The following day, my little cousin was given an appropriate Catholic burial, and afterward my mother stayed with Tía Ana for several days before returning to Havana.

A few months later, on a cool afternoon, my mother was sitting on the porch of our house in Santos Suárez, singing, as was her custom. Suddenly, a strong breeze began to blow. Ollita told me she felt so cold, she began to rub her arms with her hands, and just when she was about to get up and get a shawl to warm herself, she heard a voice whisper my name in her ear. From that moment on, my mother knew I was going to be a girl and that my name would be Celia Caridad.

There are only two seasons in my beloved Cuba, the dry season and the wet one, and both are equally warm. At the end of October, the pounding rains let up a bit. Nonetheless, it's then that everyone begins to prepare for the impending damp heat. I decided to enter the world on one of those warm days, surrounded by song and prayer.

Because she felt so heavy, Ollita couldn't help but stare at her belly all day long. With all the black beans and white rice that we ate in Cuba, newborns tended to be quite big. On the day I was born, Ollita later told me, her belly seemed so large and heavy that she could hardly stand. She knew I would soon be born, and in a matter of hours, I was.

My mother's water broke the morning of October 21, followed by acute pains in her back. In an attempt to ease her discomfort, my mother started pacing, with her hands on her hips, in the back passageway that linked all the homes on the block. Soon they sent for my grandmother Dolores, Tía Ana, and a midwife.

It was often said in Cuba then that when women give birth they find themselves on the threshold of death, and that's why they need the services of a midwife. When I was older, I met the midwife who helped my mother give birth to me. She was a heavy, strong black woman with thick lips and large, straight teeth. She was very involved in the occult, and even though she was present at my birth, and a very warm person, she always frightened me.

When my mother couldn't stand the pain anymore, she returned to the house so she could lie down. Drenched in sweat, she pushed with all her strength. Since they knew it would be a hot day, the bed had already been placed in front of the window to make the most of the outside breeze. As she stared at a nearby kapok tree, watching it sway in the wind, my mother's eyes rolled up into her head and she pleaded with God to help her deal with the pain. As the contractions came in rapid succession, my mother's moans turned to screams of desperation. She shut her eyes and pushed with all the strength she had, and finally, I was allowed to pass into this world. I announced my arrival with a cry.

My grandmother Dolores immediately placed me on my mother's chest. Tears streamed out of Ollita's eyes as she sang the lullabies I now remember so well. I've heard that when a child is in its mother's womb, it can hear its mother's voice, and I agree. Given that my mother spent all her time singing, I was familiar with her voice even before I was born. Throughout my childhood, the timbre of my mother's voice always calmed me. As an adult, even the memory of her voice soothes me.

They soon washed me, wrapped my newborn body in a white cotton sheet, and put me back into Ollita's arms, where we both fell asleep. Someone went to get my father at work and informed him of my birth. When he arrived, he asked Ollita what name she had chosen for me, and she told him that I would be christened Celia Caridad. A neighbor who was present interrupted, "But today isn't Saint Cecilia's Day. That's not until November 22, and it's only October." It was then the tradition in mostly Catholic countries to use the name of the saint that corresponded with the day of a child's birth as at least *one* of the christening names. But Ollita responded, "It doesn't matter. Her name is Celia." My name is derived from Cecilia, and Saint Cecilia is the patron saint of music. God had plans for me, that much was clear.

After I awoke, Ollita began to breast-feed me and asked for Tía Ana to come to help her. When I finished feeding, they cleaned and dressed me. They inspected me from head to foot with the firm decisiveness of a mother and protective aunt. They checked my arms, my long, skinny legs, my feet, and my hands.

They counted the fingers on one hand and began to count the others. Given that newborns' hands are usually clenched into tiny, determined fists, they didn't notice anything out of the ordinary.

A few weeks passed, and one day as Ollita was washing me, she inadvertently opened my left hand and noticed that my pinkie fingers were oddly twisted. Later, she told me that her heart almost jumped out of her chest. She called to my grandmother Dolores, who ran into the room to see what was wrong. My mother showed her my hands, each marked with its twisted pinkie finger. Both began to simultaneously cry and praise God. They immediately called for Tía Ana so they could tell her that her daughter had returned. From that moment on I had two mothers, Ollita and Tía Ana, who upon my christening had officially become my godmother.

I've been told that all in all, I was a quiet infant. Still, I shrilled like a whistle and had the habit of waking up in the middle of the night, and that, of course, would wake up the entire house. What's more, I hummed constantly while my grandmother and my mother tended to me. Once my grandmother said to my mother, "Ollita, do you see how this girl wakes up in the middle of the night only to wake up the rest of the house? That's because she's going to work at night. She's going to be an entertainer. Just you wait and see."

I have few personal memories of my grandparents. Dolores was relatively young when she passed away. I was still a child. Even though my grandfather Ramón Alfonso died much later, he lived in Pinar del Río and not Havana, where my family lived. We didn't grow up with him, but when he came to visit us in the capital, he'd tell us story after story about the war for Cuban independence from Spain. He was what Cubans proudly call a *mambí*, a title of African origin applied to all Cubans who rose up against Spanish rule between 1868 and 1898. All the same, I don't think he ever ranked higher than a foot soldier in the Cuban army. He used to tell us that the *mambís* were so underfed that to keep from starving, they resorted to eating cats. I think my dear grandfather was so traumatized by that experience that after the war he ate only beef. I've heard today that things have gotten so bad in Cuba that many are now eating cats again. That is, of course, if there are any cats left.

My mother's children are, by order of birth, Dolores (or "La Niña"), me, Bárbaro, and Gladys. Two other siblings were born between me and Bárbaro. The first one, who was named Japón, was very tiny, and his lips shook when he cried. Ollita took good care of him and often cried because she noticed how weak he was. Japón was still an infant when he passed away, although I don't know what caused his death. My mother then had a very pretty baby, and they named her Norma, but she also passed away at a young age. I was very young when Japón and Norma died, but my mother's suffering was so obvious during this period that it left its mark on me forever. Even though I was too young to understand, I'll never forget the pain I saw on her face. But time passed, as did her grief, and Ollita got pregnant for the last time, bringing my baby sister, Gladys, into the world.

Many people lived in our modest Santos Suárez home: my mother, my father, my grandmother Dolores, when she was alive, and depending on what time of the year it was, one relative or another and their children. There was a lot of love in that modest home. It had a small living room with a door that faced the sidewalk, two bedrooms, a dining room, and a bathroom. All the windows had bars on them meant to protect the house. When the windows were open, the cool Cuban breeze would

flow through the bars and into every room of the house. The air in our home was also always filled with my mother's singing, the aroma of the food she cooked for us, and the laughter of children. We always had enough white rice and black beans to eat, and every so often we had papaya and fried ripe plantains. I remember that on special occasions my mother would make a delicious *ropa vieja,* literally "old clothes," a typical Cuban dish made of shredded beef. It smelled so good and was so juicy that I get hungry, and sad, just thinking about it. I have never had anything else so delicious in my life, and I've eaten food that's been cooked in the best kitchens of the world and in the homes of friends renowned for their culinary expertise. I guess I'm saddened when I remember my mother's food because nothing on earth compares with what is served to you as a child. My Ollita's *ropa vieja* is as good as it ever got.

I was enrolled in school when I was about six or seven years old in Santos Suárez's Public School No. 6, called República Mexicana. When I first started, I didn't want to go. I never wanted to leave my mother's side. However, I soon grew to like school. I always enjoyed learning and was a very serious student. I knew an education would help me go far in life. Since my father wanted all his children to have professions, and I always loved children, being a teacher would be the most natural professional step I could take. I honestly believe then that the route toward making my father proud of me was in my becoming a teacher. It was only later, taking the advice of a teacher I revered, that I realized how to make myself happy and at the same time make my father proud of me (something that back then, I thought impossible).

One day I returned home from school to discover that friends of my parents, a couple, had come for a visit. Although I don't remember their names, I do remember my mother asking me to sing them a song. I sang a traditional Cuban song called "Y Tú Qué Has Hecho," which is known by many as "En el Tronco de un Árbol." The couple were so pleased with my performance that the next time they came for a visit, the husband brought me a pair of white patent-leather shoes. I was totally surprised by his gesture of goodwill. Not only had my singing made them happy, but those white patent-leather shoes, which meant so much to me, initiated my lifelong fascination with fashion.

My childhood was filled with very happy days and good, wholesome fun. I walked to school with my friends Estela, Ana Maria, Caridad, and Orlando, and besides walking to school and back home together, we played a lot, joking and laughing the entire time. Although I didn't have many girlfriends when I was a child, because I spent most of my time with my cousins, I still went to as many places as I was allowed to with my closest friends. By the time we were teenagers, we would go together to the dances held at the Sociedad de los Jóvenes del Vals, a private neighborhood social club located on Rodríguez Street in Santos Suárez. My friends and I also went for long walks in the city's parks.

I never had a boyfriend because I was very straitlaced and even shy. I spent most of my time learning and singing the songs that were in style back then. We would sing Carlos Gardel's tangos, since they were all the rage in the 1930s and he was considered the greatest musician of his genre. We also sang songs by Cuban entertainers such as Paulina Álvarez, Fernando Collazo, Abelardo Barrozo, and Pablo Quevedo. I remember Quevedo very well, since my sister Dolores was such a huge fan of his. She cried her eyes out when he died. Those were great times, and I spent them singing.

There was a *comparsa* in Santos Suárez called La Hornalera. In Cuba, *comparsas* were neighborhood-based amateur associations that work all year long preparing to perform in the pre-Lenten carnival. In Havana, *comparsas* paraded through the city's main arteries in conga lines, each wearing elaborate costumes. *Comparsas* ended before a grandstand of dignitaries who would then judge the year's winners. In any case, my mother was against us hanging around the *comparsas* because everyone would get drunk. Fights would sometimes break out, and someone could end up being knifed. This problem wasn't exclusive to Santos Suárez; it always happens in large crowds where people are drinking and dancing. My mother also worried that we would begin dancing behind the *comparsas* and, losing track of where the parade led us, would eventually get lost. Actually, that did happen to us once, and when it did, we were scared out of our wits. Still, neither my mother's warnings nor my fear of getting lost kept me from dancing behind the *comparsas*. It was something I loved and would do whenever I got the chance.

Nothing could outdo carnival in Havana. Yet even though carnival in Havana was legendary, I had never been allowed to go. But one day, all five of us—Estela, Rosa María, Caridad, Orlando, my cousin Nenita, and I—took the bus to the Paseo del Prado, one of Havana's main thoroughfares, to see the parade. Even though the bus fare was only a nickel per seat, we didn't have enough money for all of us. Since Nenita was the biggest, and I was very skinny, I sat on her lap, so we would only be charged one fare. I must have been around fourteen.

During the carnival season in Havana, I lived in fear that someone would see me dancing at the festivities. But the fear wasn't strong enough to keep me from cavorting with that wonderfully loud and festive celebration. Everyone donned a costume and let loose for a week of nonstop fun. That's where I saw my first musical extravaganza. Although I really enjoyed it, I still remember the odd combination of fear and joy—the fear of getting caught and the joy I felt in my heart. I knew I wasn't supposed to be there, but the colors, the music, the sense of energy, and living life to its fullest potential were very intoxicating. I remember the euphoria I felt when we walked home that night. We had to walk because we didn't have enough money for the bus ride back. It was the longest and best walk of my life.

I've never liked dishonesty, so that night when I got back home, I couldn't sleep. I felt terribly guilty about lying. When we left for the parade of *comparsas,* I let it be known that I was going to my friend Caridad's house, and *her* parents thought she was visiting *me.* The following morning, Tía Ana woke me up with the usual pitcher of cold milk, and after I drank it, I said, "*Tía,* what would you think of me if I told you that last night I snuck out with Nenita and the others and we went to see the *comparsas?*"

She answered, "Celia, *mi niña,* how can you do such a thing at this time of the year, when there're so many drunk people wearing costumes out there on the streets?" She said this with a smirk, and I noticed that she wasn't really angry with me. Her comment came from concern rather than anger.

"Please forgive me for lying to you, *Tía.*" I confessed to her how excited I was with all those lights and all that music, and since she was usually my accomplice, I begged her to take me back to the *comparsa* parade that same night.

She replied, "If you promise not to go out alone again, I'll take you." That same night, we both escaped from my parents' house and headed back to a second night of carnival.

I took a bath and changed, and Tía Ana did the same. At dusk, my *tía* told my mother that she was going to visit friends in another neighborhood, and because she didn't want to go alone, she would take me to keep her company. My mother had her back to me, and Tía Ana winked at me so I wouldn't say anything. I felt a little guilty that I had to hide the truth from my mother, but I must confess that I didn't feel that bad, since my aunt was like a second mother to me. If she said it was okay to go, then by all means it must be okay to go. When we said good-bye, I saw Ollita giving Tía Ana a look that let me know she suspected we were going off to the *comparsa* parade. Tía Ana smiled back at her and grabbed me by the hand, and we left. As we walked down the sidewalk, my mother yelled out to us, "Be really careful. Ana, you're responsible for her. Did you hear me? I beg of you, be careful!"

"Don't worry, Catalina," Tía Ana replied. She squeezed my hand and we giggled; we were proud that our plan had worked. We ran to catch the bus, and I remember beating her to the stop. Unlike the night before, this time we had enough money for the round-trip fare. The only walking I would do was in the actual *comparsa*.

We arrived at the grandstand in front of the Capitol building, and the place was total madness, with everyone screaming, laughing, and dancing. It was wonderful. Still, there were a few drunken men who frightened me, so I grabbed my *tía's* hand and didn't let go. All the same, we danced and sang with the *comparsas* as we followed closely behind them. We didn't stop until our feet finally gave out on us. I don't remember what time we got home, but it was definitely past my bedtime. My father was sleeping, but Ollita was up waiting for us. My dear mother was thrilled to see us and never said a bad word about our lying to her. She never even brought it up.

I barely slept that night. I dreamt I was the Carnival Queen.

In my dream—and this I'll never forget—I saw myself wearing a flowing white gown, my hair pulled back in a bun, topped off with a floral wreath. I danced with my arms outstretched to the world. It was something I never could have dreamt had I not just had such a wonderful experience. And it was all thanks to Tía Ana, my ally and confidante.

The first time I really did have a chance to wear a flowing white gown, I may not have been a queen, but I was a princess. My mother had registered me in catechism classes at the Miraculous Medal Parish on Santos Suárez and Paz streets when I was really young. She and I often went together to mass, which at that time was conducted in Latin, and women and girls had to wear veils on their heads. The day of my first communion arrived in 1935, and it was one of the most special events in my life. I felt very calm and pure when the priest gave me the host, although I remember being warned not to bite down on the host because it was the body of Christ. Oh, Lord! No one can imagine how careful I was not to touch the host with my teeth. I asked God for many favors during my lifetime, and from that moment on I have never strayed from my spiritual path and relationship with God, although I have always made it a point not to judge what others may or may not believe.

Right behind my house lived a *santera* named Chela. A *santero* or *santera* is a person who practices one of Cuba's syncretistic religions with Spanish Catholic, indigenous, and African roots, although I should note that all *santeros* also consider themselves Catholics. In any case, the fact was that my mother was always very frightened by Santería and the *santeros,* and she instilled that fear in me at an early age. From time to time, our neighbor Chela held a nighttime *bembé,* a major Santería celebration, in her backyard. One dreadfully warm afternoon, when I couldn't stand being locked in the house anymore, I wanted to go out back and get some fresh air, but I was afraid to, since Chela was getting ready for one of her *bembés.* But the heat and my boredom conquered my fear. I went out and sat under the kapok tree that grew in the corner of the backyard, and through the back corridor that linked all the houses, I could clearly hear the neighbors. I was frightened when I heard the beat of those drums and the songs being sung in honor of the saints in Lucumí, the Afro-Cuban liturgical language of Santería. Still, the music called out to me. That I sat there listening to the music surprised even me, since I have to admit that the first time I ever heard those songs and drums I ran and hid, especially when I saw how much those rituals frightened my mother. But with the passage of time, I began to appreciate that type of music as a beautiful way of expressing my African roots. As a matter of fact, I even developed a good Lucumí pronunciation, although I never learned what the words meant. It was more than that. Later, I would realize that the music during those ceremonies would forever give me inspiration.

I remember a huge black man who was always at Chela's *bembés*—he had a reputation for being possessed by the spirits during her gatherings, and when the spirits supposedly possessed him, his eyes would roll back into his head, his body would contort, and he would begin to twirl. I started calling him "El Negro Zarabanda" ("the Twirling Black Man"). I always found him frightening. Every time he passed our front door I'd run and hide under the bed. When he saw how scared I was of him, my running away never seemed to bother him; he would simply laugh. But as I've already said, I didn't always feel the music was solely about the religion, and people, associated with Santería.

Many people who don't know me well think I am a *santera.*

I'm black and Cuban, so naturally, I must believe in Santería. Some people actually swear they've seen me at Santería rituals. I remember once, years ago, while performing in the Dominican Republic, we were followed by a man as we were walking down the hall of a hotel toward our room. He stopped us as we tried to open the door to our room and said, "I know you."

"Really? I don't think I've ever seen you before," I answered.

"Don't you remember me?"

"No, I don't."

The man insisted, "But how can you not remember me? We were both initiated into Santería together. I saw you come out of the initiation room."

"Honey, you seem to have the wrong black woman," I responded, turning my back and walking into my room.

Another incident like this took place in Miami. I was performing at the Montmartre nightclub in the early 1970s when a young Cuban man accompanied by two pregnant women came to see me in the dressing room before the show. When they walked into the room, the man told me that one of the women was carrying a daughter of Yemayá, who in the Afro-Cuban pantheon corresponds to the Catholic Our Lady of Regla. The other one was carrying a daughter of Ochún, the equivalent of Our Lady of Charity. He told me that he had brought them for my blessing. I told him, "*Mi amor,* if you want my blessing, I'll give it to you. But I'm not a *santera.*"

"What do you mean, you're not a *santera?*" he asked angrily. He then turned his back on me and stormed out of the room, almost physically dragging the two apologetic women with him.

I respect all belief systems and all religions, including Santería, but I am not a *santera.* I won't deny that I am somewhat versed in it. There is no such thing as a Cuban, regardless of his or her background, who doesn't know *something* about Santería; but my knowledge of Santería is fairly superficial. For me, it's a matter of Cuban folklore. Still, many people insist on classifying me a *santera*. Again, I think it's due to their prejudices, since I am both black *and* Cuban.

I'm a fan of all types of Cuban music: Lucumí songs (which we also call "Afro"), *son,* rumba, cha-cha, bolero, mambo, *danzón,* and so forth. As a matter of fact, Cuban music, from the Baroque to the atonal, is so varied that it has something for every taste. I truly believe that music is Cuba's greatest gift to the world, and I learned to appreciate it at home, since music was very important in our family. Music and dance are integral factors of the Cuban national character; my family was only an extension of this core Cuban relationship with music.

In my family, my mother and my brother, Bárbaro, sang the most. My mother used to sing me a song I really liked that she once performed with a *comparsa.* I would sit at the table and say to her, "Ollita, sing me that song from the *comparsa,*" and she would always oblige with a smile on her face. My dear brother, Bárbaro, who always helped me in any way he could, also had a fine voice, but unfortunately, the regime currently in power in Cuba never allowed him to develop his skills. Because he is related to me, and I am not exactly a favorite personality of the government's, he has, sadly, never been allowed to pursue a career in music.

Even before I entered the world of music, I was lucky to have met many of the Cuban musicians who would eventually become giants in their field. Since we loved to dance, we used to go to the dances at Club Antilla and at the Jóvenes del Vals, and it was there that I met Arcaño and His Maravillas, the great musician Israel López ("Cachao," brother of Orestes López, the legendary father of the mambo), and the musicians of the Melodía del Cuarenta Orchestra. But the singer I idolized most back then, and whom I tried to emulate the most, was named Paulina Álvarez.

I met Paulina when she performed at Jóvenes del Vals, before the club moved in the late 1930s to Correa Street in Santos Suárez. Since my aunt Nena loved to go out dancing, she would take her children, Nenita, Papito, and Minín, and she would also take me along because she knew how much I loved Paulina Álvarez. Paulina was a trailblazer who began performing in public in the 1920s, when women rarely performed Cuban dance music in public.

In Cuba it was legal for minors to enter establishments that served alcohol, so we were all allowed to go see good music, no matter where the band played or how old we were. We would always sit near the front, and I would make my way, alone, toward the stage and stand where I could get a clearer view of Paulina. She always held her claves—two cylindrical pieces of wood that when struck together set the basic beat in most genres of popular Cuban dance music—as she performed with the Neno González Orchestra. Since Paulina was always photographed with claves in hand, and since I wanted to be just like her, I was soon given two claves as a gift. I can honestly say that I admired Paulina so much that I modeled my performance technique on hers.

There are those who are adamant in their belief that it was Paulina who in performance used to yell, *"Azúcar!"* ("Sugar!") from stage. I never heard her say that. If I had, I'd admit where I got it from and would never try to deny that the word did not originate with me. Paulina was my idol, so how could I not admit it if it were true? I'm not saying that someone is being dishonest, and if they wish to say that I stole my trademark *"Azúcar!"* from Paulina, well, to each his own. If it's true that Paulina yelled, *"Azúcar!"* from the stage, the only thing I can think of is that she said it during one of her performances at the Sugarcane Festival, since she always performed at those types of Cuban national events. Maybe there's where the confusion lies. But my history with *"Azúcar!"* which I will explain in more detail later on, had its origins many years later in a Miami restaurant.

I remember a song that Paulina sang called "Dulce Serenidad." I loved it, and I always wanted to record it in her honor, but for one reason or another I never had the chance. Still, many years after I first saw her perform on stage, I was blessed to be able to share the stage with her.

The Riveros Orchestra, the singer Xiomara Alfaro, Paulina, and I all performed in Havana's Tropicana nightclub in a show produced by the renowned choreographer Rodney. Performing with Paulina was a wonderful experience, and I was finally able to tell her in person how much I had idolized her. She complimented me on my voice, and I was thrilled.

I may have inherited my voice from Ollita, but I got my love for the stage from Tía Ana. There was a time when I went to live with her and her husband, Pancho, in Pinar del Río. I don't remember exactly how old I was, but it was sometime before I turned sixteen. All the same, Pancho was a very kind man, and I loved him as much as I did his wife. He was always very supportive of me. He gave me money for my books and other school expenses and always treated me very well. He loved me like a daughter. I don't know why Tía Ana left him, but after she did, I stayed with her for a while longer in Pinar del Río so she wouldn't feel so lonely. I have wonderful memories of that period, since Tía Ana made sure to feed me my favorite Cuban dishes. We talked about everything, took long walks, and once in a while, when we had some extra money, we even went shopping.

I was always singing during the time I spent in Pinar del Río, but I was also very shy. My aunt constantly encouraged me to sing without any apprehension or fear. To let go. She used to say, "Celia, when you were born, the angels blessed your vocal cords, so you should never be afraid to sing. Sing, *mi niña,* sing. God blessed you with this voice you have, so use it."

I would sing to please her, but while I did, I moved nothing but my mouth. The rest of my body remained as still as a statue. Then she would say to me, "*Chica,* move your body! How do you expect to liven up a crowd if you just stand there, stiff like a statue? Let the music take you away." I loved being with my aunt in Pinar del Río, but I began to miss my mother and wanted to return to Havana, which I did soon thereafter.

In Santos Suárez, every member of the household chipped in the best way he or she could. Since I am very nearsighted, there were certain chores I just couldn't do. As a result, one of my responsibilities was to put the younger ones in the house—my brother, Bárbaro, my cousins Minín and Papito, and all the others—to sleep. I was in charge of rounding them up, bathing them, and getting them ready for bed. Once I tucked them in, I would always sing to them. Although I sang the same lullabies my mother sang to me, my voice was so loud that it kept them awake instead of lulling them to sleep. Not only could I not get them to sleep, but the neighbors would stand at the front door, which we always left open, so the outside breeze would cool the house. Because I was so shy, one day I decided it would be best if I closed the door. That proved useless, since the kids still didn't go to sleep and the neighbors then began standing by the open window so they could hear me sing.

Life for us was very simple back then. My days were filled with good clean fun and school. I finished my secondary studies at the Las Oblatas, Havana's Academy of the Oblate Nuns, and during that time I had a group of friends that included my cousin Nenita and my friend Orlando. When we could, we used to go to a dance club called Los Tulipanes in the La Víbora neighborhood of Havana. Although we passed by, we never actually went inside. We just watched what was going on from the outside.

Even the scene along the street was lively at Los Tulipanes. Since La Víbora was a bit far from where we lived, our male friends would walk us home, and since Nenita and I lived farther than they did, we were the last ones to be escorted home. As I said, life was good. We never imagined anything bad could happen until the day the sea decided to unleash its fury.

I'll never forget those awful days just after the hurricane of 1944. The hurricane was so brutal that it destroyed almost everything in its path. The gale-force winds turned the rain into what seemed like blinding sheets of water. Havana's seaside boulevard, El Malecón, where we normally strolled and enjoyed the magic of life, became a very dangerous place. The waves unleashed all their might and seemed like gray fists, mercilessly beating the stone walls and docks along the bay with such strength that it seemed everything was on the verge of collapse. The royal palms, which usually dance in the breeze, were bent so far down toward the pavement that eventually they were pulled out by their roots and blown into the wind.

The thunder deafened me, and it seemed as if our little home were going to be torn to pieces at any minute. I convinced myself that Mother Nature had released this frontal attack on Cuba because she was upset, and although I hadn't a clue as to why she was upset, she punished us without pity. The force of the hurricane was so great that I was able to realize then the greatness of God's power, as well as the limitations of man. When it was finally over, a pleasant calm arrived in Havana, although debris and destruction were everywhere. Many people were left homeless, and others had their businesses totally ruined.

Many years later, when I met the wonderful gentleman who became my husband, he told me how difficult life became for him because of that hurricane. At that time, Pedro Knight played the trumpet for a traveling circus that was torn to shreds by the storm. There was no money for the circus employees since there was no audience to perform in front of, and there was no audience because there was no money. Pedro didn't even have enough money to buy food for himself. All the circus employees went hungry. They ate only once a day, and what they consumed came from a large pot of boiled water with a sprinkle of brown sugar served with a slice of bread. It was an awful time for him. But eventually everything was rebuilt and many buildings ended up looking new, although, sadly, others disappeared forever. People started going back out to the streets, but for quite a while all they did was talk about the hurricane and how it had devastated our lives.

I had a wonderful cousin, my dear Serafín, may he rest in peace. He was very clever and very aware of how my voice attracted people. One day in 1947, when I was already a registered student at Havana's Escuela Normal de Maestros (Teachers College) Serafín signed me up—without my consent—at an amateur show called *La Hora del Té* (*Tea Time*), which was then broad-

cast from the Radio García Serra Studios, located on Felipe Poey
and Estrada Palma streets, about twelve blocks from my house.
After registering me in the contest, Serafín came to me and said,
"Celia, I want you to get dressed really nicely this coming Satur-
day, because I'm taking you to an amateur contest. Am I making
myself clear?" I was overjoyed, and nervous, because I knew that
people won wonderful prizes in those sorts of competitions, especially in *La Hora del Té*.

Finally, the day I was to participate in the competition arrived. I woke up extra early that day. I have never liked being late
for an appointment, so when I have one early in the day, I always
get up as early as possible so I won't be late and look bad. I remember stepping out to the backyard and being greeted by a
cool yet damp morning. Everything was covered in dew. The sun
reflected off the beads of moisture gathered on the plants and
trees throughout the neighborhood, making everything shine like
a sequined dress.

I put on a white dress, white stockings, and my white patent-
leather shoes, which were then all the rage. My mother combed
my hair into a bun and held it up with a beautiful clip. I felt very
calm, which even I found odd. I really didn't know why I was so
sure of myself. Maybe it was because I was taking my claves with
me, those same claves that linked me to my musical idol, Paulina
Álvarez. Maybe I thought that somehow they gave me power.
They certainly seemed to that morning.

I left for the studio with my dear cousin Serafín, who would
eventually become my unofficial agent. We usually went everywhere by foot, but that day we took the bus. When we arrived, I
noticed that there were other people waiting and that most of
them were older than me. They called us in and divided us into
two groups, one for the younger performers and one for the

older ones, since the contests were classified according to the age of each participant. When my turn came, I sang a tango called "Nostalgia," accompanied by my claves. "Nostalgia" wasn't one of those typical accordion tangos, and apparently my use of the claves was so well received by the judges that I won the contest. As a result, I was invited to return the following month and then they gave me my prize: a beautiful cake.

The cake came in a very pretty box that read "La Casa Potín," which was a well-known Havana bakery. On the bus home, we carried it carefully on our laps so that it wouldn't get crushed. Still, Serafín and I couldn't help ourselves, and we opened the box so we could smell that mouthwatering, stunning cake, decorated with white frosting and colorful, delicate flowers. The cake looked as though it were made of lace.

We were very excited when we finally made it home. In fact, Serafín was more excited than I. When we walked up to the door of the house, we found everyone waiting for us on the porch. They greeted us enthusiastically with applause and cheers. They all wanted to see what I had won, and after Serafín and I showed them our prize, we soon devoured the cake. Incredible as it may sound, after all these years I can still taste that cake in my mouth. Lord, it was wonderful! Afterward, we discussed which song I should perform in the following month's elimination round. Of course, each member of my household had his or her favorite. When I won in the next round, my prize was a beautiful necklace. From that moment on, I knew that these talent contests were good for me. I entered as many as I could.

After winning at the Radio García Serra contests, I took part in a radio contest sponsored by Los Curros Enríquez, a club for Spanish immigrants located on San Indalecio Street in Santos Suárez. Since the club did not have its own radio studio, the show was broadcast from somewhere else, although I don't remember exactly which studio it was. However, I do remember the program director, Adolfo Ruiz, and the main host, Mario Degne. Both men emceed the show together. Sometimes I won, sometimes I lost, and on one occasion they even rang the gong to throw me off the show. Although I should have been humiliated, it wasn't my fault. I showed up that afternoon to rehearse, and the pianist, whose name was Candito Ruiz, decided that he didn't want to rehearse with me. Lots of singers were scheduled to perform that day, and I guess I just wasn't his favorite. He said to me, "No, I'm not going to rehearse with you. The number goes out as is." When I arrived for the broadcasting of the show that night, I couldn't get the song, entitled "Chiquilla," to sound right. We tried it three times, but it just didn't sound the way it was supposed to. And on the third try, they gonged me off the show. Still, the audience graciously applauded. Given that they were familiar with me and knew I could sing well, they were nice to me. That experience served as a good lesson. From that moment on, I would never record or perform anything if I hadn't gotten the tone right. It's amazing; that happened years ago, and I still haven't forgotten what I learned. I'll never, ever forget being gonged.

One day, after she returned to Havana, Tía Ana accompanied me to a contest at another radio station. I performed well and even won, but while I sang, I stood there like a flagpole. When I finished, Tía Ana asked me, "Celia, why don't you shake a little, honey? You have to understand that you have to let the public feel everything you're carrying inside through your entire body. Not just your voice. Next time, I want to see you move. Am I making myself clear?"

And that's what I've done since. Thanks to Tía Ana's advice, I added the famous zing to my performances through the way I move. Tía Ana's advice has served me well.

I was also a contestant on *La Corte Suprema del Arte* (*The Supreme Court of the Arts*) on the Havana radio station CMQ, which was under the direction of José Antonio Alonso. The greatest Cuban entertainers of yesteryear appeared on that show. Sometimes I'd win money, and other times they would give me boxes full of prizes that Serafín and I happily took home. Those packages were filled with soap, chocolate, bread, La Lechera brand condensed milk, and other necessities. In other words, those boxes were chock-full of everything you could imagine, and Serafín and I always left content with what we had won. After every contest, our home became a party. Everyone, with the exception of my father, seemed to laugh and talk at once, they were so excited that I had won.

My father would always get quiet after I came home from a competition. I can't deny that his attitude hurt me, and I just couldn't understand why he didn't want me to perform. It was then that I realized just how opposed he was to my becoming a singer.

Simón Cruz, my father, was much older than my mother. He was very traditional and, let's say, a bit old-fashioned. He worked hard and had very long days. He was always tired and hungry when he came home from work. He wasn't the affectionate type. Maybe he was closer to my siblings, but I'm not too sure about that, either. Although he was cold when dealing with me, the support I received from my mother and Tía Ana made his attitude bearable. I could forget his distance when everyone else around supported me. Simón wasn't the type to give compliments or make positive comments about anything. He definitely let it be known when something displeased him, though, that was for sure. Needless to say, I loved him a great deal and respected him because he was my father. Still, I always placed my trust in my mother. I was just closer to her. Yet even though my relationship with my father was not affectionate, we still loved each other deeply. The love between us was never in doubt.

Now I understand why my father felt the way he did about my budding career. I didn't then, but I do now. My father spent all his time on the railroads and actually worked inside the railcar where, by using huge shovels, all the coal was scooped into the furnace. It was a hard job, and the days were long. Many of the men he worked with had rather sordid ways of enjoying themselves during their time off, spending their free time in bars and nightclubs filled with musicians and showgirls (or, as they were known then, *mujeres de la vida,* meaning prostitutes). Since my father wanted all his children to be professionals, and his dream for me was that I become a certified teacher, when he saw the path I was on as an entertainer, he feared I would disregard my teaching aspirations and fall prey to the *mujeres de la vida* culture.

My father detached himself from me, and we spoke very little once I began entering contests. The more I won, the more we drifted apart, until the day came when he angrily said to me that the only women involved in show business were *mujeres de la vida.* His comment hurt me so much that I went to my mother and addressed the issue with her. She said, "Don't pay attention to him, *mi niña.* You just keep on doing what you're doing, and I'll deal with him." My mother saw things differently because she really knew me. She knew everything about me. My mother had no doubt that I was a decent young woman and that I was blessed with strong values. She trusted me and wasn't worried about me. She was sure that all I needed to achieve success was to make the most of my talents. She said that if I did that, everything else would fall into place.

I want to make it clear that my father spent his whole life working as hard as he could to give us the best within his reach. He made sure that all his children were educated, and although he was a "grumpy old black man," as my mother used to call him, he loved me with all his heart. I also loved him back with all of my heart. He was an excellent father and husband, and I'll always stand by this.

I stayed in school and entered only those contests that didn't conflict with my schedule. With the money I won in talent competitions, I managed to have enough for my books at Teachers College, where I had wonderful professors and also made some good friends. As a matter of fact, there's where I met my friend Esther, who before graduation fell in love with the famous Cachao, whom I had met at the dances at the Jóvenes del Vals, where he performed. Esther eventually married him.

During the late 1940s, I also performed with a neighborhood band called El Botón de Oro (the Golden Button), headed by a gentleman named Francisco Gavilán. He made each of us wear a small gold button in the shape of a flower, which was how the group got its name. My sister Dolores was already singing with El Botón de Oro before I even began performing with them. Because they didn't pay us, we worked with them for fun, at parties and other neighborhood events. If we were lucky, my sister and I were rewarded with soft drinks. Mostly, though, our only payment for singing with the group was all the water we could drink. Still, we didn't complain, since we loved the chance to perform in front of a live audience.

I soon became well-known at several major radio stations.

Radio Cadena Suaritos, CMQ, RHC-Cadena Azul, Radio Progreso, and Radio García Serra, the same radio studio where I entered my first talent contest, were all familiar with my name and voice. I performed at so many radio stations, though, that I don't remember all their names. Most times, my stint at any particular radio station lasted no longer than a day.

My forte was performing at school and Cuban patriotic events. I had been doing so since I was in grammar school. At Teachers College there was often some show or another, and my professors and fellow students would always ask me to perform in them. The last time I sang for a school was on graduation day in 1949. After the commencement ceremonies ended, and most people had left, I remember speaking with one of the most beautiful and talented teachers in our school, Miss Marta Rainieri. I asked her how I should go about becoming a teacher and having a classroom of my own one day, and she looked straight into my eyes and said in a serious tone of voice, "Celia, God gave you a wonderful gift. With the voice you have, you can make a good living. If you pursue a singing career, you'll be able to make in one day what it takes me one month to make. Don't waste your time trying to become a teacher. You were put on earth to make people happy—*by using your gift.*"

I was surprised to hear my professor speak so candidly, but I can't deny that I was thrilled to hear what she had to say. It was that moment when I decided to pursue a singing career for good. Although I knew I would have to deal with my father's disapproval, I felt I had no other choice but to follow my fate, my *destino,* and use what God blessed me with.

Immediately, I began looking for someone who could help me conquer the music business. My search led to my initial study of *solfa,* piano, and music theory at the Academia Municipal de Música, the Havana Music Academy. In addition, I took private piano lessons with a teacher Tía Ana hired for me. Poor thing, I just couldn't stand her. I had no real reason for disliking her, since she was friendly and elegant, but I had such a negative reaction to her that I have somehow blocked her very name from my memory. Finally, one day after one of my lessons, I returned home and announced to Tía Ana that I didn't want to see my piano teacher anymore. It was the end of my private piano lessons. Fortunately, I also studied piano with Oscar Muñoz Boufartique, the renowned composer of one of my greatest hits, "Burundanga." Oscar was a dedicated and energetic man. He used to say to me, "Celia, you have to cut those nails of yours if you want to learn how to play the piano well." I always refused to cut them. I now regret never having learned how to play as I should have. Nails grow back. I didn't value the chance I had at the time to learn to play the piano, and it's one of my greatest regrets. Still, I met so many people at the academy who worked in the music business, that I began to collaborate closely with all of them. Owing to these contacts and the amateur contests that were growing in popularity throughout Cuba, of which I won many, more and more radio stations began to hire me.

I have great memories of the CMQ Radio Studios, which was located on L Street and Second in El Vedado. Every day when I arrived, I had to sit on a bench in front of the reception desk, which had on it a notebook where the freelance entertainers, or *boleros* (or *bolos*), as we were called, had to sign in. The notebook specified all the entertainers' names, program names, rehearsal times, show times, and any other relevant information.

Radio talent would arrive and check the notebook to see if they had anything programmed for that day. Naturally, we spent a lot of time waiting on that legendary bench at CMQ.

During the long hours I spent on that bench, I made a lifelong friend in Juan García Rojas. Known today as Johnny Rojas, Telemundo's director of talent, Juan was the godson of Mimi Cal, who died in exile and who in Cuba was highly esteemed for her role as "Nananina" in CMQ's show *La Tremenda Corte* (*What a Courthouse*), in which the unforgettable Leopoldo Fernández, popularly known as "Pototo," played the lead role. I should note here that another version of this same program later passed to Cuban television in the 1950s and is still broadcast throughout the Spanish-speaking world, with the sad exception, of course, of Cuba. In any case, Mimi felt great affection for me, and she gave me a nickname, "La Muñequita de Chocolate" ("the Little Chocolate Doll"). Since I was skinny back then, and had good posture when I walked, they also started calling me "El Cisne Negro" ("the Black Swan"). I felt adored with all the terms of endearment people handed me. The people at that radio station made me feel so at home that I always wanted to do everything I could to please them. They taught me so much of what I now know. Since I spent hours sitting on that bench, I would use the time to observe and study all the other performers. I studied their warm-up techniques and the way they carried themselves as they belted out songs. Whenever I was unsure about anything, no matter how small, they all did their best to guide me with honest, good-hearted advice.

That bench was known as "the bench of dreams," since it was there where we dreamed about all the possibilities and goals we had for our futures. I must point out that of all we thought the future might hold, the only thing that never occurred to us was that one day we would be forced into exile.

Johnny used to say to me, "You'll see, you'll be a great star someday," and I would answer, "Do you really think so, Juanito?" Like any young person, I hoped and hoped that all my hard work would someday pay off big. Back then, Johnny was also making the rounds as an actor. He had to sit for hours, waiting for his turn as a *bolo*. We always encouraged each other. Sometimes he would get really frustrated because he'd arrive, rehearse all day, and then the show he was scheduled to appear on wouldn't air. One must remember that everything was broadcast live and without the aid of teleprompters. In other words, we had to memorize everything. If we allowed ourselves to be distracted by the smallest thing, we'd make mistakes and get a bad reputation, and then we just wouldn't make it. We had to know how to concentrate on what we were doing at all times. We didn't have the luxury of doing take after take, as actors and singers do now. If you made a mistake, that's how it was broadcast over the airwaves. Being nervous was just part of our lives.

Sometimes, though, we slipped up hilariously, and Johnny and I would crack up laughing, secretly hoping that our missteps weren't bad enough to cost us our jobs. But if our errors *were* worth worrying about, we would later joke about them to try to make ourselves feel better in order to bolster our confidence.

Once in a while, Johnny would be selected for a major role but would get so nervous, he couldn't handle it. Nevertheless, I never doubted he would do just fine. Every time he finished a performance, I would remind him, "You see, Juanito, I told you everything would be fine." We would both laugh and smile. Juanito knew I was right.

Those experiences in the studios were my best performance education. I learned that things don't always work out on stage. You have to know how to cover your mistakes or make a different choice in your performance when you have no other option. We couldn't lose our cool and let the audience know we had gotten it wrong. I am not an actress, but what I learned at CMQ helped me immensely. Yet the best thing I got out of my experience at CMQ was my friendship with Johnny Rojas, which has lasted more then fifty years.

One day in 1950, when I was working at CMQ, I met a choreographer named Roderico Neyra. He had invited me to join a show he was working on. Everyone knew him as "Rodney," which was why people thought he was American. This was far from true: he made up his stage name using the first three letters of his first name, then added a "y" to the first two letters of his last name—and "Rodney" was born.

The production he was working on was to be an Afro-Cuban dance-and-music extravaganza. I'm not sure if this production was the first of its kind, but I do know it was the most successful one ever produced in Cuba. Actually, it was a sensation. The production was called *Sun Sun Ba Baé,* which I think means "the pretty bird of dawn" in Lucumí. "Zun zun," with a "z," is what Cubans call the bee hummingbird, the smallest bird in the world and native only to Cuba and whose name is derived from the sound it makes in flight. Still, there are those who say that in this case, "sun sun," with an "s," comes from the word *owl* in Lucumí, and *ba baé* comes from the Yoruba word for Saint Lazarus, known as Babalú Ayé in the Afro-Cuban pantheon.

Sun Sun Ba Baé debuted in 1951 and was truly a stunningly entertaining Afro-Cuban celebration. Structured as a musical revue, with a theme song with the same name as the title, *Sun Sun Ba Baé* was over an hour and a half long. It presented several Afro-Cuban tableaux, with me as the lead singer. I should note that the show's title song was a *guaracha,* a popular genre of Cuban music born out of Afro-Cuban religious rituals with which I would always be closely associated.

The show opened with modern dancers, singers, and Cuban dancing icons such as Olga Chaviano, who would famously emerge on stage reclining on a palanquin carried by black men, one at each corner. It was certainly a sight to see. Everyone thought so.

There was another scene in the show with a stunning American blonde whom everyone called "Skippy." I never knew her real name, and for that matter I never saw her again after the show closed, but Skippy would appear on stage sitting at a table, as if she were a tourist, listening to *batá* drums (very resonant drums used in Afro-Cuban religious rituals) while watching a group of blacks dancing to their rhythm. Suddenly, a *santo* would overtake her—or, in other words, she would be possessed by a spirit—and she would begin dancing with the other blacks on stage. As she did so, she would strip down to a bikini. Of course, those bikinis covered a lot more than they do today, but in those days, *ay,* it was scandalous.

I would then walk onto the stage, singing in Lucumí. The drums reverberated throughout the nightclub while dancers filled the stage, wildly performing their acrobatics. It was such a dramatic sight that the audience would always reward us with a standing ovation when we were through. I was told that the composer of the piece, Rogelio Martinez actually consulted with *santeros.* Rumor had it that he asked them to request permission, on his behalf, from the *orichas* to perform the music that he composed for the show. I believe I was told that the *orichas,* the gods of the Afro-Cuban pantheon, gave their approval on condition the music be somewhat different from what is played at an authentic *toque de santos,* one of the *santeros'* core percussion-based ceremonies. But who knows if this is true. Maybe it was all made up by someone in order to add more mystery to the show.

   Sun Sun Ba Baé was first staged at the Sans Souci nightclub, located on the outskirts of Havana, but was soon moved to the Tropicana, located in Havana's sister city, Marianao. It was when the show moved over to the Tropicana that it became all the rage. Rodney's smashing success with this revue actually landed him the job as director of choreography for the entire nightclub. The show made him a legend.

   Nothing could compare to the Tropicana back then. As a matter of fact, in its heyday during the 1940s and 1950s, the Tropicana was the most famous nightclub in the world. Some of the most innovative music of all time was first performed at the Tropicana. Originally, the actual club had been a weekend resort called Villa Mina, but Victor Correa and his wife, Teresita España, converted it into an outdoor nightclub and opened its doors to the public on New Year's Eve 1931. It was such an amazing place that it was known as "El Paraíso Bajo las Estrellas" ("Paradise Under the Stars"). When Rodney was put in charge of the club's choreography, he became world-famous.

   When I started working at the Tropicana in its glory days, it was already under the ownership of Martín Fox, who in 1953 enclosed part of the outdoor nightclub under dazzling arches made up entirely of colored glass. I still consider it one of the most beautiful places I've ever performed in. I've heard that the regime that governs Cuba today has recently tried to revive the look and feel of those days, but in my opinion, they're just wasting their time. Sometimes trying to recapture the glory of the past is simply impossible.

Apart from the visual spectacle of *Sun Sun Ba Baé,* Rodney created the all-female performance group Las Mulatas de Fuego (the Blazing Mulatto Women) in 1948. This was one of his most groundbreaking and successful endeavors. Those women could stop traffic anywhere. Rodney made sure to recruit the most gorgeous mulatto women who ever graced this earth. Even today there are people who are fascinated with Las Mulatas. I should note that there was more than one troupe of Mulatas. For instance, when the original Mulatas and I were touring in Mexico, back in Cuba Rodney formed another troupe to perform in our absence, and when we returned to Havana, he formed yet another troupe, which he sent off to perform in Argentina. The original Mulatas were Vilma Valle, Elena Burke, Olga Socarrat, Marta Castillo (whose mother didn't allow her to travel outside of Havana), Mercedes Montaner, Anita Arias, Meche Lafayette, and Fefa, whom we called Simaya. With the passing of years, I have been reunited with some of them, and once in a while I hear how one or the other is doing. But after the current Cuban regime took over my country, everything fell apart, and as a result, the four Mulatas troupes ceased to exist. In my opinion, it was a real shame. The world would be a better place if a new generation of Las Mulatas was to perform once again.

Las Mulatas actually launched their career in Havana's Fausto Theater. I sang, they danced. I still remember some of the songs I performed with them, such as "La Puntillita," "Meneíto pa' Aquí, Meneíto pa' Cá," and "Pulpa de Tamarindo." I don't remember who was the orchestra conductor in that theater, but I do remember that Fredo Vargas was the pianist. The show began with an instrumental overture. I would then walk onto the stage singing, with the Mulatas following. One by one, they would glide behind me and onto the stage, wearing plumed costumes. Not only were they a beautiful sight, they were also unique: there was nothing like them anywhere. With a full house every night, we were very lucrative for the club. When our run at the Fausto was over in 1949, we were such a success that we were invited to tour Venezuela. While there, I took the opportunity to record a few songs with the Sonora Caracas Orchestra, with the singer Luis Alfonso Larraín, and with the Leonard Melody Orchestra.

Things went pretty well for the Mulatas and me in that luscious Andean country. However, I do remember a promoter named Guillermo Arenas who hired us and had the brilliant idea of booking us at a theater in the middle of carnival. God only knows what he was thinking when he scheduled us, given that during carnival, people want to enjoy themselves out in the street, not in a stuffy theater. There were some lonely nights where we had to applaud ourselves because we didn't have a single person in the audience.

Our experience at Venezuelan nightclubs was the exact opposite. We were hired by a nightclub called La Taberna del Silencio (the Quiet Tavern). I always found that name to be strange, since it was a nightclub and was far from silent. In any case, we performed there for three months to a packed audience every night. Las Mulatas and I performed so many times that I memorized all their numbers. One day, one of the Mulatas got sick, and I told Elena Burke, "Don't worry. I know all the numbers. I can take her place." In retrospect, I'm not sure why I ever came up with that idea. Elena answered, "Will you, *negra*? Thanks a lot. Here's the outfit." I got dressed and put on my makeup, and just when I was about to go on stage, I froze. I couldn't go on. I just couldn't.

I stood there for a while, and then I ran back to the dressing room. When Elena came backstage, she asked, "What happened to you? Why didn't you come out?" and I answered, "*Negra,* forgive me, but I couldn't. I felt naked. There were so many people out there looking at us. Sorry, honey, but I just couldn't." Elena couldn't stop laughing at me. Needless to say, I never offered to play the role of a Mulata again. I sang the songs. It was what I was good at, and I stuck to it.

While touring with Las Mulatas, I always managed to find small side engagements. I had such an opportunity with a gentleman named Victor Saulman, a major player in Venezuelan radio. Mr. Saulman booked me for Radio Caracas. After they auditioned me, I performed in four shows sponsored by a Venezuelan cigarette company. At Radio Caracas I also met a renowned young tenor named Alfredo Sadel. We met in the foyer of the radio studio as we waited for our respective programs to air. It was a studio that would be the setting for many of the most enduring relationships in my life.

I should note that I had already been to Venezuela before I toured there with Las Mulatas or, later, with the Sonora Matancera Orchestra. In 1949, I toured Maracaibo with another all-female orchestra, Anacaona. Conchita Castro founded Anacaona in 1932 with her three sisters and four friends and named her band in honor of a legendary Cuban Indian princess of the Siboney tribe. Conchita had ten sisters, and as the years passed, all eleven of them became part of the troupe. In the 1930s, there were other all-female Cuban ensembles, such as the Loló Soldevilla Orchestra, the Edén Habanera Orchestra, and the Ensueño Orchestra, as well as many others whose names I don't recall. I performed only with Anacaona. It was a marvelous experience to work with a large group of women like that. It was like having ten sisters whom you could count on for anything. All doors opened for us wherever we went. Like my time with Las Mulatas, my experience with Anacaona would remain in my soul forever.

In 1949, Las Mulatas and I traveled to Mexico City, where we performed in the Folies Bergères Theater and in a nightclub called the Zombie. There was a club with the same name in Havana, but I don't know which came first. A Cuban named Heriberto Pino, who would later flee Cuba for exile in Spain, owned the one in Mexico City. Our shows at the Zombie club were always well received, and we spent a total of five months there, from July to the end of the month of November. It was during that time that I met Don Vallejo, the (then) major star of Mexican radio. Many years later, I would become godmother to his son.

After we returned to Havana, we began to tour frequently. Most entertainers tended to travel by ship, but we traveled on Cubana Airlines, because going by sea took too long and our schedules were too tight. Back then, traveling by air was a real luxury. Even though the seats weren't as comfortable as they are today, we were given excellent service on those flights. Have things changed! The food they serve nowadays doesn't compare with the Cuban sandwiches they fed us back then. Granted, they do treat you better in first class these days, but it still does not compare at all with the friendly service we were given on those Cubana flights.

All this happened before my time with the legendary Sonora Matancera Orchestra. I should note briefly that I also recorded before I began performing with the Sonora Matancera. I don't remember exactly what the circumstances were that gave me the chance to record for the first time, and maybe it was just destiny, but I recorded my first record in Cuba in 1950 with a group called Puchito. The group was renowned for its *batá* drums. I followed that recording with a couple of songs I sang with a group with which I had already performed at Radio Cadena Azul called La Gloria Matancera. I also recorded with a gentleman they called "Don Galán," who I think had something to do with the Venezuelan Sonora Caracas Orchestra. I remember him well because he never paid me, and at the time, I really needed the money. No real harm was done, but I suppose it says a lot that I remember him so clearly. Although things like this do happen in show business, I still think it is a wonderful business. Although not an easy one, the business has more rewards than drawbacks. I don't deny that it has a shady side, but like everything, it depends on the character of the people you choose to surround yourself with.

Everybody in show business seemed to respect me, but the only person I had yet to win over was my father. I thought it was important that he know more about what I did for a living. Because women in show business were frowned upon, it wasn't unusual for girls to run away from their parents when they wanted to be entertainers. Back then, people used to say, "We're terribly humiliated. One of the girls in our family has become an entertainer."

Nowadays, child performers are taken to work by their own mothers. Times have changed, and in that respect, I'm glad they have. I never believed that female entertainers couldn't be decent, not even when my father was a young man. When I first started performing in Cuba, all you needed was talent and self-respect. One had no need to bed a bandleader or a radio station manager. I once knew a young woman in the business who got involved with an *alleged* businessman and did a lot of stupid things with him. It turned out that the man wasn't who he claimed to be. Poor thing, she really believed in him. She got into trouble and died during childbirth. Unfortunately, there are too many impressionable young women who make terrible mistakes in their attempt to make their dreams a reality. This pains me tremendously. All you have to do is respect yourself and everyone else will respond in kind. I've always held to this belief.

Thank God I realized at a young age that good manners are more important than beauty and that perseverance is more important than connections. With this mantra, I continued down the path I was on and, with the exception of my father, my family always supported me. My father was ashamed of me and wouldn't tell anyone I even existed. Fortunately, all of that changed one day.

My father was at work, and one of his co-workers showed him a newspaper and said, "Look, Simón, this girl has your last name! Is she related to you?" When my father saw that the newspaper article talked only about my talent and nothing else, he finally realized I never was what he thought I had become. He realized I was still a good girl and that no matter how filled with "nightlife" my world became, I would always remain the good girl both he and my mother had raised. That evening, when he returned home, the two of us had a long, one-on-one conversation. He explained why he had been so opposed to my artistic career, and for the first time, I was able to understand his position. He finally told me he trusted me, and from that moment on he would never again deny I was his daughter. This happened in 1949. To this day, when I remember our conversation, tears come to my eyes.

At the beginning of 1950, I started working at Radio Cadena Suaritos, where they already knew me, and I stayed there for about a year and a half. The station's headline attractions were Amelita Prades and Candita Batista, who also recorded exclusively for that station. I was hired as a backup singer for Amelita and Candita and was never allowed to sing solo. Once, Mr. Laureano Suárez, the owner of the station and best known as "Suaritos" in the industry, did let me do a number with a singer named Charles Burke, but I was never given another opportunity to do anything special. Even that one song was barely broadcast. I don't think I was ever Suaritos's favorite.

Obdulio Morales conducted the orchestra that played on Radio Cadena Suaritos. His specialty was the *batá* drums, and he was the one responsible for teaching me so much about Lucumí music. It was during this period that I met Rodney, and after we did *Sun Sun Ba Baé,* I hoped that something else would come my way. Not in my wildest dreams did the thought of my joining the Sonora Matancera Orchestra ever cross my mind. I didn't even know who they were back then.

The first person who mentioned that orchestra to me was my cousin Nenita, when one day she told me, "Celia, do you want to hear a good band? Turn on the radio at eleven o'clock in the morning, and you'll get an earful." I did as she instructed. The moment I heard them play, my dream of performing with the Sonora Matancera was born.

After hearing the Sonora Matancera play on the radio that first time, I just couldn't get them out of my mind. Still, I remember forcing myself to bed, and when I finally fell asleep, I had a dream. I was on stage at Havana's Campoamor Theater wearing a white gown, with the Sonora Matancera playing behind me. I remember that the dream seemed so real to me at the time. I took it as a sign that someday it would come true. Luckily for me, I didn't have to wait too long.

Dos

MY GOLDEN YEARS WITH THE
SONORA MATANCERA

El tiempo y la memoria juegan juntos en nuestra historia.
Time and memory are intertwined in our common history.

—Emilio Aragón and Oscar Gómez.
Celia Cruz, "La Cuba Mia."

$\mathcal{J}n$ JUNE 1950, I WAS AN OVERWORKED EMPLOYEE AT Radio Cadena Suaritos when a gentleman known simply by his last name, Sotolongo, came to see me at the studios. He invited me to perform with the Sonora Matancera Orchestra. When I heard him utter his request, my heart almost flew out of my chest. Instantly, I remembered the dream I'd had when I saw myself performing at the Campoamor Theater, and I almost choked at the realization that it could come true.

At that time, the renowned Sonora Matancera Orchestra had a famous Puerto Rican soloist, Myrta Silva. Myrta had a successful career in Cuba, but she decided to leave the Sonora Matancera and return to Puerto Rico. With the money she had made in Cuba, she could build an enormous new home in her country, and she decided to do just that, leaving open the lead singer's spot in the orchestra. The directors of Radio Progreso, the station that broadcast *Cascabeles Candado,* a variety show sponsored by the Candado Soap Company, decided they weren't going to leave their orchestra without a female lead. It was then that they authorized Sotolongo to go to Radio Cadena Suaritos to inform me that Radio Progreso wanted to audition me for a show sponsored by a toiletries company. I remember Mr. Sotolongo saying to me, "Go to the studios, and ask for the director of the Sonora Matancera, Rogelio Martínez, and tell him I sent you." I thanked him and said my good-byes. I had a few songs left to perform before the end of the day, but I remember feeling so nervous and excited about possibly joining the Sonora that I almost couldn't finish them. Once I was free for the day, I decided to speak with Rodney and ask him for advice. Since it was Friday, I knew where to find him: Havana's América Theater.

Since we had become good friends, I remember asking Rodney, "You're Rogelio Martínez's friend. Please, introduce him to me. He's actually invited me to perform with the Sonora Matancera. Could you believe it?"

Rodney answered, "Go to the Blanquita Theater tomorrow. We'll be performing there. I'll introduce you to him."

The following day, when I arrived at the Blanquita, Rodney, Rogelio, and some other people I didn't know were waiting for me. I explained to Rogelio that Mr. Sotolongo had come looking for me and asked me to work with the Sonora in *Cascabeles Candado*. He told me, "Well, Celia, we'll be waiting for you at Radio Progreso. We rehearse there Monday through Friday, from nine to noon."

I went to mass the following Sunday so I could thank the Lord for giving me the opportunity to realize my dream. After mass I stayed to say the rosary for the good health of my mother, Tía Ana, and the rest of my family.

That Monday I got up very early. I didn't want to wake up anyone else in the house, but my mother was waiting for me in the kitchen with a cup of very sweet *café con leche*. I left the house wearing a raincoat and an umbrella. It was the rainy season, so if I wasn't careful, I could find myself soaked, which wouldn't be a great way to start my day and could prove disastrous for my audition. I arrived at Radio Progreso at a quarter to nine, nice and dry.

When I entered the studios, the first person I saw was my future husband, Pedro Knight. I later learned that he was always the first to arrive, whatever the event. When I think about those days, I am amazed by how things just fell into place. The Sonora not only made me well-known throughout the world, it also gave my Perucho, the love of my life, my "*Cabecita de Algodón*" (or "Cotton Head," as I call him since his hair turned white). Who would've imagined life would work out like this.

When I first saw him, Pedro was rehearsing his trumpet. I didn't even know his name, but he looked familiar. After I had that dream where I wore the white dress, I went to see the Sonora play at their three p.m. Radio Cadena Azul show: I think that on two or three occasions we saw each other as I left the studio and the Sonora Matancera entered. In any case, I introduced myself to Pedro and explained to him what Rogelio had told me when we met. Pedro then asked me if I had brought any musical arrangements with me, and I had. Since I was constantly looking for work with different bands, I had a repertoire and my own arrangements, which I took to all my auditions.

Pedro looked at my arrangements and noticed that I brought scores for fourteen musicians. The Sonora only had nine. He told me it would be best if I waited for Rogelio, who then pointed out the same problem. Even so, they asked me to stay, and when the other musicians arrived, we tried rehearsing a few numbers. We tried "No Queremos Chaperona" and "El Tiempo de la Colonia," but they just didn't sound right. We decided that the best thing would be to give the scores to Rogelio, and he would pass them on to the Sonora's arranger, Severino Ramos, who would adapt them to the Sonora's style.

About two weeks passed, and I was still at Radio Cadena Suaritos. An article soon appeared in a newspaper saying that

Myrta Silva was leaving the Sonora Matancera to return to Puerto Rico and that a woman by the name of Celia Cruz was replacing her.

When Mr. Suárez, the owner of the station, found out, he fired me with the following words: "This coming Friday is your last day here." By throwing me out on the street, Suaritos was, in effect, leaving me to starve. The job with the Sonora wasn't concrete yet. Suaritos paid me next to nothing, but back then any money was good money to me, since I had to help my family with all the finances. Given that I didn't have a phone at home, I had to go to the corner grocery store to call Radio Progreso to check on the status of my singing with the orchestra. Each time I called, I'd ask the receptionist, "Excuse me, ma'am, has Mr. Rogelio Martínez asked that someone call for me?" And she would answer, "No, not yet. Wait a little longer." I was becoming a bit desperate, since my family was going through some tough financial times.

Finally, the day arrived. It was the end of July 1950 when I got Rogelio on the phone. He said to me, "Please come in. The arrangements are ready for your audition." Oh, Lord! I was so relieved and happy! I ran home to tell Ollita and the family that, at last, I was really going to audition with the Sonora.

I debuted with the Sonora Matancera Orchestra on August 3, 1950. My entire family sat in the studio's front row. My cousin Serafín, who had been so instrumental in the building of my singing career, was thrilled that afternoon. Sadly, Serafín never lived to see me blossom as a singer with the Sonora. He passed away shortly after my debut.

The Sonora Matancera changed my life. Musically, the band was excellent. People still listen with awe to the music the

Sonora recorded back then. I have always said that the Sonora was a great orchestra way before I joined it. I will always consider the members of the band my brothers. I have to make it clear that I never officially joined the Sonora, I was simply their invited guest. When they went on tour, they not only took me along, they usually invited the Puerto Rican singer Daniel Santos to come along as well.

Some people are confused as to my role with the Sonora because they don't understand that I was under contract to Radio Progreso, and not the Sonora, to perform on their *Cascabeles Candado* show. The program included a comedy segment, starring "Mamacusa Alambrito," a character created by the comedian Echegoyen. After he performed, we'd perform three songs between segments. I first sang together with Bienvenido Granda, and then Daniel Santos would arrive and all three of us sang together. It was on that same program that the greatest male voice of Cuban popular music, Beny Moré, performed with the Sonora.

When I began with the Sonora, Bienvenido Granda was the orchestra's singer. He had a huge mustache, and that's why people called him "the Singing Mustache." He joined the Sonora the same year Pedro did, in 1944. Pedro joined the orchestra on January 6 of that year, and Bienvenido joined in December. When Humberto Cané, the Sonora's previous singer, retired, he recommended Bienvenido, and the Sonora hired him immediately.

Pedro once told me that the night Bienvenido debuted with the Sonora, they were set to play for a dance at a place very holy to Cubans. El Rincón was a former leper colony and a sanctuary dedicated to Saint Lazarus. It was located in a town close to Havana called Santiago de las Vegas. The Sonora had been hired to play at the celebration of the eve of Saint Lazarus Day—that is,

December 16. Back then, the Sonora had a Buick that became famous throughout Cuba, since in the 1950s there were only two cars of that make on the island. The car sat seven, but all of us managed to squeeze in. On the way to Santiago de las Vegas, it ran out of gas. All of them, except for Rogelio—who was driving—had no choice but to get out and push. Nine of them, dressed in tuxedos, had to push that heavy car a long way. Pedro was so frustrated that he kicked it. The kick hurt Pedro far more than it did the car. His kick didn't even leave a scratch, but poor Pedro ended up with a bad knee that nagged him for quite a long time. It was on that trip to Santiago de las Vegas that Bienvenido debuted with the Sonora Matancera. When he left the orchestra, Celio González and Estanislao Sureda (whom we all called "Laíto") replaced him.

Daniel Santos joined the Sonora the same way I did. In other words, the radio station hired him as a special guest of the orchestra. Daniel was a true master of music, but there was something strange about him. Although we worked so closely together, he never talked about his family. He mentioned absolutely nothing about his personal life, although I knew he had children. I remember him feeling passionate about his country, Puerto Rico, but he seemed to have something of a tormented soul. He and I performed together in the Blanquita Theater in Mexico City a few days before he passed away in Ocala, Florida, on November 27, 1992. It tore me apart to hear of his passing, and although we couldn't attend, I heard his funeral in Puerto Rico was an official event of the state.

Cascabeles Candado was very popular because it was the best thing on the radio. Radio Progreso had a powerful antenna that broadcast to the whole Caribbean basin, which was a blessing for the Sonora and anyone who worked at the station. Having a live show transmitted daily from such a powerful radio station enabled a band to be introduced to millions of listeners instantly. Because of the popularity of the show, as well as the strength of the antenna, people already knew who we were in Trinidad, the Netherlands Antilles, Haiti, and Santo Domingo before we even toured there. I should note here that whenever we were invited to tour the Dominican Republic, we were always asked to parties given by that country's most beloved singer, the legendary Casandra Damiron, whom I will forever admire.

Yet even with the excitement of the time, not everything was perfect. I had my fans and detractors at Radio Progreso. There were many people who applauded me, but there were others who were still Myrta Silva fans and, as a result, didn't want me there at all. They'd call the station, they'd write letters to the station manager, Manolo Fernández, to Rogelio, and to me, saying that my voice didn't match well with the Sonora sound. I was given the letters addressed to me, and if they had constructive criticism, I would find a way of improving, but if all they did was insult me, I would immediately throw them out. Still, those negative letters did sadden me deeply. It hurts when you give the best of yourself and people illogically reject you just because you're not who they want you to be. Oh, Lord, only You know how helpful Tía Ana's advice was to me! She used to say, "Don't be insecure, mi niña. Only God understands why He does what He does. You just keep going. If there're people who reject you, love yourself even more. Never bow your head to anyone." I found strength and love in her advice every day. I learned to thank God for everything, even the hard times, since that's the way He chose to teach me about life. What I needed to know to make me the person I wanted to be, He would provide.

Since my family counted on my financial support, I couldn't even consider giving up. I concentrated on what I had to do. I learned my numbers, I never missed any rehearsals, I always arrived early, I worked well with others, and I wore the best clothes I could afford. God may not have given me a pretty face, but He gave me many gifts. I learned how to make the best of those gifts. Actually, I think my core values and work ethic have been my life's best assets.

The 1950s were a special time for me. It was a prosperous and hopeful time. Everything seemed to have reached its zenith. There was a lot of artistic energy flowing around Cuba back then, and composers were dying to have the Sonora play their pieces on the radio. What's more, Rogelio had a good ear for what would work, and he had the knack for matching great songs with the appropriate singers.

He was responsible for my first recording with the Sonora. Rogelio had already told me that he wanted to record with me, so I just had to wait for him to tell me when. One day, I arrived at Radio Progreso and was told that a man named Mr. Siegel was visiting.

Sydney Siegel was an American who worked with the Seeco label, the same recording company that had the exclusive rights to record the Sonora. We called him "MEE-ster SEE-gol." He went to hear the program, and when he spoke to the Sonora's conductor, Rogelio informed him he wanted to record with me. Siegel told Rogelio that he was crazy and that he didn't want to give me a recording contract. But Rogelio insisted, and he told Siegel that it was he who decided whom he recorded with and nobody else. Siegel insisted that women didn't sell records and were good only for live performances. He told Rogelio that even sales for an important singer like Libertad Lamarque, the Argentine tango singer who became one of the greatest entertainers in the Spanish-speaking world, had been declining. How did Rogelio expect to get anywhere with me when an entertainer on the scale of Libertad was not selling well?

But Rogelio knew Siegel was wrong, since Mexican female singers such as Toña La Negra, Eva Garza, Elvira Ríos, and Maria Luisa Landín were selling extremely well. He tried explaining to Siegel that he shouldn't mix apples and oranges. Siegel wouldn't budge. Still, Rogelio insisted. Finally, they agreed that if the record didn't sell, Seeco wouldn't have to pay out, that Sonora would be responsible for paying me. I recorded a single with two songs, "Cao, Cao, Maní Picao" and "Mata Siguaraya." The record was a hit throughout Cuba. After recording that first single, I never had a problem with either the public or Sidney Siegel again. Rogelio later told me that after I recorded that record, Siegel gave him full creative control. As a result, I recorded a total of seventy-four albums with the Sonora Matancera and Seeco. We recorded a new record every three months for fifteen years. I thank Rogelio for the opportunity he gave me. In the beginning, it was a challenge for me to perform with the Sonora, since they were so famous and I was relatively new to the industry, but Rogelio helped me all he could. He truly believed in me. I may be a determined, hardworking woman, but it was the dream that God sent me, which continued to inspire me, along with Rogelio's backing, that allowed me to reach the success I had back then. I will be grateful eternally to him for all he did for me.

The Sonora kept performing on the radio and in nightclubs

until we had the opportunity to tour Haiti. Bienvenido and I were the singers who went. We had a wonderful time, and we sold out everywhere we performed. My greatest memory of our trip to Haiti was meeting the marvelous Haitian singer and dancer Marthe Jean-Claude. I invited her to visit Cuba, and she honored me by coming to see me in Havana. In 1952, she performed at the Tropicana, and while in Cuba, we recorded a very popular duet called "Chaque Une."

From day one it was a pleasure to work with the guys from the Sonora. It was like having nine brothers. They took good care of me and were always helpful. They were perfect gentlemen. Whenever we traveled together to another Latin American country, no man ever dared to cross the line with me, because if he did, all nine of the Sonora men would come to my defense. Those guys, my brothers, didn't care who it was; they would protect me from anyone who tried anything. It could've been a general or a president, and they'd still defend me.

One day, when we were on tour in another country—I won't say which one—there was a powerful general who insisted on not leaving me alone. I started walking faster toward our car, but he kept following me. Suddenly, the Sonora's car doors opened, and all at once, out came nine talented black guys poised to protect me. Needless to say, the general almost had a coronary. When I traveled with the Sonora, I didn't need a chaperone, although my cousin Nenita did chaperone me on trips I took without the orchestra. I remember that when she and I traveled alone, we would secure a chair against the door before falling asleep or even use the bed to jam the door shut, so no one could get into our room. A single girl could never be too careful on the road.

Apart from the protection and professional support they all

gave me, the guys from the Sonora and I became close friends, especially Pedro, Caíto, and Lino Frías. Caíto used to call me "Herma," short for *hermana* ("sister"). In all, the experience of working with the Sonora was a daily education in Cuban musical history. Without the Sonora, I wouldn't be where I am today.

Many opportunities came my way thanks to the Sonora. Back in the early fifties, it was not uncommon for singers to record jingles promoting cigarettes, juices, and other commercial products. But what they tended to show the public on television was a blond woman or a white man singing with dubbed voices. Blacks were not on television.

I recorded jingles for Candado soap, Barcardí rum, Coca-Cola, H. Upmann cigars, Guarina cheese, Colonia 1800 cologne, Pilón coffee, Jupiña pineapple soft drink, Partagás cigars, and Hatuey beer and the theme song for the variety show *Casino de la Alegría* (*The Happiness Casino*). A few years back, a man named Omar Marchánt gave me a cassette recording of most of the jingles I recorded. It was a wonderful surprise. The jingles themselves were marvelous, but they paid us virtually nothing for recording them. I remember that the owners of Colonia 1800 cologne paid me only twenty-one pesos for recording their jingle. We were usually paid fifty. I'm not even sure why I agreed to do it. In those days, though, one did what one was told. I loved to sing, and any opportunity to do so was great to me. Even twenty-one-peso opportunities.

Someone once said that I was a "pioneer jingle singer." Before I was given a jingle, it usually had passed through four or five other singers. For instance, there was an actress named Frances Nápoli who once said to me, "Look, Celia, they've asked me to do this ad, and they want me to sing it the same way you would, but, *chica,* I just can't." Poor thing, in the end, they hired me and not her. Every time any producer tried to dub my voice using someone else's face, it just didn't work. The public wouldn't accept it. Yet they wanted my voice in the ad. I have an unusual contralto voice, and people were familiar with it, so it was effective in selling products, but the public wasn't happy hearing it come out of someone else's mouth. The producers who insisted on using a model when they thought I didn't have the look they wanted had to show their models dancing or doing something else while my voice played in the background. That's how I made it on Cuban television, which already existed by 1950, just after it had premiered in the United States. It's amazing how things happen! In two years I went from being criticized by segments of the public because I wasn't Myrta Silva to doing jingles on television, which was then the most exciting medium around.

By the mid-1950s, I had started branching out from recording and performing live on stage, radio, and television, to film. Although I have never claimed to be an actress, I made my big-screen debut in 1955. That year, God blessed me with the opportunity to work with the great Argentine comic actress Niní Marshall in a Cuban film entitled *Gallega en La Habana* (*A Spanish Woman in Havana*). Pedro also appeared in that film. I loved seeing my Perucho on the big screen, since he looked so handsome (and quite honestly still does).

Throughout that decade, I appeared in many television specials and several more movies filmed throughout Cuba, such as 1957's *Affair in Havana* with John Cassavetes and Raymond Burr. I also modeled for Allyn's, a hair care company whose products were marketed to black women. Those ads appeared in most of Cuba's major magazines.

Through it all, I kept touring the island with the Sonora. I remember during carnival in Santiago de Cuba, which used to take place at the end of July, the Bacardí Corporation always hired the Sonora and me for two weeks as their exclusive act. We also often performed in the Casino Español, in the city of Camagüey, in the Casino of Camagüey itself, in the Vertientes Sugar Plantation, and in Trinidad. We traveled throughout Cuba, with Rogelio at the wheel of the Sonora's Buick. If the trip took longer than five hours by car, as in the case of Camagüey or Santiago de Cuba from Havana, we flew. Life seemed so simple then. Everyone seemed to be having the time of their lives.

There were many people who represented entertainers then, although I didn't have an agent until much later, after having worked with the Sonora for some time. As a matter of fact, I didn't have much luck with agents. Someone later told me it was because I was ugly. Yes, I did have a pretty voice, but I didn't have the look many agents wanted to represent. I did everything without the help of an agent. Back then I learned a tremendous amount. Finally, when I started to record with the Sonora, Tito Garrote agreed to represent me.

In 1957, God gave me the privilege of traveling for the first time to the city where I would live for half my life, although I would never have dreamed it at that time. I was invited to go to New York City to perform and receive a gold record award for my recording of "Burundanga." Ironically, Sydney Siegel, the same man who did not want me to record in the first place, was going to hand me the prize.

The concert took place at the Saint Nicholas Arena in the Bronx. Machito and His Orchestra were on stage. Machito, whose real name was Frank Grillo, with his vocalist sister, Graciela, were seminal figures in the popularization of Cuban music in New York. In any event, during the concert, I suddenly heard

screaming and yelling. Everything turned into chaos. I was backstage, frightened, and a woman covered in blood ran up to me
and said, "Celia Cruz, look at me! Is this what I get for coming to
see you?"

I felt terrible. I didn't know what to say to her. The police
arrived and we were all thrown out of the theater. I have no idea
what happened. There are too many versions of the events that
inspired the mini-riot. Some people say that the Saint Nicholas
oversold tickets and the crowd got upset. Others say that we had
sold so many tickets and were so overcrowded that a nearby club,
angry at losing so much business, reported us to the police, and
for some reason the large crowd panicked (which is what I think
really happened). The whole evening was a real mess. There were
shoes left everywhere, and the following day people came to
claim their shoes and other items they'd left behind after being
hurriedly escorted out of the club. It was a terrible experience. I
have never been that frightened again. The next day, the New
York Spanish-language daily *El Diario* ran the following headline:
ANARCHY AT A CUBAN SINGER'S CONCERT. I was devastated.

The wonderful thing about show business is that
you have the opportunity to meet great people. I have met all
kinds of entertainers, composers, actors, and even heads of state.
I also got to meet the best musicians and composers of my time
when I first started out professionally in Cuba. Many of them are
still my friends.

One of the first entertainers I befriended at an early age was
Cuco Martínez. I think he originally lived in Santos Suárez, since
I remember saying hello to him from my porch as he often
walked by my house. It's frightening how small the world can
seem on an island as large as Cuba. I later met one of the greatest

of all Cuban singers, Beny Moré. Beny and I worked together in several radio shows, although I regret that we never recorded together. When you hear us singing today, what you're actually hearing are reproductions of radio shows we recorded. He was a simple and generous man who loved gardening and raising animals, among which there was a black hen he christened Celia Cruz. Beny was a wonderful individual and a great musician. Unfortunately, he was only forty-four years old when he passed away in 1963. His death saddened me for a long time.

Thanks to Beny, I met my very close friend Rolando Columbie, his pianist. We worked together a great deal back then, and I remember how he used to ask me to go to stores that sold women's clothes so I could buy presents for his secret girlfriend. What I didn't know was that this woman was my dear friend Gilda Columbie, who is now his wife. When, thirty-five years later, I found out what their link had been, I said to her, "*Chica, if I had known that the things I was buying for him were for you, I would've spent even more of his money.*" Rolando and Gilda now live in Spain, and not only do we see one another whenever Pedro and I visit, we phone one another several times a week.

As a matter of fact, people in Las Palmas think Rolando is my bodyguard, since when I'm visiting, he never leaves my side. He began doing that because there are so many fishing trawlers traveling between Cuba and Spain that, once, a ship flying the Cuban flag kidnapped two Cuban exiles right off the beach. When they whisked them away, the Cuban exiles in Miami mobilized all their resources and were able to intercept the Cuban ship when it stopped in Canada. I don't know how they managed to do it, but they were able to free the Cubans from their kidnappers, and it all ended happily. Still, Rolando worries that it may happen again, and that's why he never allows anyone near me when we stroll on the beach.

Back in the days of yesteryear's Havana, I had the great pleasure of meeting Dámaso Pérez Prado—the man responsible for turning the mambo into a worldwide craze—during one of my tours across Cuba. Many promoters, like Conde Meyrelé, hired him to play piano in the entertainment caravans that toured the island. He was an excellent pianist and arranger, and many times he accompanied me on the piano. I think he also arranged music for Cascarita, the Casino de la Playa Orchestra, and many other bands. We worked together often. As a matter of fact, the first time Pérez Prado toured Mexico, he, Las Mulatas, and I flew on the same plane together. Of course, we spoke and enjoyed each other's company during the flight, but once we arrived, he went his way, and we went ours. It was just his manner.

Ninón Sevilla, the Cuban actress and dancer who in the 1950s was so famous in Mexico that she actually made more movies than most Mexican actresses, loved to have get-togethers in her Mexico City home. That woman loved to cook! Her home was like a Cuban embassy, where politicians, writers, poets, and all kinds of crazies used to gather. I've heard that sometimes Fidel Castro and Ernesto "Che" Guevara used to go visit her at her home. Thank God I never bumped into those two while I was visiting! In any case, Ninón invited us to eat, and a few of Las Mulatas and I accepted the invitation, and again we ran into Pérez Prado. Afterward, I returned to Cuba, and I saw him once more. I asked him, "So, Prado, how are you? Anything new?" And he answered, "Everything's okay, *chica*. But I'm leaving soon. Ninón Sevilla is taking me back to Mexico." It was then that Pérez Prado left Cuba for Mexico for good.

During this time, many Cuban entertainers lived in Mexico,

since that country was—and still is—an important Spanish-speaking market. From the 1920s through the 1950s, Cuban music reigned supreme in Mexico, and that's why Cuban performers were constantly traveling between Cuba and Mexico. Among the Cuban entertainers I knew who were living in Mexico in the 1950s were Humberto Cané, Silvestre Méndez, and Joaquín González, may he rest in peace, who was the husband of my dear friend Yolanda Montes, better known as the entertainer Tongolele.

I first met Tongolele when we were both performing at the Folies Bergères Theater in Mexico City. We later started doing caravan tours together, and as the years passed, our friendship blossomed. There was a time when Tongolele, or "Yoli," as I called her, and I worked so much together that she would even fix my hair and do my makeup. We have shared many experiences together. I feel like another member of her family. Every time I arrive in Mexico, I go to her house to cook and eat good Cuban food.

I also had the pleasure of working in Mexico with the great Cuban musician Carlos "Patato" Valdés, although I had already met him in Cuba, since he had worked at Havana's Zombie club while I was performing there. I should note that I never knew that he played with the Sonora until ten years ago, when we mentioned him to a journalist, and Pedro told me that he had played with him. This surprised me, since after working so many years with the Sonora, I thought I knew everything about them. According to Pedro, Patato left the Sonora for Alberto Ruiz's Cuba Habana Orchestra. As a matter of fact, Patato was instrumental in taking Cuban music to the world. In any case, we had an intimate circle of Cuban entertainers working in Mexico at that time. We were all friends, most of us extremely close.

I also grew to admire and befriend musicians from other countries during those early years of my career. There was a Peruvian composer I respected whose name was Chabuca Granda, although her real name was María Isabel Granda. I finally met Chabuca in 1982, before she passed away, although I had been a fan of hers since the 1950s. Before joining the Sonora, I had already performed in Peru when her song "La Flor de Canela" was very popular. I liked it so much, I learned it by heart. From Peru I traveled to Mexico, where I was on my way to perform in a theater, whose name I don't recall, with several other entertainers. One day while I was waiting in their dressing room, I started to sing "La Flor de Canela," and the Peruvian band Los Hermanos Silva (the Brothers Silva), who were performing in the same show, began to accompany me. They later recorded the song on their own, and they were very successful with it. As a matter of fact, I remember that when I first heard it, I thought it would be perfect for Olga Chorens and Tony Álvarez, a married couple who were singers and who in the 1950s had their own family variety show on television. The show starred their young daughters, Lisette, who today is a singer in her own right, and Olga, who is now a news anchor for the New York affiliate of the Univision television network.

That song had such an impact on me that I spent years hoping to meet the woman who wrote it. Fortunately, Felipe Leatherstein, the sculptor and son of the owner of the Pacific Fair in Peru, the largest festival in that Andean country, knew how much I wanted to meet her. Every time I was in Peru, he would throw a party in my honor and invite celebrities from Lima's bohemian class. So in 1982, at one of these parties, Felipe surprised me by inviting Chabuca. It was wonderful to meet her, and she was very kind to me. We sang together, and she told me how happy she was that I had recorded her song "Fina Estampa." Five months after that, Chabuca fell ill and died. Sometime later, her daughter came to visit me in New York, and we reminisced about how gifted her mother had been. Chabuca's talent touched me greatly.

I also had the great pleasure of meeting and befriending the famous Franco-American singer Joséphine Baker. Joséphine was performing at a nightclub called El American, although I don't remember if it was in 1956 or 1957. What I do know is that we performed at El American together for a week, and then together we performed in Venezuela. I should note that poor Joséphine was not well received during her tour of Venezuela. Nobody seemed to want to see her perform. She spoke Spanish well, but with a heavy accent. She just couldn't understand why she didn't have a large audience in Venezuela. One day while we were on tour, Joséphine asked me, "Celia, is Venezuela always like this?" I told her yes. We had been hired to perform at Caracas's Coney Island, which, like its New York City namesake, is an outdoor amusement area not known for booking quality entertainment. For Joséphine the apprehensive reception was very unusual, since she was used to performing before adoring crowds in France. Joséphine and I toured with the great Cuban musician and my friend Miguelito Valdés, the original "Mr. Babalú," and the singer Evangelina Elizondo.

Joséphine's show in Venezuela was more or less the same one she always performed in Paris and New York. Her signature songs, like "Merci Beaucoup," were the same, and she couldn't change it much in Caracas, since the stage we were given wasn't up to it. Her show was just too beautiful and her costumes too regal for the kind of people who were attracted to the Coney Island in Venezuela. All you had there were a lot of young people running around, dancing, and carrying on. Joséphine was a refined singer. Although she had a pretty voice, it wasn't very strong, so the audiences in Caracas didn't pay any attention to her. She would leave the stage, go through a costume change, and return, and still the audience ignored her. People went to Coney Island to rumba, merengue, and dance Cuban *guaracha*. It was not the kind of place for an entertainer of her caliber. Poor thing. She had an awful time in Venezuela.

On the other hand, Mexico went very well for her. There she worked closely with the Cuban choreographers Roberto and Mitsuko, a married couple whose names are actually Roberto Gutiérrez and Mitsuko Miguel and who are still dear friends of mine. Roberto and Mitsuko, whom I lovingly call "Los Misukos," choreographed a fantastic show in Mexico City for her in 1961. It was so successful that Joséphine herself asked them to stage it for her in Paris's Lido nightclub. Years later, we were reunited when she performed at the Westside in New York. I had great admiration for Joséphine Baker.

When I recall my life, I realize just how many people I loved like siblings who have passed away. It used to make me sad, especially when I thought of my brothers from the Sonora Matancera who are also gone. But I've come to realize that this is just a temporary separation. We will meet again in the afterlife. I thank God, however, that there are a few people from that time who are still living.

Among them is my dear friend Matilde Díaz. In Cuba, I used to listen to a radio station called Radio Continente. Since I've always been an early riser, I would listen to a Colombian band called the Lucho Bermúdez Orchestra at seven o'clock. They played very nice music, mostly with clarinets, and Matilde was their singer. I eventually became a big fan of theirs, so one day in 1951, when I found out they were performing at Radio Cadena Azul, I ran to see them. When I arrived at the studio, I was informed that they'd already left but that I could find them at a nearby hotel. To the hotel I went.

I arrived at the hotel and asked if I could speak to them. Lucho came down to see me. I told him my name and that I was a great fan of theirs. I remember Lucho being very kind. I didn't meet Matilde that night, though. I say we met in 1950, but Matilde says it was in 1952. In any case, it really doesn't matter, since regardless of when we met in Cuba, we immediately became the best of friends. When Matilde and the Lucho Bermúdez Orchestra didn't perform in Havana's Tropicana nightclub and were off to work in Mexico, Matilde and I would even write to each other. We became pen pals.

Throughout the 1950s, my recordings could be heard everywhere, but it wasn't until "Burundanga" became a megahit throughout Latin America that I was invited to perform in Colombia. Lucho and Matilde originally were from Medellín, although they later lived in Bogotá. Every time we toured Colombia we started in Cartagena and from there went to Medellín. When we ended up in Bogotá, we would spend time together. All four of us became close, and even after they separated, I continued being friends with both of them. I am even the godmother of their daughter, Gloria María.

In 1993, Matilde celebrated her fiftieth anniversary as a stage performer, and at that celebration, we both sang "Burundanga" together. Lucho passed away in 1994, but Matilde and I both recorded a duet, "Las Pilanderas," in 1996. As far as I'm concerned, Matilde is the best Colombian singer of all time.

The list of the friends I made during my professional days in Havana is very long, since my work with the Sonora allowed me to associate with many wonderful people. By the end of the 1950s, I was already known as "La Guarachera de Cuba," which of all the titles ever bestowed on me is the one I hold closest to my heart. I believe that it reflects my roots as a humble singer of Cuban popular dance music. La Guarachera had become a success, so I finally had the financial means to realize one of my greatest dreams: building a brand-new house for the woman to whom I owed it all.

I wanted to give my mother all I could, because if it hadn't been for her, I would never have realized my artistic potential. First she gave me life, then she encouraged me to pursue my dreams wholeheartedly and even helped me to face my father. I purchased two plots of land at 110 Terraza Street in Havana's Lawton neighborhood solely for her. The plans were to build the house on one plot and to have the other one turned into a garden. Unfortunately, the construction process didn't go very well. I was in charge of the project and would get so upset when, every day, the contractors gave me a new story about why materials were so hard to come by, given the country's political instability. Since I couldn't wait for my mother to move, I was becoming increasingly desperate.

But God always comes to the rescue. One day, my friend María Hermida invited me to perform at a party in a ranch some distance from Havana, and I went and performed. To my surprise, the president of Cuba, General Fulgencio Batista y Zaldívar, was among the guests. Since my house in Lawton was only half-built, I decided that the president would probably have some idea how I could go about completing it. When I was finished performing, I came down from the stage, and "El General" approached and congratulated me. I decided that it was now or never and explained the problem I was having with the contractors. Batista immediately called one of his aides and asked him to make sure I was allowed to buy, without delay, all the materials necessary for the completion of the new house. Finally, Ollita's new home would soon be finished.

I will never forget the day we moved into that house. Once it was completed, we had it cleaned and furnished. I remember spending a few weeks in Havana's most elegant department store, El Encanto, buying everything one might need for a new house. Although I must admit that I've never liked shopping in department stores, I wanted Ollita to have everything she needed. I also had it beautifully decorated so it would look perfect when she first stepped foot in it. We planned a party, and we had a priest come and bless it.

When my mother entered her new home, her surprise and joy were so great that my eyes welled with tears. Oh Lord, it was such a wonderful moment! And since I have always been as devoted to Our Lady of Charity—the beautiful mulatto patroness of Cuba and my namesake—as I was to my mother, I had a shrine erected for her in front of the house. I made a vow that from that day on, September 8, on the eve of her day, I would throw a party every year in honor of Our Lady of Charity. The celebrations that I held for Our Lady of Charity in the Lawton house became famous throughout Havana.

We lived a comfortable and calm life in that house in Lawton. Unfortunately, the blessings we were enjoying were about to end, although when change did come, most of us simply couldn't believe it.

One day in 1958, after noticing she looked drained, I took

Ollita to the doctor for a few tests. Although she obviously looked ill, I was stunned when the doctor told me she was gravely ill. I remember the doctor saying, "I still have to confirm it, and I want you to get a second opinion from Dr. Manuel Doval Valiente at the Mercedes del Puerto Hospital for Special Surgery."

I felt panicked. I stared into his eyes, and I realized he was dead serious. We were alone in a small room so that my mother wouldn't hear our conversation. "Look, Doctor," I said, "I don't understand what you're trying to say. What's really going on with my mother?"

The doctor said, "Celia, your mother has cancer, and she won't be able to beat it. Please, go and talk with my colleague, and see what he has to say."

I grabbed Ollita by the hand, and off we went to see Dr. Doval.

We didn't hear good news from him, either. He explained, "Indeed, Celia, your mother has cancer in her bladder. But you're not going to lose her right away. She'll live another two years. And if you take really good care of her, she might live four."

I asked the doctor what I had to do, and he gave me detailed instructions. The most important thing was to be mindful of her nutrition. Although Ollita loved to eat pork, I wanted her to nourish herself with better food. I started feeding her lobster, shrimp, rare fish, and other seafood she loved. We fed her fruit shakes and vegetable juices. We fed her anything that might make her stronger. We made sure that she had no reason to get upset, and we all took turns caring for her. She was never alone. When it became necessary to give her injections and medicine, we hired a nurse. We followed the doctor's instructions to a T. My beautiful mother lasted four years and a few months.

As expected, my mother's health became the focal point of my life. That—coupled with the increasingly unstable political situation of Cuba in 1958—convinced me that I had to secure a steady income. Although tours took me away from my mother, I had to take them when the opportunity arose, since they paid better than performing in Havana. When Batista left Cuba and the *barbudos* ("bearded men") took over in January 1959, I was performing in Mexico in a nightclub called El Afro. I read the details of the turmoil unfolding in Cuba in the Mexican press, and I immediately called home to find out what was really happening. It was too radical a change for Cuba, and everyone was extremely frightened. I decided then that as soon as my contract with El Afro expired, I would return to Cuba. I left Mexico for Havana on a sparkling new Braniff airplane on January 28, 1959.

Cuba was in an exceptionally chaotic state of affairs. I was shocked when I descended the stairs from the plane at Havana's José Martí Airport, the same airport through which I had departed and returned so many times, and saw that it had been totally militarized. A few minutes later, I knew that things had really changed when the customs agents rudely asked to see my passport. Pedrito, one of my chauffeurs, was waiting for me outside the terminal. As soon as he saw me, he pushed me into the car and told me that Cuba would never be the same. He was actually the first person to say something like that to me.

The following months were terrible. It was like living in a state of agony. People began losing their jobs, the regime closed all the casinos, and all corporations and companies were expropriated by the state. Cuba's growing prosperity was being systematically destroyed. It seemed that the *barbudos* had set out to destroy the Cuban people's innate good nature and solid standard of living.

In the early months of 1959, I tried to live as normal a life as possible, but it was impossible to do so. I was soon invited by Miguel Ángel Quevedo, the publisher of *Bohemia*—at that time the magazine with the highest circulation in the Spanish-speaking world—to perform at a party he was throwing in his home. He hired me to sing, accompanied by a pianist, on a terrace overlooking the pool. In those days, Fidel, "El Diablo," still conducted himself as if he were an honest person and continued living the good life in many places throughout Havana. As I was performing, I saw everybody running toward the door. I immediately realized what all the commotion was about when I saw Fidel Castro. All the guests ran off to greet him, because at that time many people still supported him. But something inside me kept saying he wasn't to be trusted. Mr. Quevedo approached me and said, "Celia, Fidel wants to meet you. He says that he used to clean his gun to your song 'Burundanga' while he was in the mountains during the insurgency."

Without being curt or rude, I answered, "With all due respect, Mr. Quevedo, you hired me to sing and stand next to this piano, so I think my place is right here. If that man wants to meet me, let him come to me." When Fidel realized that the pianist and I were the only ones there who weren't giving him the red carpet treatment, his own arrogance kept him from approaching us.

When the regime began confiscating all private businesses in 1959, all radio and television stations were taken over by government agents, and their programming changed radically. Once they started exclusively to broadcast propaganda, the situation became unbearable. Our professional future in Cuba seemed bleak. Freedom of artistic expression did not seem to rank high on the regime's agenda. It was soon after realizing this that the

Sonora and I began preparing to leave for Mexico, where work was guaranteed.

In early 1960, I was informed through official channels that there would be a show at Havana's Blanquita Theater in which several bands and singers were to perform. I was expected to be there. After rehearsal, the show's director suddenly gathered us all to one side and told us that we would have a very special guest that evening and that after we were finished on stage, we had to go down and greet him and his entourage. Apparently, these people thought they deserved to be honored in such a manner. Almost all the entertainers who performed that night—whose names I won't mention, since almost all of them are now living in exile—went to greet him and even had their pictures taken with him.

Minutes before I went on stage I was asked to sing "Burundanga," but since I was friendly with all the musicians, we made believe that none of them knew the number and that we didn't have the score. I went on stage, and I think I sang "Cao, Cao, Mani Picao." When I finished, the audience applauded, but I didn't wait for them to finish. I turned and walked off stage. I knew Fidel was sitting in the front row, but I can't say whether or not I saw him, since I tried to avoid looking in his direction. His presence revolted me. As I was walking down the steps back to the dressing rooms, the artistic director approached me and said, "Celia, I'm sorry, but I can't pay you. You're the only one who hasn't shown El Comandante the respect he deserves. You should know that this show was produced by the new regime."

I answered, "If I have to belittle myself to make money, I'd rather not have any."

It was upon leaving the Blanquita Theater that I finally understood why El Diablo repulsed me so. I realized that by way of his arrogance and despotism, he was destroying all free expression and artistic freedom in Cuba. He had turned what once was beautiful into a weapon to prove how he could control others. As the months passed in that year of 1959, I realized just to what extent he wanted to control everything, and I refused to become another act in his circus. The regime would actually send its agents to fetch me at home to perform at their events. My poor brother, Bárbaro, would answer the door while I hid in an armoire and would tell them I wasn't in Havana. By the end of 1959, people were in fear of one another; all trust had vanished. Some people who had been my friends, and even some relatives, had become spies for the regime. It was brother against brother, and all due to the fear that people had of that demon, who would be nothing without the terror he inflicted on others. Demons like Castro aren't born, they're made, and they get their strength from manipulating and destroying others. I just don't understand why Cubans didn't realize that earlier in the revolution, before it was too late to do anything.

I remember that one day early in 1960, as I arrived to perform one of my last shows at CMQ Studios, I saw my friend actor Amaury Pérez leaving the building. When Amaury saw me, he ran toward the car I was exiting. Anyone who's seen pictures of me from back then knows that I used to collect gold coins, and I actually had around twenty bracelets made from them. When Amaury approached me, he said, "Celia, they want you to donate your jewelry to the revolution in the middle of the TV show." As soon as he walked away, I removed all my bracelets right there as I stood on the sidewalk and wrapped them in newspaper; then I crossed the street in the direction of an old lady I recognized because I bought coffee from her every day. I handed her all the jewelry I had on and asked her to hold it for me until I returned to pick it up. When I entered the CMQ Studios, someone asked me why I wasn't wearing my bracelets. I answered, "Because everything's changing too fast in Cuba, and you never know when you might bump into someone who suddenly wants to take away what belongs to you." I wasn't able to wear jewelry again until I left Cuba.

By the end of 1959, traditional Cuban entertainment had taken a backseat to politics. The regime used the media exclusively to promote its agenda. Virtually all of the written press had been suppressed and replaced by government-run publications, and since the regime had taken over all television and radio studios, they dedicated their programming almost exclusively to Soviet-style propaganda, long-winded speeches, hate speech, show trials, and executions of "enemies" by firing squad, the majority of which were conducted under the direction of Che Guevara. As a result, most of the entertainers who wanted to keep performing had to sing the praises of the regime. Sadly, for people such as my brothers from the Sonora and myself, who did not agree with what was happening to Cuba, the future looked bleak. I was worried, since I had to work to ensure that my mother continued to receive excellent care. But God had mercy on me, and I was finally offered a contract for a few months at Mexico City's La Terraza Cassino nightclub. The Sonora was offered a contract in that same city's Lírico Theater. I was torn about leaving because of my mother, and she knew it. That's the kind of relationship we always had. Whatever I felt, she felt, too, without my having to say one word.

I believe that all mothers are good, and we should always thank them for having given us life. But there are those mothers who are truly special, and mine was one of those. My Ollita knew how to love me unconditionally. She understood what made me happy and what was good for me. She never wanted to monopolize me, like many mothers. My mother gave me wings, and although she knew that one day I would leave her nest, she never asked me to give anything up for her sake. I have no way of thanking her for that now, but I hope she feels my gratitude.

One afternoon, I returned home and found her sitting in her rocking chair. I approached her and gave her a kiss. I remember her asking me to sit down. I did, and she said, "Honey, don't worry about me. You can't stop that right now. Your future is calling you. If you have to take that job in Mexico, do so. Of course, I would love for you to stay with me, but since that's impossible, I give you my blessing. Go." I started crying and began to hug her. Although she felt so tiny in my arms, I knew that she was the strongest person in my life. She taught me how to persevere and not to give up if life threw me curves. That's what my mother was like, tough and resourceful. I think of her every day.

I accepted the offer from La Terraza Cassino in Mexico, and Rogelio took charge of all the bureaucratic procedures so that the Sonora would be allowed to leave Cuba. We had all the documents we needed, except the exit visa requirement that the regime had imposed because so many people were desperately fleeing the country. Of course, the process to secure the exit permits was becoming increasingly complicated. I never found out exactly what Rogelio had to do to get approval for all our exit visas, but he got them. It's only in retrospect that I now realize Rogelio was the only one among us who knew we would never return to Cuba.

When you go on a long trip, you always have a lot of things to get done before you leave. Leaving Cuba for Mexico on that occasion was no exception. As could be expected, Ollita was doing more or less well. Tía Ana, my guardian angel, would give me advice, look out for me, and cheer me up when my mother's condition saddened me. Ollita had her good days and her bad days, and it was those bad days that made me so despondent. Thank God Tía Ana was with us, since I couldn't afford the luxury of crying or behaving like a coward in Ollita's presence. She had always been a brave woman, and I didn't want to let her down. I would sit with Tía Ana and have long talks with her. Sometimes I would lay my head on her lap and she would stroke my hair as I wept quietly. Once or twice I actually fell asleep on her lap as I had when I was a little girl.

A few days before I left Cuba, my father took a turn for the worse. He had gotten something that we in Cuba called "old people's disease." I don't know exactly what it was, but there was no doubt that my father was on the verge of dying. He had always been a man of strong body and character, and that's why it saddened me so to see him in such bad shape. When we were told that there was no hope for him, I planned his funeral and paid all the expenses. Since Ollita was also so ill, I didn't want to leave her with anything that could worry her. My brother, Bárbaro, accompanied me to Havana's Colón Cemetery to finalize the arrangements.

Right after we finished having lunch on July 14, 1960, Rogelio called to tell me that everything was set and that we were leaving on a Cubana Airlines flight for Mexico City the next day. He didn't say anything else, nor did I detect anything different in his voice.

My luggage was packed, and I spent the rest of the night

peacefully with my Ollita and my brothers and sisters. We made jokes and talked about all sorts of routine things until bedtime. The next day, we had to be at the airport at noon. I like arriving early because I hate having to rush. I called our driver, Domingo, before going to bed. Everything was set. My stay in Mexico was going to turn out fine. So I told myself.

On the morning of July 15, we drank coffee and I said my good-byes to Ollita alone. I told her that I would return for *Nochebuena,* or Christmas Eve dinner. She gave me her blessing, and then we all got in the car and left for the airport. As usual, we arrived much earlier than the others. Actually, we were there two hours before the scheduled departure. We made ourselves comfortable in the Havana airport and talked and made jokes. The whole family went to see us off, except for my father, who was just too sick to go. Ollita looked fine; she even seemed happy.

After about an hour, the guys from the Sonora arrived with Rogelio, who was carrying all the travel documents (he was always in charge of those things). We greeted one another with big smiles on our faces and many hugs. Since back then it was normal for whole families to see people off at the airport, the terminal was packed; some people were crying, others were laughing, while others were giving messages to be conveyed to friends or relatives abroad. The children were behaving as children do: some were playing, while others cried.

Tía Ana gave me her blessing and told me not to worry about Ollita, since she would make sure to follow the instructions for Ollita's care. That's when I heard Rogelio calling for us. Since everything about leaving Cuba had changed, he wanted to explain the official process to us. We heard the boarding call over the loudspeaker and made our way through customs. After we were sure that our luggage had made it onto the plane, we exited the terminal. Although at that moment I didn't know it, it would be the last time I'd feel the Cuban sun as it shone in that beautiful sky. I can still see it in my mind as if it were a picture. I then turned and saw my Ollita smiling from the observation deck. I remember blowing her a kiss. Tía Ana stood behind her and put her hand on her shoulder, letting me know she wouldn't abandon her. That gesture calmed me a bit. Now I'm glad that I didn't know then that I would never see my mother again. If I'd known, I wouldn't have been able to leave her.

The line kept moving. I turned, and the plane was about fifty yards in front of me. I saw the stairs full of passengers waiting to board and kept walking, clutching my hand luggage until I reached the stairs. I grabbed on to the handrail and walked up the steps. Before entering, I turned to get a last look at my two mothers. I blew them a kiss and entered the plane.

The doors closed, and we all looked out the windows so we could wave good-bye. The engines roared and we sped down the runway. In just a couple of minutes we felt gravity push us against our seats, but we still kept looking out the window. I remember a man who began to pray. I assumed he was simply afraid of flying. Who knows, maybe he wasn't afraid; maybe he just knew he wasn't returning to Cuba. I still hadn't a clue. I couldn't take my eyes off the window. As the airplane climbed, Havana's skyline became smaller and smaller, until it disappeared from sight and all we could see was the ocean. When we were safely out of Cuban airspace, Rogelio turned to us and said, "Guys . . ." Then he turned and looked me straight in the eyes. "This is a one-way trip." His words shocked us. Some of the members of the Sonora began to cry. I remember Pedro having a somber look on his face. He squeezed my hand, and I too began crying. I was struck by the enormity of what I had just lost forever. In my heart, I knew I would never see my country again. All I could think of was what I had left behind: my mother, my whole family, and so many friends. My life, as I knew it, was gone.

Tres

EXILE

Cuando salí de Cuba, dejé enterrado mi corazón.
When I left Cuba, I left my heart buried in its soil.

—Luis Aguilé. Celia Cruz, "Cuando Salí de Cuba."

Celia at home, 1972, Mexico City.

I DON'T REMEMBER ANYTHING THAT HAPPENED ON that flight to Mexico. The idea of leaving Cuba forever was about all my mind could handle at the time. I was totally lost in my thoughts. As a matter of fact, I came to only when I saw Mexico's mountains.

It was the first time I flew to Mexico without getting inspired by those majestic peaks. On that day, they seemed cold and barren. They somehow seemed to reflect the deep pain I first felt when I heard Rogelio's fateful words, that we were never, ever going back home. My body froze and I became sick to my stomach. The chills actually stayed with me for several days. Thank God I have the stage to help me deal with my pain. If it wasn't for my performing, I might have been lost. The sadness I feel when I think of my beloved Cuba stings every time.

I immersed myself totally in work. I do so whenever I feel pain. Even at rehearsals I give it my all. This total devotion to craft helped me professionally, especially in Mexico, where we were extremely popular and our schedules were fully booked. Actually, the Sonora Matancera was so popular that we were hired to perform every day of the week, sometimes several shows a day! With all the chaos that was unfolding in Cuba in the early 1960s, my worrying about Ollita, my father's illness, and the reality that we no longer had a country to return to, singing became my only escape.

Before my first month in Mexico was over, I received word that my dear father had passed away. He was seventy-eight, may he rest in peace. I can't really articulate exactly what I felt when I heard the news. So many emotions exploded in me that I couldn't distinguish one from another. I had no other option but to resign myself to the pain. I was always taught that it's unhealthy not to. Feeling it, whatever "it" may be, is the only way to work through life's really tough moments.

We debuted as residents of Mexico at Mexico City's La Terraza Cassino nightclub on July 22, 1960. The crowd there was so large that they had to put tables out on the sidewalks to accommodate the overflow. It was wonderful. The Sonora's schedule conflicted with mine because we were both hired to perform at the Lírico Theater while I was performing at La Terraza Cassino. Eventually we adjusted our performance calendar so we could work together as much as possible. Our public in Mexico demanded it.

We were soon hired for a five-month-long stint at the Los Globos nightclub, where we performed together several times with the Luis Trápaga Ballet, which was known throughout Latin America for its wonderful performances. I had met Luis in 1957 when we performed together with the Cuban entertainers Manolo Torrente and Ana Margarita Martínez-Casado on a Cuban television show known as *Noche Cubana* (*A Cuban Evening*). The show appeared on Channel Four in Havana, the first television station in the Spanish-speaking world. Luis Trápaga's troupe was the main attraction, and it was quite a spectacular event. As time went on, we became great friends.

During one of our performances at Los Globos, Quique, the

son of the great Mexican film star María Félix, arrived and asked to speak with me. He said it was urgent. I was more than willing to see him, having been a huge fan of his mother's. He explained that his mother was throwing a party in her home and one of the invited guests was the Mexican president, Gustavo Diaz Ordaz, so she wanted to invite the Sonora and me to perform. I was very flattered by the invitation, and of course, I accepted.

My brothers from the Sonora couldn't perform with me that evening because they were already booked elsewhere. All the same, they managed to help me out. They juggled their schedule and made it to the party to accompany me. We arrived at María Félix's home and performed. After we finished, María Félix, her agent, Fanny Schatz, President Diaz, and I sat at a table to talk. The president was very cordial with me, and he told me that he was delighted with my voice and our performance. Later he even gave me a present, which I kept and still have: a Piaget watch with an engraving on the back that reads: "For Cuba's voice. With high regards, Gustavo Diaz Ordaz." I was eternally grateful to receive such a beautiful piece of jewelry. It was a truly memorable moment.

During the year we spent in Mexico City, we lived in an apartment complex called the Pennsylvania. All the musicians from the Sonora lived there, as did other Cuban performers, like the dancers Sonia and Miriam. When the Franco-American singer Joséphine Baker and the greatest of all Spanish performers, Lola Flores—known as "La Faraona" ("Pharaoh's Queen") because of her dark, gypsy features—performed in Mexico, they also stayed at the Pennsylvania. I should note that my dear friends the choreographers Roberto and Mitsuko lived in the Pennsylvania as well. They were responsible for coordinating the logistics of bringing Joséphine Baker and Lola Flores to Mexico. While there, these international legends would stay in their home. It's how we all became such close friends.

I continued working at La Terraza Cassino until November 20, 1961. The whole group, including Las Mulatas, then went on tour to Miami, New York City, and Chicago. When we returned to Mexico City, we performed in the Lírico Theater, the Blanquita Theater, and the Los Globos nightclub, among many other places, and wherever we went, we continued to pack the house. Celia Cruz and the Sonora Matancera became all the rage in Mexico. During that period, apart from connecting with so many future legends of the Cuban and Mexican music world, stage, and screen—including Javier Solís, María Antonieta Pons, Rosa Carmina, Olga Guillot, Tongolele, María Victoria, José José, and Carmen Salinas—we were also reunited with many Cuban friends and fellow entertainers who were also fleeing Cuba. It was a momentous year for me, both exciting and extremely sad.

At the beginning of that year, I was informed that Ollita had taken a turn for the worse. I was told that she was so feeble, she would never leave her bed again. I decided I would try to return to Cuba the following April. I would never make it in time.

I booked my flight to Cuba for April 17, 1961. As I was ready to leave for the airport, I was told I couldn't leave, since the Bay of Pigs invasion made the trip too high a risk. No flights were landing on the island. After the Bay of Pigs fiasco had passed, the political reality in Cuba changed so radically that I never returned. Still, I was able to speak to my mother on the phone, since thank God they still allowed Cubans living abroad to call home. I called her once a week while she was in the hospital, mostly on Sundays. Every time I spoke with her, she would say, "Honey, I would love to see you, but we're not allowed to now," and then we would change the subject, since we knew the phones were tapped. I would tell her what I was doing, and I even told her that I was dating Pedro. She had met him in Cuba, so I assumed she remembered him. But after a couple of minutes, her voice seemed to lose its energy. My relatives would take the phone from her and tell me that she needed her rest. I would always start crying then. My mother could've easily begged me to go see her before she died, but she didn't. That's one of the things that made her such a saintly and selfless woman. She made me feel at peace. She made our horrible situation as bearable as she could by not complaining about her pain and suffering. I wasn't allowed to see my Ollita when she died. I swore to never set one foot in Cuba again as long as the Castro regime remained in power. And just in case the regime doesn't fall before God calls me home, I've made arrangements to buy a plot in a New York cemetery. As long as Castro's in power, I refuse to be buried in Cuba, even if it means that I won't be buried next to my mother.

Since television was not accessible to most Mexicans in the early 1960s, the best way for performers to reach the masses was by touring. With caravans such as Las Caravanas Corona, which covered the whole country and took us to small towns where we dealt with the audience directly, we saw almost every inch of Mexico. These tour caravans were lucrative for their promoters, since we traveled to as many places as possible in a short period of time. I enjoyed working that way because I was allowed direct access to the people. Nothing compares with the personal relationship that develops between the public and an entertainer. The caravans were a wonderful way of giving one's all to an audience and of cementing strong bonds with the people we toured with. Performing with the caravans was tough work, but it was worth every minute. I always had a great time.

Since all the entertainers touring with the caravans worked so closely together, we tended to become tight, like a family. The caravans also allowed us to become reacquainted with performers we already knew but hadn't seen for some time. As hectic as those times were, they were happy years for me. Those caravans also prepped me for the extensive touring I was later famous for. When people ask me now where I get my stamina and energy, I tell them that it's how I was trained. I thank my time in Mexico for that.

This exhausting touring method of performing also allowed us to share and celebrate life's joys, as well as its troubles, with other entertainers. During my time with the caravans, I became close with the legendary Mexican entertainer Toña La Negra, although I had met her years earlier when she had first performed in Cuba. We not only worked in the caravans, we also performed duets in Mexico City's Blanquita and Lírico theaters.

Toña loved to cook, and every time Pedro and I went to visit Mexico, she would make us a very spicy *guajolote* mole. Although it's a delicacy in Mexico, my system just couldn't take it. I used to say to her, "Toña, remember that I can only eat baked chicken or something along those lines. I can't eat spicy food." Spicy food just doesn't agree with me. I don't like to suffer while I'm eating. I admired her greatly and had great affection for her, may she rest in peace, but her mole was just too much for me.

One of the drawbacks of traveling with the caravans was that we barely had enough time to eat and change. While one group performed, the other one ate. The promoters rented out restaurants on the condition that at such and such a time, a group of entertainers would arrive and eat, with the whole place reserved just for them. When we were finished, we would get on our bus and travel to another town, and then another portion of the caravan would come and take their turn in the same restaurant. And so on. It was an assembly-line operation.

Fortunately, Celia Cruz and the Sonora Matancera were having so much success in Mexico that promoters were looking to hire us everywhere. I thanked God for that, since it's much better to be able to choose where to work than have to scrounge for a gig.

Back then, the Mexican film industry was at its peak. It was truly a wonderful movement, so I was thrilled when I was offered a role in the film *Amorcito Corazón* with the Mexican actors Mauricio Garcés and Rosita Quintana. I sang the *bolero* "Tu Voz" in the film. It's been years since I last saw that movie. I was never given a copy of it. I don't know what happened, although I've been told that it's still available. I'm not sure if that's so, since I've heard that many of those older films are decaying and some have even been lost forever.

I later heard there had been a fire at Churubusco Studios, the most important production center of the golden age of Mexican cinema, where *Amorcito Corazón* had been filmed. When the firefighters arrived, their water hoses did more damage to the studio than the flames. That saddened me deeply. I associate that film with the period in my life in which my relationship with Pedro was forever cemented.

By the time we left Cuba for life in exile, Pedro and I were already best friends. We still are. He would tell me what was on his mind, and I would tell him what was on mine. We were friends for almost twelve years before we really started dating. I never imagined that one day we would be married. I swore when I was young that I would never marry a musician. They're too promiscuous. While we were just friends, Pedro had at least eleven girlfriends. Eleven! But with the trust we eventually shared, and by dealing with each other on a daily basis, we realized that we could always count on each other. I don't know how, or exactly when, things began to change between us. One day, though, I suddenly realized that Pedro was trying to court me.

My mother was alive when Pedro and I started dating, although she was very ill. I remember a particularly vulnerable time when I cried every day for hours. Pedro was very supportive. I don't know if I would've been able to hold up during the final stage of my mother's illness without him. Pedro made me laugh. There are people who reflect their names perfectly, and Pedro is one of them. His name comes from the Latin for "rock," and he is my Rock of Gibraltar. And his last name, Knight, couldn't be more appropriate, since he is a perfect gentleman. He sweeps me off my feet on a daily basis with his thoughtfulness and wonderful manners. He brings me coffee every morning. He always holds the door for me. He offers me his arm wherever we are. He is my protector, my best friend, and the love of my life. He is the knight who saved me from a life of bitter loneliness. When I found myself exiled and orphaned in a foreign country, Pedro helped make my life bearable.

Pedro and I are always joking around. Humor is definitely the base of our bond. When we used to stroll down the streets and through the parks of Mexico City, all we did was make each other giggle. That's why Mexico City holds a special place in my heart. It was the first place I went to after I left Cuba, and it was where I first fell in love with Pedro.

I'll never forget the day he came to me and said, "Celia, I have a problem. I think I'm falling in love with my best friend, and I don't know what to do."

"And why don't you tell your best friend what you're feeling?" I said.

"Because I don't want to lose her friendship."

"But, Pedro, if she's your best friend, don't you think she knows you well enough? Why should you have to lose her?"

I remember feeling my heart begin to pound in my chest. Pedro took my hand and kissed me for the first time, right there. He then embraced me, and I remember feeling as if I were going to faint. My stomach did flips, and it felt as though thousands of butterflies fluttered inside me. I stood there in his arms with my head on his shoulder, the tears streaming from my eyes. I must have looked horrifying with my mascara running and smearing onto his shoulder. I said, "Oh, Pedro, look what I did to your jacket," and he said in his special way, "Don't worry about it, *mi negra*." From that moment on, my heart belonged to him.

We were very discreet. Not even the other members of the Sonora had any idea we were dating. It actually took some time before they were aware of it. Our courtship was unique, a personal and sacred relationship. That's why we kept it to ourselves. We didn't want the gossip to take off before our relationship had a chance to really get started. As a matter of fact, Rogelio used to say that when he first found out we were dating, he couldn't believe it, he was so surprised. He said that Lino Frías, the Sonora's pianist, overheard someone say that Pedro and I were dating. After that, the whole Sonora found out about our courtship, and we couldn't keep our precious little secret from anyone any longer.

My joy was tempered only by my mother's illness and the worsening situation in Cuba. People were desperate to get out of the country. Fidel was getting impatient because people were openly defying the regime he was imposing on them. He declared that all Cubans living abroad who wanted to continue being Cuban citizens had to return to the island before October 1960. Even if I had considered going back, I couldn't with all the work I was being offered in Mexico. I totally disagreed with his approach to things; I just didn't want to live in a country ruled by him. He was a Cuban citizen, as we all were, and as far as I was concerned, he did not have the right to strip anyone of his or her citizenship. He had no divine right to take my Cuba away from me. People belong to their country, not to a specific dictator's ideological regime. If I had to ask his permission to return to Cuba, that would be equivalent to recognizing his authority, and I would never do that.

In July 1961, I secured a contract to perform alone without the Sonora at the Los Angeles Palladium with the Mexican promoter Chico Cesma. While in California, my travel documents expired, so I couldn't return to Mexico, and quite honestly, at that moment I didn't want to. My reason for not wanting to return to Mexico had nothing to do with the Mexican people, whom I loved and still do. My reason was based solely on my issues with the Mexican government. Becoming a naturalized Mexican citizen was just too complicated and too long a process. If you weren't a Mexican citizen, you couldn't buy any type of real estate. Even worse, the Mexican government was too sympathetic to the regime in Cuba for me to seriously consider living there permanently. Another issue I had with returning to Mexico was that I was tired of the daily grind. Singing "El Yerbero Moderno," "Tu Voz," and "Luna Sobre Matanzas" every single day!

Granted, they are lovely songs, but I just didn't want to keep singing the same thing over and over again.

As an entertainer, I had a deep desire to be creative. Unfortunately, it was just too difficult for me to do so in Mexico at that time. I feel great affection for the Mexican people, and I know they feel the same for me. The Mexican people did not want me to leave. Even Agustín Lara, the great Mexican composer, cried when I told him that I wasn't planning on returning from Los Angeles. In tears, he said to me, "*Negra,* please don't leave. I'll even get you your own band." But my mind was made up. There was no going back. Yet again I left a country I had come to think of as home.

Once I finished my contract with the Los Angeles Palladium, the famous New York club of the same name hired me to perform. I flew alone to New York, the city that would eventually become my home. I was soon able to secure permanent residency in the United States. Because the regime in Cuba publicly declared its Communist nature in mid-1961, and with the increasing presence of the Soviet Union in Cuba, the American government began allowing Cubans refuge in the United States. With visa waivers, and after waiting through a grace period, any Cuban could apply for permanent residency status.

In early 1962, I was reunited with the Sonora, and Pedro, in New York City. By the middle of the year, the promoter Guillermo Arenas gave us a contract in New York, and that's how we were professionally reunited in exile. He promised to take care of all our needs as we settled in America, and he was true to his word. Another person who helped me secure work was my agent, Catalino Rolón, who also represented the great Cuban singer and my friend Rolando Laserie. Thanks to Catalino and Guillermo, I was able to make La Gran Manzana my new home.

I rented an apartment on Seventy-fifth Street and Broadway, in the same building where Rolando and his wife, Tita, lived. We used to see one another every day. They were wonderful to us. Orlando, my childhood friend, and his wife, Dalia, had also fled Cuba to New York. They were very kind and eventually became good friends to Pedro and me. We shared many wonderful moments during our first year in our new home. During our first snowstorms, we would go to Dalia and Orlando's apartment and pass the time watching the snow fall. We also became good friends with Vina and Nancy, two members of a wonderful Puerto Rican family. Because our apartments were so tiny, we couldn't all fit in one apartment, so we'd go sightseeing throughout the city. It was then that I befriended a wonderful fellow Cuban exile named Zeida Arias.

What I did find difficult during my first year in New York were the beauty parlors. I was very excited because American black women had a new way of doing their hair. They first ironed it, and then they would weave artificial hair into one's own relaxed hair. It was a time-consuming process, so I would show up at the beauty parlor at seven in the morning, and I wouldn't leave until four in the afternoon. The beauticians would ignore my appointment and let their friends go ahead of me. They took advantage of me because I didn't speak English. They knew I couldn't speak up for myself. That helpless feeling I had when I waited to get my hair done inspired me to learn English, although I still have a terrible accent whenever I speak it. As I always say, my English is not very good-looking.

———

Among my favorite memories during those early years in New York are the surprise road trips Pedro got into the habit of taking us on. We usually traveled with our friends Gloria and Luis Díaz. We all enjoyed the spontaneity of those trips. I remember driving all the way up to Buffalo and Niagara Falls once. On another trip we ended up in Philadelphia. Who knows what got into Pedro back then. Maybe he just missed the wide-open spaces of Cuba.

We were settling into our lives as exiles in New York. As I said earlier, I had already been to New York when I came to perform and to receive my first gold record in 1957. But living in a city is much different from visiting one. New Yorkers were different from anyone I was used to. The language and customs of the city were alien to me. All the concrete and total lack of nature always seemed odd. The buildings were so tall that I sometimes got dizzy just looking up at them. The buildings seemed like gigantic fingers jutting out of the ground, each finger pointing toward heaven. I used to be afraid of getting lost when I was out alone, yet the sheer enormity of the city excited me.

While I always liked the cold weather and loved the snow, I had never experienced anything like the first winter I spent in New York. My ears were so cold, they felt as if they were going to freeze and break off my head. I always kept my scarf on. Thank God I've never been sickly. I never, ever caught a cold. The one thing I admired about New York City from the moment I arrived was its ability to embrace so many different types of people. There's everything in New York. No place in the world can make that boast.

I never experienced any major racial barriers or prejudice in New York or, for that matter, anywhere else in the United States.

Racism exists everywhere, and its victims can be found the world over. Racial prejudice and discrimination even existed in the Cuba I came from, although it was much less virulent and manifest than what I'd heard could be found in America. I am not a product of a community rife with racial animosities, though. The Cuba I came from was a cosmopolitan place, and its people came in all shapes, colors, and sizes. We were first Cubans, and then we were white, black, mulatto, Chinese, Catholic, *santero,* Jewish, or Protestant. In my country, I was never denied any of my rights because of my skin color. Ever since I was a child, I've always befriended people of all colors and backgrounds. I have been fortunate in continuing this experience as an exile in the United States.

I have always given the best I can in my work, and as a consequence, opportunities have always knocked on my door. From the moment I arrived in the United States, I was fortunate to have never lacked a gig somewhere. Luckily, I always had enough money to send to Cuba for my mother's care when she was still alive. Granted, I needed to be on the road a lot, but I didn't mind it, since I was so used to it. As soon as Rogelio brought the whole Sonora to New York—except for Jarocho, who chose to remain in Mexico—we were immediately hired to perform at the Puerto Rico Theater in the Bronx. I was happy to have Pedro near me, since I missed him terribly after I left Mexico and he stayed behind; I was truly thrilled to be reunited with the whole band. Even though we had performed together for years, Rogelio was a perfectionist and made us rehearse every day. He wanted to make sure that all our arrangements were perfect.

The opening at the Puerto Rico was a major event, and we made sure we were ready. The performances headlined me with the Sonora Matancera, along with the Puerto Rican singer

Lucecita Benítez, my friend Rolando Laserie, the Mexican singer and songwriter Armando Manzanero, and the Chilean singer Lucho Gatica. Our run there was quite special. It felt amazing to perform with the Sonora again.

In September 1961, my sisters, Dolores and Gladys, my cousin Nenita, and other relatives checked my mother into Havana's Mercedes del Puerto Hospital for Special Surgery for the last time. She was admitted to the intensive care ward on the sixth floor. I called her there several times a week and could tell from her voice that she was getting weaker. I was very concerned, but I was powerless to do anything other than tell her I loved her more than anything and that she would be in my heart forever. At the end of March 1962, I remember returning home very tired. I went straight to bed, and while I slept, I had a dream I'll never forget. In the dream, I ran toward my mother, and she said, "*Niña,* don't forget that I'll always be with you." I felt very lucky that Ollita promised never to leave me.

The next morning I woke up with a smile on my face. It was April 7, and that night was our debut at the Puerto Rico Theater. I was very excited, as I always am before an opening night. I went to get my nails done that morning and returned home immediately after. I entered the apartment and saw Pedro on the phone. His back was to the door. I was going to tell him something, but when I heard the serious tone in his voice, I decided not to let him know I was there. I wanted to hear what he was saying. Since he didn't notice I had come in, I remember him saying the following words into the receiver: "Look, Celia's mother passed away last night, but she still doesn't know." When I heard him, I froze.

It was a terrible shock. I suddenly felt out of breath. I ran down the stairs. As I ran, I felt a knot in my throat and started to choke. I felt as if someone had stabbed me in the heart. I just kept yelling, "Ollita! Ollita!" All I could do was repeat her name over and over again. I wanted to feel her next to me. I wanted to see her. I just didn't want to believe she was gone. Not being by her side when she died was a nightmare come true. I knew she was very sick, but I never thought she would die without my seeing her again. I understood right then why she had come to me in a dream. She'd known she was going to die. I still couldn't control myself. I returned to the staircase landing and sat there sobbing. After a few minutes, Pedro came down to get me and took me back to the apartment. Soon after that, all my brothers from the Sonora, Rolando, and Dalia came to console me. I wouldn't let them.

Pedro kept repeating, "*Negra,* that's why I didn't want to tell you anything. I didn't want you to suffer so much." I told him that I didn't want to cancel the performance that night since no power in the world was going to bring my mother back to life. Locking myself up wasn't going to change things. I went to the Puerto Rico Theater and performed, but I still couldn't get the knot out of my throat. I don't know where I found the strength to sing. I hid behind the curtains and cried between numbers. As I cried, I thought of how Ollita appeared to me in the dream. Since her passing, I always feel she's with me when I perform. On that night I literally learned how to turn my tears into song.

The following day, April 8, 1962, I began the bureaucratic process required to ask permission from the Castro regime to return to the island for my mother's funeral. But since the dictator never forgave me for having fled Cuba, he denied my request. I was not allowed to bury my mother. The day my mother was buried in Havana's Colón Cemetery, I felt so much rage and despair that I feared I was going mad. I could barely see, since my eyes were sore from my constant crying.

But as usual, God did His best to soothe my pain. On June 18 of that same year, He blessed me with the opportunity to be the first Hispanic woman to perform in New York's Carnegie Hall. I performed there with the man who would later become one of my closest friends and brother, Tito Puente, and the Count Basie Orchestra. When I walked on stage, I felt as if I were walking on a cloud, with Ollita by my side. As a matter of fact, I could hear her voice ringing in my ear: "I'm proud of you, *niña*. I'm so proud of you."

That night was one of the most memorable of my life. Never did I dream back in Santos Suárez that one day I would sing on one of the world's premier stages, especially only two years after having fled my country with nothing but a suitcase.

Through everything, Pedro never left my side. Soon after my mother's death, he proposed marriage. As he spoke, I hugged him and thought how blessed I was to have a man like him, who loved me so much that he would never leave my side. Rather than saying yes, I told him, "Pedro, you're my friend, my brother, my cousin. You're the only family I have left."

We were married on Bastille Day, July 14, 1962, in a civil ceremony in a judge's chambers in Greenwich, Connecticut. Pedro jokes that he took me the way the French took the Bastille. My retort to him is that I said yes not to him, but to the judge in front of us. It's an ongoing joke between my Perucho and me.

The affair was very simple. My friends Tita and Rolando Laserie served as witnesses. My agent, Catalino Rolón, was also there. Afterward we had dinner in a diner. Yes, my wedding reception took place in a diner.

Pedro and I often celebrate our anniversaries abroad. During our newlywed years, we usually spent our anniversaries performing with the Sonora Matancera. Many years after we were married, we were performing in Paris around Bastille Day. I don't remember what year it was, but I remember what happened because it still makes me laugh. Pedro had forgotten to buy French francs before leaving the United States, and since we arrived on a national holiday weekend, he couldn't find a place to buy local currency. We did have American dollars and credit cards, so we didn't try very hard, and Pedro decided instead to spend his energy looking for a nice place to celebrate our anniversary. He found a charming Argentine restaurant where we had a wonderful time. But when the bill arrived and Pedro went to pay with American dollars, he was told that the restaurant accepted only francs. Pedro began to pull out every credit card he had, but they didn't accept any of the ones he pulled out. He then said, "*Negra,* they're going to arrest us," and I jokingly said, "Don't worry, Pedro, I'll wash dishes to pay for our meal."

Fortunately, we were saved when Pedro finally found one card they did accept. We were very embarrassed at the time, but whenever I remember that night, I just can't help laughing.

After my mother passed away, my sister Gladys, who was single at the time, felt lonely in Havana. The situation in Cuba was becoming so unbearable that she couldn't stand living there anymore. The regime's henchmen would arbitrarily strip away any rights they chose to, and since Gladys likes to speak her mind, we were worried that she would end up in one of Fidel's prisons. In 1963, we requested that the regime grant her permission to travel to Mexico. Once she arrived in Mexico, we arranged for her to seek asylum in the United States. I was thrilled once she was on American soil and I was able to see her. From that moment on, Pedro and I would no longer have to live without a close relative living nearby. It was comforting having my sister around me.

In 1964, I had the opportunity to debut on the greatest stage in black America, Harlem's famed Apollo Theater. I felt honored to perform on the same stage where the greatest figures in African American entertainment had delighted crowds for decades. I performed there with Machito and his sister, Graciela, in a Cuban music production staged by my friend producer Jack Hook. Jack was instrumental in taking Tito Puente and me and our music to Japan several years later.

My relationship with the Seeco label and the Sonora Matancera came to an end in 1965. I was tired of recording the same thing over and over again, and I wanted to try new things with other musicians, which my contract with Seeco didn't allow for. I also felt that Seeco's Sydney Siegel wasn't doing enough to promote my recordings. I decided to leave the label, and as always, Pedro supported my decision. I went to Mr. Siegel's office and asked him to relieve me of my contract. He told me that if my request was based on the fact that my records weren't selling, he shouldn't be held accountable. The problem, according to him, was that my records just didn't sell, period. So I asked him, "So why do you want to keep representing me if I don't sell?" He proceeded to show me some papers, trying to prove to me that he'd been promoting me. I told him that my mind was made up. A few days later, he sent me a registered letter stating that I was under contractual obligation to record five more albums. I recorded three. After that, Mr. Siegel released me from my contract. I didn't leave the Sonora, but because they stayed with Seeco, I couldn't record with them anymore. When I finally went to Mr. Siegel's office to say good-bye and pick up my contract release, the poor man started to cry. And with that, my fifteen-year formal relationship with the Sonora Matancera also came to an end.

We did continue to tour together. We traveled to Venezuela and Mexico, and we also toured throughout the United States. As a matter of fact, we had so much work in Mexico that Pedro and I kept a rented home there, since as foreigners, Mexican law barred us from buying one. I was so blessed with the love of the Mexican people that I won their Premio Heraldo for Best Interpreter of Tropical Music in 1967, 1968, and 1970.

Before I continue, I should mention my relationship with Venezuela in the 1960s. Joaquín Riviera, a good friend of mine from Havana who fled Cuba to Caracas in the early sixties and was in charge of recruiting talent for Venevisión, the country's major television network, hired me as much as he could. Throughout the 1960s and 1970s, I traveled extensively throughout Venezuela, performing on television specials. I was also invited many times to perform for the Miss Venezuela beauty pageant, which in that country is a major national event. Since I first toured there in the early 1950s, Venezuela and its people have also always held a special place in my heart. It saddens me that the last few years has seen so much political and economic upheaval in that country, but with the grace of God, I hope that Venezuela will soon again be the great and promising nation that back then gave me so much love and so many opportunities.

In New York, I had no problem securing a new contract. God has blessed me with having ended up in a country where earlier pioneers of Cuban music paved the way. Cuban music had been all the rage in New York since the 1930s, when Cuban musical pioneers took the city by storm. From the 1950s through the 1960s, the Palladium was the mecca for all the best Cuban musicians. The Palladium became so popular that it stopped being an exclusively Hispanic club and became a focal point for all glitterati, Hispanic or not. It wasn't unusual to find Sammy Davis Jr., Dean Martin, and Peter Lawford of the famous "Rat Pack" at the Palladium, dancing to Cuban music.

Mario Bauzá, Arturo "Chico" O'Farrill, Ramón "Mongo" Santamaría, Carlos "Patato" Valdés, Miguelito Valdés, and many others all played a major role in bringing Cuban music to New York. Xavier Cugat, born in Spain but raised in Cuba, took Cuban music to Hollywood, and in the 1950s, Desi Arnaz became an American household name. Cuban music, be it cha-cha, rumba, or conga, had become part of the American scene. But with the installation of the Castro regime in Cuba, the free back-and-forth flow of Cuban musicians to the United States came to an end. Because of politics and Cuba's isolation, Cuban music ran the risk of disappearing from the American consciousness.

Born in Harlem, New York, in 1923 of Puerto Rican parents, Tito Puente, "El Rey de los Timbales" ("the Kettledrum King"), would be instrumental in keeping Cuban music alive in the United States. His real name was Ernest Anthony Puente, but everyone knew him as Tito. He was raised during a time when Cuban music was entering the American mainstream; Cuban music was a staple of life to this first-generation Puerto Rican American growing up in East Harlem. I first met Tito in Havana in the early 1950s on one of the many trips he made to Cuba. Tito was an expert in Cuban music, and his contact with the island and its musicians made him only more of an authority.

Tito had already been collaborating with the renowned Cuban singer Lupe Yoli Raymond, known to all as "La Lupe," who had also fled to New York in the early 1960s. La Lupe had an extraordinary voice and a style all her own. She was truly unique.

Tito and she were a team from her early years of exile in New York, but in the mid-1960s they decided to part ways.

One day in 1965, I received a call from Tito. He told me he would like to work with me on a steady basis, and I told him that I would be honored to. He told me to wait for a phone call from a man named Morris Levy, and a few days later, Mr. Levy signed me to record for Tico Records. In January 1966, I began working with Tito on our first album. The album was called *Celia y Tito*. In all, I think we recorded eight albums. None of them were big hits, although we did have a few successful singles. I think the lack of commercial success with those albums was due to lack of advertising, since the albums themselves were wonderful.

I recorded "Acuario" with Tito, which was our version of the Fifth Dimension's "Age of Aquarius." Our adaptation of that song was a hit around the world. We also rerecorded a song I first did with the Sonora, "Dile Que por Mi no Tema." It too became a hit. I recorded many new songs with Tito, but we also worked on many songs I had first recorded with the Sonora, such as "Cao, Cao, Mani Picao," "Tatalibaba," "Algo Especial," and "Moncó." I recorded another Sonora piece, "Sahara," with Tito when we first went to Spain in 1967. He always wanted to record an album that sounded just like the Sonora, but it was impossible. Nothing can compare to the sound of the Sonora Matancera, although Tito tried.

Tito was always in charge of the musical arrangements. He liked to work alone and through the night. Sometimes we would go out for dinner, and then he would go on working until four o'clock in the morning on whatever we were going to record the following day. Although we may not have had much luck with our recordings, Tito and I did extremely well on tour. We traveled to many countries together, and it was during these trips abroad that our friendship really developed. I cherished my friendship with Tito, and it broke my heart when God took him in 2000.

Thanks to the efforts of my producer, Jack Hook, we visited Japan twice. Tito was a star in Japan, so we were always received well by all the adoring fans. It was fascinating for me to witness how well the Japanese could sing in Spanish. That intrigued me to watch, since our languages are so different. There is a Japanese singer named Aimée Kai who has been my fan since my early tours of Japan with Tito. Whenever I returned to Japan, I've helped her with the pronunciation of my songs, which she performs but does not understand. There is a Japanese salsa band known as Orquesta de la Luz that became a hit throughout the Spanish-speaking world in the 1990s. Its lead singer, Nora, who I believe is married to a Cuban or Panamanian, claims she patterned her act on my performance style. I also have a Japanese friend named Yoshiro Hirohichi who told me in 1995 that there were about fifteen to twenty popular salsa bands in Japan. In great part, Tito deserves much of the credit for trailblazing Cuban music in both Japan and the United States.

While Tito and I toured, Pedro continued performing with the Sonora, and as a result, he couldn't always travel with me. Our obligations took us in different directions, but on occasion, Pedro and I would manage to meet up in one city or another. The constant touring made our home life difficult. Finally, the moment arrived for Pedro and me to sit down and discuss how we were going to handle our careers. Pedro was my agent, but that didn't mean he had stopped touring with the Sonora. Still, he never wanted me to be alone, since he always worried that something could happen to me if he wasn't there to help. Pedro says that I don't know the meaning of the word *no*. And he's right; I can't say no to anyone. Pedro doesn't have any problem saying no.

Pedro and I are a committed couple, and that's why he had to tell Rogelio what he needed to do. Pedro told him, "Rogelio, I have a problem. I leave Celia and I travel all over the place with the Sonora, or I leave the Sonora and go with Celia. But I married Celia, not the Sonora. If I have to pick between the trumpet and Celia, I'll take Celia. I have to leave the Sonora to be with her." Rogelio assured him that if he ever changed his mind, the Sonora would always welcome him back. With that, Rogelio gave him his blessing.

So great is Pedro's love for me that he finally left his beloved Sonora and trumpet on April 30, 1967, in order to build all we now enjoy together. He soon began traveling with me, and since then, we have almost always worked together. Pedro is often asked why he left the Sonora and why he doesn't give interviews, to which he answers, "Celia needs me to do a lot of things for her. She has a million things to do, but she has no time. That's what I'm here for. If I spend five minutes speaking to reporters, those are five minutes I have to take from getting things done for Celia. That's why I don't pose for pictures, nor do I do interviews. I don't want any attention for myself. Use your time with Celia."

I have said I owed my career to my mother, because she supported me. Now I believe that she left me in Pedro's hands so I could continue the career path she helped start. From those early days when he reviewed my scores until today, Pedro has been my greatest supporter.

The end of the 1960s and the early 1970s brought great changes to our personal lives and to our music. Regardless of the efforts of people like Tito Puente, young people—the major target audience for the music industry—began to turn their backs on our music. They saw it as old-fashioned. As a result, we went through a couple of slow years, but with God's grace, we always managed.

It was during this salsa slump that Pedro and I began to talk seriously about starting our own family. Pedro had seven children from two previous marriages, but I wanted a child of my own with him. The problem was, I just couldn't get pregnant. I saw several doctors and underwent several procedures, some of which were painful, but I still couldn't get pregnant. The doctors had no idea why. This saddened me immensely, but Pedro said to me, *"Negra,* don't worry about it. I don't need any more children. God's already given me plenty of them. I don't want to see you upset about this."

At first, it was hard for me to accept the fact that I would never have children of my own, but if it wasn't an issue for Pedro, I would just go on with my life as God willed it. It was then that I began "adopting" children wherever I went. Pedro and I have christened over fifty children, and I truly love them all. I have photo albums full of their pictures. They consistently write to me and send me their report cards and drawings. I keep all of them. I write to all of them on a regular basis, and I always send them cards on their birthdays. I like sharing time with them, spoiling them, and returning them to their mothers with smiles on their faces.

Sometimes I wonder what kinds of parents Pedro and I would have been. I don't think I would've been a very strict parent, while I think Pedro would have been too strict. I have no doubt that if we had children, I would've retired for good, since I would not want to tour with children. Every child needs his or her own space, his or her schooling, and most important, stability. As far as I'm concerned, I think that's impossible to maintain when parents are constantly on the road, performing.

God also blessed me with nieces and nephews. I love them dearly, especially my sister Gladys's two daughters and her son, since they have been the closest to me. Gladys gave birth to her daughter Linda in 1969, and then she had twins in 1972, her second girl and her only boy. Gladys had the twins christened Celia María and John Paul, and I am extremely proud of them. John Paul, whom we call "Johnpy," was a special boy. God put him on this earth to spread joy. He came into the world on his own time, since he was born twelve hours after his twin sister, Celia María. From the first moment I held him and looked into his eyes, I knew we would be the best of friends. Thanks to the love I've been able to share with my nieces and nephew, I am at peace with the fact that I was never able to bring life into the world.

Around the time that my nieces and nephew were born, I had the privilege to perform at a show called *Cuba Canta y Baila (Cuba Sings and Dances)* in the newly inaugurated Lincoln Center for the Performing Arts in New York. *Cuba Canta y Baila* assembled many Cuban performers who had fled Cuba in the previous ten years or so. It was wonderful to be reunited with so many artists who, like me, had been torn from our homeland. It was a blessing to resurrect our country's joy on Broadway, in front of several thousand fellow Cuban exiles, if only for a couple of hours.

I really believe I have been extremely lucky in life. Only God knows why I've been so fortunate. In the late sixties, many Latin musicians were struggling, but I always had an audience that wanted to see me. My career moved ahead slowly then, but it still had momentum, and I kept touring Mexico, Costa Rica, Ecuador, El Salvador, Panama, Nicaragua, Honduras, Guatemala, Belize (which back then was known as British Honduras),

Celia as a student at Public School #6, "Mexican Republic."

Studio photograph taken after Celia received her First Communion at Santos Suárez's Our Lady of the Miraculous Medal Church in 1932.

Celia, her siblings, and her mother in 1948. *From left to right:* Catalina Alfonso, Bárbaro Jimenez, Gladys Jimenez, Dolorez Ramos, Celia.

Celia with her cousin, Evangelina "Nenita" García.

Celia, Christmas, in Santos Suárez, Havana, Cuba.

An elegant Celia in a 1955 publicity still.

An autographed photo of Celia that she dedicated to a friend. The inscription reads:
"To Margarita E. Mendoza and your family. A token of my friendship. Celia Cruz."

Celia performing at the
Tropicana Nightclub,
January 20, 1957,
Marianao, Havana.

Celia and the Sonora
Matancera in "El Teatro
de La Habana," 1957.

Celia and the Sonora Matancera.

Celia and Myrta Silva in the
Valencia neighborhood of Río Piedras,
Puerto Rico.

Celia and the great Mexican singer
Pedro Vargas appearing on *El Casino
de la Alegría,* a variety show broadcast
over CMQ Television, channel six,
Havana, October 12, 1955.

Celia with Las Mulatas de Fuego, Cabaret Bambu, Havana, Cuba.

Celia dancing with renowned Cuban vocalists. *From left to right:*
Jorge (dancer), Celia, Beny Moré, Rolando Laserie, and Celeste Mendoza.

Celia with Tito Puente, when she met him in Havana in the early 1950s.

Chino Hassán (in a white short-sleeve shirt), Celia, Pedro Knight, and the Sonora Matancera.

Celia and Pedro arriving
at Barajas Airport,
Madrid.

Celia at the beach,
El Condado, Puerto
Rico, 1976.

Celia and Pedro at home.

Celia, Pedro, and Lady
Liberty, 1965.

Celia, La Habana Cuba, 1959.

Yolanda "Tongolele" Montes, Celia, and
Las Mulatas de Fuego.

Celia performing at Los Globos in Mexico.
María Félix, the great Mexican screen star,
is sitting at the far left.

Celia in concert in Bogotá, Colombia.

Celia in "El Teatro Blanquita," 1967.

The great Mexican actor and comedian Mario "Cantinflas" Moreno, Maria Victoria, and Celia in Mexico.

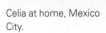

Celia at home, Mexico City.

Celia and Pedro Knight with her nieces and nephew, the children of her sister Gladys. *From left to right:* Linda Becquer, John Paul Becquer, Celia Maria Becquer.

Celia and the Fania All-Stars in Nice, France.

Celia and Johnny Pacheco.

Celia at the unveiling of her star on the Hollywood Walk of Fame, 1987.

Celia album cover.

Celia at the 2003 Grammy Awards.

Celia with President George Bush at the commencement ceremony of Florida International University, which awarded her an honorary doctorate.

Celia with President Bill Clinton on the White House South Lawn after receiving the National Endowment for the Arts Medal, October 14, 1994.

Celia and Thalía at the opening of Bongo's Cuban Café in Walt Disney World, Orlando.

Mary J. Blige, Tony Bennett, and Celia.

Plácido Domingo, Celia, and Juan Gabriel during Univision's Premio Lo Nuestro Awards, Miami, 1990.

Celia and Luciano Pavarotti during the rehersal of "Pavarotti & Friends" concert, Modena, Italy.

Cristina Saralegui, Celia, and Gloria Estefan at a party for *People en Español* in Miami Beach.

Emilio Estefan Jr., Celia, and Mario "Don Francisco" Kreutzberger, Beverly Hills Hotel.

Celia and Antonio Banderas at the opening for *The Mambo Kings*.

Celia, Patti LaBelle, and Omer Pardillo-Cid in Miami Beach's Jackie Gleason Theater at the Telemundo Network's 2003 special tribute "Celia Cruz: ¡Azúcar!"

Celia and Grace Jones in Galicia, Spain.

Celia and Aretha Franklin during "VH1 Divas" concert, 2000.

Celia in concert at Miami's Calle Ocho Festival, 2000.

Previous page: Celia in the National Auditorium
of Mexico during a tribute to her, October 2002.

Celia during the shooting of the music video for her single "Mi vida es cantar" in Mexico City's Chinatown.

Celia in concert.

Celia, in her role as Evalina Montoya, owner of Club Babalú, in the 1991 movie *The Mambo Kings*.

Celia performs to the largest audience ever recorded by the *Guinness Book of World Records,* Tenerife, Spain, 1987.

Celia and Pedro in Amsterdam.

Celia and Johnny Pacheco, 1978.

Harlem's Apollo Theater, with Celia headlining.

El Campín Stadium, Bogotá, 1999.

Lincoln Center, New York City.

Madison Square Garden, 1994.

Maracaibo, Venezuela, 1993.

Madison Square Garden.

With Oscar D'León in the Miami Arena, 1996.

The Olympia, Paris.

Miami's James L.
Knight Center, 1997.

CELIA IN CONCERT

Carnegie
Hall,
New York
City.

The Hollywood Bowl, 1998.

Thierry Mugler's
fashion show,
Los Angeles, 1992.

The JVC Jazz
Festival,
Carnegie Hall,
New York City,
1993.

Celia with President Ronald Reagan at the White House.

Celia with New York Mayor Ed Koch on Fifth Avenue
during the Hispanic Parade in 1988.

Olga Guillot, Lola Flores, and Celia, Madrid, Spain.

From left to right: Pedro Knight, Johnny Pacheco, Tito Puente, Celia, Rogelio Martinez, Jose "El Canario" Alberto.

Jerry Masucci, Celia, Ralph Mercado.

Celia with Oscar de la Renta.

Celia and Naomi Campbell at the
Dolce & Gabbana Party in Los Angeles,
June 14, 2001.

Celia and Desi Arnaz, 1982.

Celia and Bill Cosby at radio station WQBI, February 9, 1992.

Celia and Pelé in Mallorca, Spain.

From left to right: Andy Garcia, Celia, Marlon Brando, Tito Puente, and Ralph Mercado at Hollywood Bowl, Los Angeles.

Celia, Paul Simon, and Rita Moreno.

Celia and Pedro, at their twenty-fifth anniversary, August 1987.

Celia in Venice, Italy, August 2003.

Celia during the exhibition of "Cuba Nostalgia," Miami, 1999.

Pedro and Celia with her niece and nephew, Celia Maria Becquer and John Paul Becquer, Miami.

Celia during the recovery from her surgery.

Celia and her aunt, Ana Alfonso,
New York City, 1995.

Celia's brother Barbaro Jimenez,
her friend Maria Hermida, and Celia
in New York, 1998.

Celia in Paris, August 2002.

Celia with a bag of Cuban soil she collected by putting her hand through the barbed-wire border fence at the U.S. naval base at Guantánamo Bay, Cuba. This soil was deposited in her casket.

During the visit she made in 1990 to sing to the Cuban refugees held at Guantánamo Bay, Celia stares across the fences and barbed wire that divide the base from the town of Caimanera, Oriente Province.

Venezuela, and Miami. It was during one of my tours to Miami in the late 1960s that I met the three women who would become my closest and dearest friends.

In Miami, we regularly performed in a nightclub called Montmartre. In the late 1960s there was a motel on Biscayne Boulevard and Thirty-fourth Street called the Sandman. The owner, a Cuban with a beautiful voice named César Campa, had arranged for entertainers performing at the Montmartre to stay in his hotel. César and I became very close friends, so much so that I am the godmother of one of his grandsons, who happens to share his grandfather's name.

César has a wonderful ability to improvise lyrics, and on more than one occasion, I've asked him to join me on stage to sing the Cuban classic "Guantanamera." As a matter of fact, we're so close that on his birthday, August 31, 1998, during a concert at Madison Square Garden, I interrupted my performance to sing "Happy Birthday" to him. Those were wonderful years in the late sixties and early seventies, when Pedro and I stayed at César's Sandman Motel while performing in Miami. We would stay for a few weeks at a time with Rolando Laserie, the Gran Combo Orchestra, and other brilliant performers and artists, and we would throw wonderful parties in the motel's courtyard. We sang, danced, and dined under the stars. Other people joined us and partook as if it were a block party. At times we made believe we were back in Cuba.

On one of our trips to Miami, we arrived late at night and went straight to the Sandman. The next morning, I met a beautiful young woman, Mary García, the motel manager. We immediately hit if off, and soon thereafter, I also became friends with her friend Elia Pérezdealejo.

Both Mary and Elia had a friend named Zoila Valdés, who owned a travel agency close to the motel. One day they asked her to come and meet me, and it was then that the wonderful friendship among the four of us began. We exchanged numbers and promised to keep in touch. We didn't simply maintain a friendship, we became family.

My friendship with Mary, who calls me "Ceño," began to flourish when she started helping me with my hairpieces. Mary is an extremely intelligent woman, so her company is always a pleasure. I encouraged her to dress in bright colors and eat plenty of fruits, since I knew they were good for her. She hates eating fruit. As we became closer, we began to travel together, and in 1978 we vacationed in several European countries together.

One of the most memorable moments of that trip was when we received the papal blessing in the general audience of His Holiness Pope Paul VI. On another trip to Europe in 1983, we visited what was then West Berlin, where we immediately made a pilgrimage to the infamous wall that separated east from west. Someone asked me if I wanted to have my picture taken in front of the crosses that stood as memorials to the East Germans who were murdered by their own border guards as they attempted to reach freedom, but I refused. I found that whole scene so disgraceful that I just could not stand there smiling for a camera. As far as I was concerned, posing for a picture in front of that horrifying wall—which, thank God, no longer exists—would be equivalent to me smiling for a picture in front of one of Castro's prisons. My visit to the wall was a moving and memorable moment for me, and I shared it with my beloved friend Mary.

Now for Elia. Everyone calls Elia "Bruja" ("Witch") or "Brujita" ("Little Witch"). I thought it was an interesting nickname, to say the least, so I asked her where it came from soon after meeting her. She explained that as a kid, she liked wearing kerchiefs and other things on her head. The more her mother took them off, the more she looked for something else to cover her head. People said she looked like a little witch, and that's how the name stuck. Bruja is a wonderful person and is always very helpful to me. She never says no. She's one of those people I trust so much that if I closed my eyes and fell backward, I'm sure she'd be there to catch me. I also had great affection for her mother, América Quiroz, who before she died gave me a beautiful image of Saint Lazarus.

My beloved friend Zoila is the kind of woman who always dresses to the nines, and so am I. Together, we are very fashionable women. My style is feminine, and so are my clothes. Some people say I'm too extravagant, and they may be right, but that's just the way I am. I like to shine on stage. I love makeup, clothes, shoes, and wigs—which were in vogue in the late sixties and early seventies—and long nails. As I said earlier, my obsession with my nails even cost me learning how to play piano as well as I should have. When it comes to feminine tastes, Zoila is my twin sister. She loves makeup, false eyelashes, and everything else that makes us feel glamorous. I always loved the way she put on her makeup. Until I met her, I almost always did my own makeup, since I didn't have a personal makeup artist. When we became friends, I asked her to do my makeup, and she did such a good job that she has done me the great favor of being my makeup artist for many of my performances and for special occasions.

Before I continue, I think I should address the issue of my hair and my wigs, since much had been said on the subject. During all the years I performed with the Sonora Matancera, I did my own hair and almost never wore a wig, but at the end of the 1960s, they became fashionable, which was good for me because it helped me change my look, and since then, I continue proudly to use them. I own many wigs, and I always travel with a few of them. I also travel with an emergency wig, and I love it because it's short, practical, and looks good on me. The reason I keep it with me is that sometimes I have last minute interviews or news conferences, and I have no time to do my hair. Wigs always help when I need to get ready fast.

Now, getting back to my three dear friends Mary, Bruja, and Zoila. Every time Pedro and I go to Miami, we let them know when we're arriving. Sometimes all three of them come to meet us at the airport. From there, we usually go straight to the Shrine of Our Lady of Charity in Coconut Grove, and then we have lunch or dinner. A while back, I made a vow to Our Lady to visit her shrine every time I was in Miami, and almost always, one of the girls, out of their love for me, accompanies me to the shrine. Even Zoila, who is a Cuban Jew, has waited for me in a back pew at the shrine while I pray the rosary. The girls have helped me keep my vow to Our Lady. And sometimes keeping this vow can be difficult, given that fans come up to me in the shrine and ask me for my autograph. I never turn away a fan, but a church is God's house, and when I'm in His home, I'm there to please Him only. I've never signed an autograph while I've been visiting the Shrine of Our Lady of Charity. On more than one occasion, my friends have had to tell fans that I'm there to spend some time alone with my God, and they ask them to please give me some time alone. Fans have always honored this request.

My association with using *Azúcar!* began in the early 1970s. One evening we were dining in one of my favorite Cuban restaurants in Miami, and after we finished eating, I asked for coffee. The waiter asked me if I wanted sugar with my coffee, and stunned, I turned to my friends and said, "Could you imagine that? Cuban coffee without sugar?" I then told the waiter, "Look, *chico,* you're Cuban, and you know Cuban coffee is really strong and bitter. So give it to me with *azúúúcar!*"That night, while I was performing at the Montmartre, I told the audience what happened, and everyone burst out laughing. After that night, everyone wanted to keep hearing the story, but I got tired of repeating it, so one day I just yelled out, *"Azúcar!"* and all the people jumped to their feet. From that moment on, *Azúcar!* became part of my repertoire.

Life in exile forced me to lose my childhood friends Estela, Caridad, and Ana María. But God replaced them with Elia, Mary, and Zoila. Of course, childhood and adult friends are not the same. When you're a child, a friend is more like a buddy, but when you're an adult, that's when you get to really develop a true friendship. The four of us are so busy that we don't get to see one another as much as we want. We have, however, traveled extensively together and speak on the phone several times a week. We also visit one another whenever we can. In those early seventies at Miami's Sandman Motel, Elia, Mary, and Zoila became my sisters, and to this day, I cherish the roles they've played in my life.

I should also note that Tongolele and I performed together often in the Miami Montmartre and stayed together at the Sandman, and that's when we also became close, although as I said earlier, we had worked together many times back in Cuba and Mexico. We often talked about taking a vacation together, so we came up with the idea of going to Hawaii. Our plan was for Tongolele, her husband, Joaquín, Pedro, and myself to take a quiet vacation in a place where few people knew who I was. I enjoyed the idea of just walking down the street without anyone stopping us or eating in restaurants without having to sign autographs. After two years of planning, we finally went on our trip in 1976 and had a wonderful time going to Hawaiian dance revues, since Tongolele was looking for new ideas for her own dance routines. From Hawaii, we went on to Las Vegas, where I had a great time playing my luck on the slot machines, for which I must admit I have a certain weakness. All four of us had a wonderful time.

My relationship with the Spanish wonder Lola Flores was instrumental in the promotion of my music, and by extension Cuban popular music in general, in her beloved homeland, Spain. As I said earlier, Lola—may God have her at His side— was Spain's premier entertainer. We both came from humble backgrounds, and we both overcame many obstacles to achieve great success, but we never forgot our roots. Maybe that's why we shared such a strong bond.

My music had been promoted throughout the Spanish-speaking world by way of pre-Castro Cuba's powerful radio stations and my tours throughout the region, but it had yet to make any headway in the *madre patria* ("mother country")—Spain, which I love as if it were my own country. After its bloody civil war in the 1930s, Spain entered a long period of dictatorship and isolation, so "foreign" influences were officially frowned upon. Even though both Spain and Cuba share close cultural and historical ties, during Franco, everything Cuban was looked upon as bad for Spanish culture.

I met Lola in Cuba in the early 1950s while we were performing there, and when I started traveling to Spain in the latter part of that decade, we reconnected. Lola then owned a restaurant in Madrid called Caripén. Whenever I was visiting, she would close the restaurant to the public and invite me to sing for a select invited few of the Spanish glitterati. Those private concerts for influential people actually helped spread my music's popularity throughout Spain. Her efforts were such a success that Cuban music is now popular in all corners of that country.

Lola and I became extremely close, and I was crushed when I heard she passed away in 1995. Unfortunately, I was performing in Los Angeles when God took her from us, so I was not able to participate in her funeral, which from what I hear was one of the greatest outpourings of public grief that ever took place in Spain. As a matter of fact, it seems that whenever any of my great friends, be it Tito Puente or Lola Flores, have passed away, I haven't been able to attend their funerals because of contractual obligations. I guess that's God's way of allowing me to remember them in life and not death. In any case, Lola's mausoleum in Madrid's cemetery of the Almudena has become a pilgrimage site, and every time I visit Spain, which I do several times a year, I make sure to visit her grave and thank her for the wonderful friendship we shared. As a matter of fact, in 1998, when I recorded my heartfelt and humble tribute to her, "Canto a Lola Flores," on my album *Mi Vida es Cantar,* I took it to her grave, and when I began to place it in the mausoleum, a sudden gust of wind picked it up and the album landed right over the plaque bearing her name. I guess the Lord wanted my gift to rest as closely to her body as possible.

Thanks to Lola's efforts, by the 1980s my music became all the rage in Spain. I will later go into more detail as to how my career there developed, but I should note that one of the greatest legacies she left me, and the world, were her two beautiful daughters, Lolita and Rosario. Lolita and I have recorded together, and when we have, the spirit of her beautiful mother always seems to be present.

Pedro and I had made the most of our lives as exiles. As I said earlier, we had left Cuba not knowing we would never return. We left everything behind. But God is great, and thanks to Him, in the first ten years in New York we were able to recoup most of my material losses. We also found love, friends, and a new life for my career. Sadly, my own country stripped me of my citizenship and erased me from its history, but I found a new country that has allowed me to flourish and granted me the honor of becoming a citizen.

I was very happy the day I became an American citizen in 1977. When we left the swearing-in ceremony at a downtown Brooklyn courthouse, I was so happy walking down the street with my naturalization papers in hand that I started to scream. A police officer saw me and became concerned. He asked Pedro if something was wrong with me, and when he explained what was happening to me, the officer smiled, turned, and continued on his way.

Regardless of the language barriers and the cultural differences, being an American citizen is something very special to me. In exile, I have learned to be Cuban in a way that might not have been possible if I had stayed in Cuba. I think being an exile has taught me to love my country even more, and as a result, I am preoccupied with what the future may hold for the land of my birth. But the United States, with its great mixture of people from all over the world, has offered me a broader perspective. This country has given me the freedom to travel anywhere I please, and I know that would not have been the case if I'd remained in Cuba. I now have fans from all nations, races, colors, religions, and belief systems. We Latin Americans have gathered in this great nation, and what unites us here is our common language, Spanish. The United States has not only accepted us, it has given us the opportunities denied to us in the lands of our births without demanding that we lose our identities. That is truly one of the uniquely wonderful things about this nation. Becoming an American citizen is one of the things in my life I'm most proud of.

Cuatro
SALSA AND *AZÚCAR!*

Lo primero que hago al despertar es darle gracias a
Dios todos los días.
The first thing I do when I awake every day is thank God.

—Johnny Pacheco. Celia Cruz, "La Dicha Mia."

It MAY BE TRUE THAT EVERYTHING HAS ITS TIME AND place, but quality never goes out of style.

The late 1960s and throughout the 1970s was the age of rock and disco, and as a result, my people's music was barely played. It was the age of young people packing discotheques to dance to the music of Donna Summer, Gloria Gaynor, and the Bee Gees. Many believed that Cuban music was something of the past and that it belonged only in the homes of Cuban exiles and at dances for older people. In other words, Cuban music just wasn't hip.

Music helps define what you are and where you're from. It allows you to express your inner being with your whole body. Hispanic youth felt compelled to dance to pop music in American clubs because it was fashionable. It may have been good music, but it just wasn't theirs. It's like dancing in borrowed shoes: no matter how nice they are, they still just don't fit.

These young Hispanics, from the moment they were small children, learned to move to the rhythms of our lands. They were lullabied with Spanish songs, and they were raised with foods filled with their grandmothers' seasoning. But once they started American school, they assimilated. The same thing happened with language, since they soon replaced Spanish for English. Young Hispanics became something new, a little bit their parents and a little bit the United States.

In 1972, several Cuban exile entertainers and I performed at
New York's Radio City Music Hall in a special concert in honor of
Beny Moré. I had already performed on the great stage in the
mid-1960s, but what amazed me at the 1972 concert was the av-
erage age of the audience. Everyone was older. I was saddened,
since I began to seriously think that Cuban music was doomed.
The regime in Cuba had turned its back on the country's traditional popular music in favor of revolutionary protest songs.
Cuban musicians could no longer travel freely, and audiences in
exile were not being energized with new talent. The prospects
for the future of Cuban music seemed gloomy, to say the least.

The great Dominican flutist and my dear brother Johnny
Pacheco came to see me in 1969 after he saw me perform at the
Apollo with the Sonora. Pacheco was very aware that Hispanic
youth carried our rhythms in their blood, but they didn't know
how to distinguish among Dominican merengue, Colombian
cumbia, Puerto Rican *bomba,* or Cuban *guaracha* or *guaguancó.*
Still, Pacheco had Dominicans, Cubans, and Puerto Ricans playing in his band, and together they played traditional Cuban popular dance music with their own flavor. There was a need for one
word to unify everyone. Cuba's music was reborn abroad and, in
the United States, called "salsa."

By 1974, Pacheco and his partner, the great promoter Jerry
Masucci, owned the Fania All-Stars, a salsa band, as well as Fania
Records. Pacheco told me once that they decided to launch Fania
Records because white people had their labels, black people had
Motown, and with Fania we Latins would have our own. The
Fania All-Stars quickly started spreading this "new" music, salsa,
around the world. And since I was the only woman to earn a sig-
nificant role on the male-dominated label, my fans hailed me as
the "Queen of Salsa."

"What do you mean by salsa?" That's the question everyone was asking. Since no new rhythm had been invented, no one knew what "salsa" meant. Some people vehemently opposed its name from the beginning. I must admit that originally we got ourselves into a mess by using that word. I remember that Tito Puente, who had done so much to keep Cuban music alive in the 1960s, was always sickened by it. Until the day he died, he would get upset when he heard someone call his music "salsa." He used to make me laugh when he would say, "What 'salsa'? You eat salsa, you don't dance to it."

There is even a controversy about where the term originated. In 1967, I performed on a Venezuelan radio program that always played Sonora Matancera recordings. The program was hosted by a gentleman named Fidias Danilo Escalona, may he rest in peace. The show was called *La Hora de la Salsa* (*The Saucy Hour*), and that's where I think salsa was born. I say that salsa is just a marketing term applied to what originally was Cuban music. Since this type of music was being played by musicians of all nationalities in the United States, it started to evolve with its own "flavor." Maybe that's why the term *salsa* ("saucy") stuck. By the end of the 1980s, almost all Latin American rhythms were categorized under that title or "tropical music." For instance, when I recorded my classic "El Yerbero Moderno" with the Sonora Matancera in 1951, it was a *pregón,* a traditional Cuban vendor's cry, set to music. But when I recorded it again with Pacheco in 1974, it became a salsa piece, although not one note had changed. My 1955 recording of "Sopita en Botella" was originally a Cuban *guaracha,* but again, when I rerecorded it in 1975 with Pacheco, it too became a salsa song.

There are many people who are still so insulted by the term *salsa* that they reject it. But as Pedro and I have always said, those

same people just refuse to understand that young people were snubbing the classification of traditional Cuban music, and the use of that term was the only way to rescue it. We used to perform in Miami in the 1960s and early 1970s, but young people wouldn't come see us. There were times back then where we performed to half-empty concert halls. Young people used to say, "Celia Cruz and the Sonora Matancera? No way! That's old-fogey music." But when they started calling it "salsa" in the early 1970s, young people began flocking to our performances again. If we called our performance "salsa," 80 percent of the audience would be composed of young people. If we called it a Cuban musical performance, young people would ignore it.

What offends me is that many people who complain about the term *salsa* make their livelihoods off it. If they are so offended by the term, then they should have some self-respect and not participate in salsa events. But instead, many of these same people perform at salsa festivals and charge for their work, while continuing to deny that they have anything to do with salsa, and when they are interviewed about the topic, they find fault with the use of the word. I sincerely believe that if they're going to complain about the term, then they should announce publicly that they are not salsa performers, and they also shouldn't perform in salsa festivals. I don't think they should make money off of what they criticize so much.

The same thing applies to singers who are still in Cuba. Many of them tout the official line that salsa doesn't exist. Nevertheless, recently I've heard that the regime began putting up signs for tourists in Havana's Tropicana nightclub that say: WE PLAY SALSA MUSIC. Also, in the last few years, the Castro regime has been exporting musicians and traditional Cuban music that they had ignored and marginalized for nearly forty years. Ironically, the Cuban government is now trying to jump on the salsa bandwagon in order to see how much hard currency they can make off it.

Throughout the 1970s, we performed in Venezuela with Pacheco, although the Venezuelans also used to hire the regime's official Cuban bands, such as the Orquesta Aragón. On one occasion in 1975, Pacheco and I were performing our salsa on the main floor of the Caracas Hilton, while the Orquesta Aragón was playing what they call "real Cuban music" in another room. By one in the morning, the Orquesta Aragón had come to see us perform, since nobody bothered to go see them. I don't think that official representatives of the regime such as the Orquesta Aragón have any right to complain about the term *salsa,* since when Fidel effectively closed the doors to the free movement of Cuban musicians in the 1960s, Cuban music abroad almost died. Salsa rescued traditional Cuban dance music. This, I'll always believe.

From 1967 until 1979, we worked seven months a year in Mexico. We were already under contract with Morris Levy from Tico Records. We performed in theaters with two separate bands, one named Guaciri and the other was named África, and both were Mexican. After our contracts with the theaters ended, we continued on caravans in the interior of Mexico. We lived part of the year in New York and part of it in Mexico City.

We were still in Mexico when someone called me to tell me that Larry Harlow, "that wonderful Jewish guy" from the Fania All-Stars, was producing a Spanish-language opera entitled *Hommy,* based on the rock opera *Tommy* but set to Afro-Cuban music. I agreed to work on it. Then Masucci decided I should sing the single "Gracia Divina" in the rock opera. When we returned

Salsa and *Azúcar!*

to New York, I was told that I was booked to record the record with Larry Harlow. I learned the song and recorded it in just one day, and the opera debuted at Carnegie Hall in 1973.

After I performed in *Hommy,* Masucci decided that he wanted to record with me. We negotiated a release from our contract with Morris Levy, since we weren't happy with the promotion he was doing for the records I recorded with Tito Puente. I then signed a contract with Masucci in which it was stipulated that if our first record wasn't successful, we would part company.

During the recording of our first album, Masucci kept every part of the bargain. The first thing he asked me was whom I wanted to record with, and I chose Johnny Pacheco, since by that time his band sounded something like the Sonora Matancera. Pacheco has always been a great fan of the Sonora, and when he sang in the choruses, he sounded just like the Sonora's male vocalist Caíto.

Our first album, 1973's *Celia y Johnny,* was wildly successful. Since Jerry Masucci kept his word when he told Pedro that he would take us to the tops of the charts, we signed a long-term contract with his label, Vaya. I should note that *Celia y Johnny* included the single that became one of my greatest successes and one of the signature songs of what was becoming known as salsa: "Quimbara."

"Quimbara" was composed by a young Puerto Rican man named Júnior Cepeda, may he rest in peace. Júnior had sent a demo tape to Pacheco at the Fania All-Stars offices, but he never heard back from anyone. So one day he decided to show up at the office and asked Pacheco if he had heard the demo tape. Pacheco said he had but that he was running to a meeting. Still, he asked Júnior if he could wait and, if he hadn't had lunch yet, to go eat something and then return, since he would be back later. The problem was that Pacheco forgot all about Júnior. By the time he remembered, poor Júnior had already had lunch and had been waiting for him for hours.

Pacheco apologized and asked Júnior which demo tape he had sent him, and Júnior told him that it was the one that went *"Quím-bara, cumbara, cumaquín bambá."* Pacheco then grabbed his arm and said to him, "Come over here, kid." And that's how Pacheco got his hands on "Químbara."

Masucci didn't like the song because he said that all salsa songs had lyrics that said *"La rumba me está llamando"* ("The rumba's calling out to me"). I explained that when Cuban music singers start getting into the music, they tend to start singing that as a natural refrain and that most probably I had sung it myself in some recording I did with the Sonora. I stressed to him how sure I was of the song and that I wanted to record it. I also explained to him that the lyrics to "Químbara" were original since they were about a series of drums talking with one another. He finally agreed, and as a result, "Químbara" was as successful for me as "El Yerbero Moderno" and "Bemba Colorá," songs I recorded for the Sonora. Sadly, Júnior died on July 29, 1976, two days before the album was released. He never knew what a great success "Químbara" became or the success I had with the other songs he wrote that I recorded, such as "Dime si Llegué a Tiempo."

After I first recorded with Pacheco, I recorded an album with Willie Colon, the great Puerto Rican musician who also joined forces with the Fania All-Stars. Since I first worked with him, I've considered him a friend. He is truly a musician of the highest caliber. I heard a while back that he said I was a good example for blacks, Hispanics, and women in general. I have never thought of myself as an example for anything. Nevertheless, I am flattered that he thinks so highly of me.

Journalists are always asking me which of the songs I recorded with the Sonora and Fania All-Stars are my favorites. To
this I always reply that they're all my favorites, since I've never
had to record a song I didn't like. Actually, there are many songs I
would like to record but still haven't been able to. I am aware that
record labels and producers often tell singers what song they
should record and when, how, and with whom they should do so;
I've been blessed in that I've always had an active role in choosing
what songs to sing, and if I don't like a specific song, I don't
record it.

With the Fania All-Stars and *Celia y Johnny,* everyone collabo-
rated and contributed their own ideas. For instance, I had the
idea of recording "Toro Mata," a pretty Peruvian song I heard
while I was working in that Andean country in the mid-1960s. I
was performing in a theater when I heard it sung by a young
woman (also named Celia) who was also performing there. I enjoyed it so much that I asked a gentleman named Alberto Castillo
to give me its score for the piano, and then I brought it back with
me to New York. I took the score to Pacheco, and he liked it for
its unique Peruvian flavor. I also brought him another song I originally recorded with the Sonora, "La Langosta y el Camarón."
Those songs were incorporated in the album along with a single "Canto a La Habana," which became an unofficial national
anthem for Cuban exiles, since the lyrics are a nostalgic trip
through our lost homeland.

Masucci once asked me to do a song called "Cúcula" for the
album *Tremendo Caché,* which Pacheco and I were recording
in 1974. I didn't want to do it since the great musician Ismael
Rivera had already recorded it, and I just didn't like the way it
sounded with its Puerto Rican *bomba plena* style. That's when
Pacheco came to me and said, "My divine goddess, let's turn it

into a Cuban *guaracha* and see if you like it that way." After I heard what Pacheco had done to it, I liked it so much that we recorded it live with Ismael Rivera, during a concert at New York's Madison Square Garden in 1975. They then edited it in a studio, and the rest is history, since it became one of my greatest hits ever.

Those first concerts in the then newly inaugurated Madison Square Garden, the most famous arena in the world, were very important in the "mainstreaming" of what was then already known as salsa music. By performing in such a respected venue, we were able to gain a certain degree of recognition and exposure for our music. And on a personal level, when I saw myself singing in Madison Square Garden, I felt as elated as I had on the day I walked onto the stage at Carnegie Hall. And of course, again I felt my mother at my side, her spirit always encouraging me to do my best.

Many people think I record specific songs with an ulterior motive—that is, I want to convey a specific message through the lyrics. But that's not the case. As far as I am concerned, what makes a song a success is the rhythm and melody. If I like them, I record the song, and that's all. When I recorded Tite Curet Alonso's "Isadora," a tribute to the early-twentieth-century dance pioneer Isadora Duncan, I had no idea who she was. I later learned about her libertine life and tragic death in 1927. I am not a composer, I am just a singer. When it comes to where I get my inspiration, though, that's another story.

I have often been asked what my secret is and why my songs become so popular. My answer is that I like all types of music, and if I am going to sing a specific song, it has to first work with my style and voice. When this combination works, the result is fantastic. My albums have also been successful because they have a little something for everyone. When we pick what we are going to record on an album, we make sure to have a *bomba* for the Puerto Ricans, a *guaracha* for the Cubans, a merengue for the Dominicans, and so on, since people tend to be delighted when they hear songs recorded in their native styles. Sometimes I've recorded a song for a specific market but it's another one that adopts it. For instance, I recorded a beautiful song entitled "La Isla del Encanto," in honor of Puerto Rico, but it really didn't have much of an impact there, although it did in Mexico.

One thing's for sure, if you're in Mexico and sing a mariachi song, you get a standing ovation no matter what. The two mariachi songs that are part of my repertoire are "Laguna de Pesar" and "La Cama de Piedra." Mexicans love when I sing those songs, but I do so only if I'm being accompanied by a group of their mariachi musicians.

Mariachis have no need to rehearse or find the key or anything of the sort; I just start singing, and they automatically know how to accompany me. I wish I could always perform with them, since they are such excellent musicians. Pedro explained to me that mariachis are able to accompany a singer automatically because they've developed a system based on the seven keys that allows them to follow the singer's lead. Mariachis know how to play in every key imaginable. When one starts singing, they go up or down half a tone, depending on what the singer's voice needs. I have no idea how they do it. Pedro is a great fan of mariachis, because they are so perfectly synchronized. Most bands take days to learn tonal variations. A mariachi band can learn them in a second. If a musician wants to be a mariachi, he or she needs to be an *excellent* musician. Apart from the fact that I enjoy performing with mariachis because of the quality of their music, I do so to please my Mexican audience or anyone who enjoys that music. I have always been a singer of the people. If my fans ask me for something, I try my best to please them, and I don't impose on them what I think they should like. That's why I think my music is still so successful after all these years.

I must make special mention of my beloved Puerto Rico and its wonderful people, both on the island and in the diaspora. The Puerto Rican poet Lola Rodríguez de Tio once wrote: *"Puerto Rico y Cuba son de un pájaro, las dos alas, y reciben flores y balas en el mismo corazón,"* meaning that our two islands are the two wings of a bird, which is, of course, the island of Hispaniola, shared by Haiti and the Dominican Republic, and that both our islands share the same emotions. There are no words that adequately describe my relationship with the Puerto Rico Borinquen, which has lasted over fifty years.

I first performed on the island in 1952, and on every one of the countless times I've visited there, I've been treated like a fellow Puerto Rican. In the 1960s, tens of thousands of my fellow Cuban exiles fled to Puerto Rico, where they were well received and allowed the freedoms we had just lost in our country. For that I will always be grateful to Puerto Rico. My relationship with Tito Puente, Myrta Sylva, and Daniel Santos began in the early 1950s, when many Puerto Rican musicians worked in Cuba. I had the pleasure of performing with many Puerto Rican artists. I have also performed with hundreds of Puerto Ricans on the island and abroad, and I have always had a wonderful relationship with them.

In New York and throughout the United States, Puerto Ricans have always been supportive of me and have been wonderful fans. From the day I first debuted on a New York stage in New York's Puerto Rico Theater, to being named grand marshal of the National Puerto Rican Day Parade along Fifth Avenue in 1988, all the *boricuas* have ever shown me is love and admiration. I am eternally grateful to them.

Pacheco and I traveled abroad several times, for example, and as I said earlier, we toured Venezuela often. We even took a memorable trip to Africa.

In 1975, Pacheco, the Fania All-Stars, and I went to Zaire, now known as the Democratic Republic of the Congo. During our visit there, the country was celebrating a national holiday. They organized a festival that lasted almost a month. They booked the top African and American performers and hired the Fania All-Stars along with the best singers from Motown to perform in a series of concerts that would serve as a prelude to the famous fight between Muhammad Ali and Joe Frazier. The whole Fania All-Stars, Pedro, James Brown, the Pointer Sisters, B. B. King, Sister Sledge, Muhammad Ali and his entire entourage, and I flew to Kinshasa on a private plane. As we were about to take off, I remember thinking that the plane was so overloaded, we might never make it to Zaire.

The flight was very long and we were so bored that we had to do something to keep busy, so Pacheco and I started joking and singing until all our fellow passengers joined in. We turned the whole plane into one big party. Pacheco took out his flute and I started singing and marking the beat with a shoe. The Americans aboard couldn't believe how much energy we had, but their shock didn't keep them from joining us in our revelry.

When we finally landed in Kinshasa, the limousines picked us up and drove us down streets that had rows of people on both sides screaming, "Pacheco! Pacheco! Pacheco!" I was amazed to see Pacheco received like a conquering king. Zaire was so far from the Caribbean and the center of his fan base. Actually, I don't think they were treating James Brown or any of the other Americans the same way. It was Pacheco's show.

The concert couldn't have been a grander event. A sea of black people dancing is a beautiful sight to see. Everyone was having a wonderful time. But we couldn't understand what the crowd was screaming at us, so Pacheco said to me, "Celia, sing 'Guantanamera,' and they'll be all yours." I sang "Químbara," and "Guantanamera," but when the crowd heard the latter, they went wild. I was amazed that my version of that Cuban classic had made it all the way into the heart of Africa.

We performed all week, and I remember how cordial Muhammad Ali was to all of us. We would see him every morning when we sat down to breakfast in the hotel. We were treated like royalty in Zaire, and we were even invited on a safari after the events ended, but since Pedro and I had an engagement in Venezuela, we had to leave as soon as our commitments in Zaire were fulfilled. Actually, I wasn't too thrilled with the idea of going on a safari, since wild animals frighten me. When we first received the thoughtful invitation, I remember telling Pedro that if I wanted to see animals, I would go to the Bronx Zoo. I really didn't want to go running around in a Jeep, with the possibility of being attacked by an angry lion a real concern.

We then left Mother Africa, and went to Caracas for a concert. We then made a quick stop in Miami, where I met Lourdes Aguila through Martha Domínguez, a friend of mine. Lourdes is a wonderful woman and friend who is dedicated to the Cuban exile charitable organization Liga Contra el Cáncer (League Against Cancer). She was the founder of its telethon, and asked me to help her. In honor of my mother, I told her that I would do whatever she needed of me, and I have kept my word to her every year since.

In the 1970s, there was a popular band that played throughout south Florida called the Miami Sound Machine, whose lead female was a young woman named Gloria Estefan. In 1977, the band was invited to perform at the telethon, and there's where I met Gloria and Emilio Estefan, who were young newlyweds back then. I'll never forget the first time I saw Gloria singing "Químbara." I went to the stage to shake her hand, after her performance. At that moment we became friends, and soon after that, family. Emilio has become a Latin music mogul and has made me a part of every special event he has put together. Along with them, I met Marcos Ávila, who was also a member of the band and would later marry Cristina Saralegui. Who would have thought then that Marcos would later write the screenplay that would put me on the Big Screen. I met my dear friend Cristina in 1978, when she interviewed me for the Spanish-language edition of the *Miami Herald*. We began the interview and were soon off on a tangent. To my surprise, she burst into tears. I asked her what was wrong, and she told me that she had just lost a baby. We stopped the interview, and I told her how badly I wanted children and how much I had gone through to get pregnant. We consoled each other, and although we spent several hours together, the interview was never published.

Our friendship flourished because Pedro and I were often on tour in Latin America then and our flights were always routed through Miami. We tended to spend time in Miami on our way to Latin America and back, and when in Miami, we always made it a point to get together with Marcos, Cristina, Gloria and Emilio.

In 1979, I went to Ecuador to perform in the coastal city of Esmeraldas. From the moment we arrived in the airport in Guayaquil, it didn't stop raining, so all we could hope for was that it would let up before our concert in Esmeraldas. Everyone was very excited, as I was, since I had never performed in that city before.

The municipal authorities of Esmeraldas declared the concert day a public holiday, and when people arrived for the event, they let all children in so they could see me better and get to know who I was. Everything went as planned, until around five in the afternoon, when the rain again began to fall. We thought of canceling the concert, since it was being held in an open-air stadium. But the spectators—about five thousand of them—stood there in the torrential rain, waiting for me to start. I felt sorry for the women who had gotten their hair done and had put on nice dresses. They stood there excitedly, with their hair ruined and their wet clothes stuck to their bodies. I couldn't disappoint them. I performed, and the show went off as best it could, considering the deluge.

When it was time for me to get off the stage, I remember an enormously obese man helping me down the rain-soaked steps. The man came up the stairs and gave me his hand, and I began to step down the stairs without realizing how much the rain had weakened each stair. I heard wood cracking, and suddenly the whole staircase collapsed. I fell hard, as did the man who was helping me. To make matters worse, he fell on top of me! I couldn't move, and all I can remember feeling was a sharp pain in my leg. Pedro began yelling for help and asked me if I was all right. They tried putting me back on my feet, but I couldn't stand. We all wanted to go back to the hotel, but I just couldn't move: the pain was too intense. We decided it would be best if I saw a doctor right then and there.

The doctor gave me a shot, but it didn't help me at all. Apparently I had twisted my ankle badly, and the doctor in Esmeraldas

Salsa and *Azúcar!*

couldn't do anything more for me. I was told that I would have to
return to Guayaquil the next day to receive the medical attention
I needed.

I had a terrible night, and when I arrived in Guayaquil, I had
no time to see the doctor before I was to perform, so I sang in
terrible pain. The following day, I was taken to see a doctor in the
city's Alcívar Clinic, and when they X-rayed my leg, they found I
had broken my left ankle. They gave me analgesics and put my
ankle in a cast. I performed at a nightclub immediately after the
cast was set.

I was due to go on to the Dominican Republic from Ecuador, but I called my manager and friend, Ralph Mercado, from
Guayaquil to tell him that I couldn't go. He told me that Johnny
Ventura, the famous merengue singer who would later be the
mayor of his country's capital city, and who always invited me to
perform in the Dominican Republic, needed me and couldn't replace me on such short notice.

So off I went, broken ankle and all. I kept the engagement.
What was I going to do? Although I felt terrible, I just couldn't
disappoint Johnny Ventura. My clothing designer, Enrique
Arteaga, may he rest in peace, made me two gold lamé boots to
cover the cast. As a matter of fact, while I was performing, I realized that I had also hurt my knee. Years later, that same injury
would return to haunt me.

Pedro and I returned home to New York, and I was
finally able to recover in the quiet of my own home. A few
months went by, until December 14 of that same year, when a
radio program I was listening to was interrupted to announce the
news that John Lennon had been murdered. I felt awful when I

heard that he had been killed. But after I heard that it had occurred in front of the building where he lived, the landmark Dakota, and in front of his wife, Yoko Ono, I felt even worse. It was a fan who had murdered him. But what kind of fan would shoot a talent like John Lennon? Pedro and I saw the candles and tributes Lennon's real fans set up in the days after his death. I felt terrible for his sons, who would no longer enjoy the blessing of having a father.

I liked the song he co-wrote with Paul McCartney called "Yesterday," and I always wanted to record it. The song made me happy, because I remember enjoying myself at an Acapulco nightclub called El Zorro when it was number one on the charts. I learned the lyrics and began incorporating the song into my show, and although my English was awful, the mostly American audiences loved it. That's why years later, when Ralphy came up with the idea that Tito Puente and I should record a tropical tribute to the Beatles in 1989, I was thrilled. Our album contained our version of Paul McCartney's 1968 song "Obladí Obladá," which became a big hit. In our version, the lyrics were changed to reflect the story of my life with Pedro, and audiences always like to join me in singing the refrain, *"Obladí, obladá, vamos p'allá, que la fiesta va a empezar"* ("Obladí, obladá, let's go, the party's about to start"). As Tito and I toured after the album was released, the song picked up a huge following.

I should note that shortly after John Lennon was murdered, another deranged young man tried to assassinate President Reagan. I was very fond of President Reagan. I was terrified when I heard the news, and I asked for God's help until we finally knew he would pull through. As I will explain in further detail in the following pages, I will always be grateful to him for helping me achieve one of the greatest honors bestowed on me. I must admit that it now breaks my heart that Alzheimer's disease has ravaged his memory and that he no longer remembers what he did for the world. President Reagan will always be in my prayers.

In December 1981, a gentleman by the name of Humberto Valverde published a Spanish-language unauthorized biography of me entitled *Celia Cruz: Reina Rumba* (*Celia Cruz: The Rumba Queen*). Both Pedro and I agree it's a pretty good book, but I really think the author talks more about his life experiences than mine. The great Cuban writer Guillermo Cabrera Infante wrote the prologue. I was moved by his beautiful words of praise for me.

Something funny happened with that book in the mid-1980s. My friend Dizzy Gillespie, the great American musician, mailed me the second edition of the book for my collection. I don't know what he was thinking, but he didn't know my address, so he just wrote, "Celia Cruz, New York, New York," on the package, assuming that the U.S. Postal Service would know how to get it to me. Amazingly, it arrived.

No matter where I traveled, New York had become home. I loved the city and its surrounding areas. Unfortunately, by the early 1980s, the city was decaying. Rampant poverty and the blight of graffiti were destroying its unique beauty. I was thrilled when City Hall contacted me to launch an antigraffiti campaign. I felt honored to give something back to the great city that made me feel so at home when my own country denied me one.

In 1982, I was performing with Willie Colón at a festival held at Miami's Flagler Dog Track when one night after a performance, just as I was about to go to sleep, the phone rang. I remember finding this odd, since I had just hung up with my sister Gladys and I wasn't expecting any other calls. I picked up the receiver before it rang again. When I said, "Hello," I heard the voice of a little boy who I thought had dialed a wrong number. I liked the sound of his voice, so I asked him if he went to school, and he told me he was a student at Miami Aerospace Academy. I told him he must be very intelligent, and then he asked me if I knew who he was. I told him that his voice didn't sound familiar, and then I asked him if he knew who I was, and he said he knew I was Celia Cruz. I remember Pedro asking me whom I was talking to, and I told him, "I don't know who he is, but it's a little boy who seems to know who I am." Pedro went back to sleep, and I continued talking with the boy, who told me his name was Luisito Falcón and that he was twelve years old. He told me his aunt had seen me at a concert where my good friend the wonderful Cuban musician Willie Chirino was performing, and that's how he knew I was in Miami. He said that a friend of his mother's told him I was staying at the Everglades Hotel. He wanted to get in touch with me, so he went to his grandmother's room, picked up her phone, called information, got the Everglades's number, and asked the hotel operator to put him through to my room. I was so impressed by how articulate and clever Luisito was that I gave him all my phone numbers, and I told him that from that moment on, we would be friends.

The next day, I called Ralphy's secretary and told her that if a boy named Luisito Falcón called for me to let him know where he could find me, just as she did with my nieces and nephew. Luisito and I maintained a phone relationship, and I always sent him postcards from wherever I was traveling. On his birthday, I always sent him a card. As our phone relationship evolved, Luisito had trouble deciphering the time difference between

Miami and wherever we were traveling, so sometimes he called us at two in the morning, scaring the wits out of Pedro and me. Pedro was always saying to me, "Why does that kid call you at such ungodly hours? Doesn't he have anyone watching him?" I used to calm Pedro down by telling him that Luisito was just a kid and that no one in his home probably even knew he was calling. Luisito later confessed to me that his family didn't know he was calling me, and when they did, they would tell him to leave me alone. But Luisito was insistent in calling me, and there seemed to be no way of stopping him. Sometimes he would put a whole group of people on the line who wanted to talk to me. It may sound strange, but his calls never bothered me. I have grown to love Luisito dearly.

I finally met him in person when I was crowned Carnival Queen at the 1983 Miami carnival. He told me he started a fan club called the Celia Cruz #1 Fan Club. Soon afterward, the twenty-five initial members started following me wherever I went.

Luisito began making the rounds on radio stations, so he became friendly with all the DJs, but I kept warning him not to pay too much attention to the fan club and focus more on school. He promised me he would. To make sure he was keeping his part of the bargain, I started making him show me his report cards. I warned him that if he tried to keep them from me, I wouldn't see him anymore. So, of course, Luisito made sure to show me his grades every semester without my ever having to ask him to show them to me.

Luisito accompanied me to many events, one of which was extremely special to me. I had become a permanent fixture in the Liga Contra el Cáncer telethon, working with my friend Lourdes Águila, the doctors, and the younger volunteers, called *cangrejitos* ("little crabs"), whom I saw grow up before my eyes. I had sworn to do anything I could in the battle against the disease that took my mother. Everything I did with the telethon I did in my Ollita's name. The telethon was broadcast by the Miami Univisión affiliate in front of a live audience at the Miami Jai-Alai Fronton, and Luisito would take his friends with him to see me.

Finally, in 1983, God helped us break the $1 million mark. What helped put us over the million-dollar mark was a Johnny Pacheco merengue I recorded entitled "El Guabá." It was so popular that I performed it four times on the show, and I believe it was because of the song's popularity that we received so many donations. It was at the telethon that the members of Luisito's fan club initiated the idea of "Celia's buckets," which were buckets they passed out among the audience in the Fronton for anonymous donations in my name. Since they started passing out Celia's buckets, we've always broken the million-dollar mark. I remember that on that day in 1983, I arrived at the show at ten in the morning and didn't leave until two in the morning of the following day. Yet I did not feel tired at all; instead, I was invigorated and proud of doing something so positive in my beloved mother's name.

In 1982, I was honored with a concert at Madison Square Garden, the same arena that helped put salsa music on the map in the 1970s. The concert was a remarkable experience, since it was arranged by my peers. Aside from being honored, I have a special memory of that night, since it was the night Ralphy introduced me to Ruth Sánchez, a Puerto Rican beautician who ran her own shop, El Yunque Obá. She did my hair and makeup, and I loved what she did so much that from that moment on, Ruthie would be the creator of all the innovative hairdos I've become famous for.

Ruthie and I have been all over the world together. She's al-

ways telling me that I'm pretty, and I'm always telling her that what she is seeing is the love she feels for me and not my real face. I've shared so many wonderful experiences with her that I bet they could fill another book. Ruthie is very respected in her profession, and she worked on the hair of many famous entertainers, especially black ones. One day, Ruthie told the R&B duo Ashford and Simpson that she worked on my hair, and they told her they were fans of mine and that they wanted to meet me. She arranged for me to meet them at Manhattan's Upper West Side Sugar Bar, and when I arrived, I found myself in a room full of R&B musicians. They performed for me, they kissed my hand, and some even curtsied. I was moved that they were honoring me like that. Thanks to Ruthie, I met some of the world's most famous R&B musicians, many of whom became my friends.

In 1983, I traveled to Finland for the first time. I fell in love with the country. I had never known Finns were such great fans of Latin American music. I went to Finland to perform with Machito at the winter carnival balls at Helsinki's Hotel Esperia. Every year, for one week in January, that hotel throws a huge ball; my friend Rolando Columbie had already been working the balls for years, and he praised my talent to the artistic manager so much that he finally decided to hire Machito and me.

We performed wonderfully, and the audience was thrilled. While staying in the hotel, I befriended a Finnish samba group that was crazy about me. They were all so sweet. They kept telling me they didn't want me to leave. But we had to, and we did so very early, on an extremely cold and snowy day. Still, all the members of the samba school made sure to know exactly when I was leaving, and when we stepped off the elevator and onto the main floor, I saw two rows of samba dancers, barely dressed in plumed bikinis, lined all the way out to our waiting car. Keep in mind, it was a fifteen-degree Finnish winter morning. Still, they escorted me out and stood there applauding as I got into my car. As we pulled out of the hotel, I looked back until I could no longer see them applauding and waving good-bye. It was certainly a sight to see.

That same year, I performed in the Peruvian Pacific Fair, the largest public yearly event in that country, and from there we worked Chile's famed Casino de Viña del Mar. For the next two years, Pedro and I traveled to dozens of countries, performing on hundreds of stages. Life was good; God had been more than generous with me.

When I heard the news on the morning of September 18, 1985, that a powerful earthquake had hit Mexico City, I was terrified for my friends. Actually, Pedro and I were in Puerto Rico when the disaster took place. Since we have such sincere love for the Mexican people, not to mention all the dear friends we have who live there, Pedro and I were devastated when we saw the destruction the earthquake left in its wake. We soon heard that a few of Plácido Domingo's relatives had been killed, but it took us hours to finally reach our friends Tongolele, Roberto and Mitsuko, and the Mexican performers Verónica Castro, Marco Antonio Muñiz, Silvia Pinal, Fanny Schatz, and Silvia Cantarell. Since the phone lines were so jammed, when we actually got through to one of our friends, we started an information chain, giving one another status reports. As soon as recovery efforts were set in place, Pedro and I offered to perform on a telethon to help the victims and survivors. We tried to do all we could for those poor people.

———

Whenever I can, I try to spend the Christmas season with my family and friends. Shortly after the Mexican tragedy, on one *Nochebuena,* or Christmas Eve dinner, my friend María Hermida, who has never allowed the pain of exile to dampen her love for parties and get-togethers, invited Pedro and me to her home for a celebration. We were looking forward to spending time with her, since María was excited that a nephew of hers was coming in from Barcelona. But who would have known that on that day God would give us the son who would become the greatest source of support for Pedro and me in these last years?

María Hermida's famous parties tended to get started at around nine at night and would last till well past three in the morning. About an hour after Pedro and I arrived, in came her friend María Luisa Bolet with a fourteen-year-old boy and his mother, Magaly Cid. I later found out that the boy was a fan of mine and that María had promised to introduce him to me. I'll never forget how his face shone when he first saw me. His expression left such an impression on me that we immediately clicked. His name is Omer Pardillo. He's a Libra, just like me.

He told me that he was dying to meet me and that he became a fan of mine when he was a little kid. Omer explained that back in Cuba, when he was six or seven years old, he found a picture of me that appeared in an old copy of *Semana* magazine in the home of the baby-sitter where his mother left him when she went off to work. He was so impressed by the picture that he asked the baby-sitter who I was, so she took out a few old albums I recorded with the Sonora Matancera and played them for him. He says that he would always calm down when he heard my voice, which according to his mother was quite a feat, since Omer was a hyperactive child.

After we met, I began writing letters to Omer and sending him postcards and pictures of the places I traveled to. Omer was a special child, since while his peers were out enjoying themselves and listening to club music, he was studying and listening to my recordings.

A few years later, I was surprised when I heard that Omer had begun working for my agent, Ralphy, at only seventeen years of age. Later, when Ralphy realized how much of a fan of mine Omer was, he started giving him more and more projects related to me. Back then, Ralphy's daughter, Debbie Mercado, was in charge of publicity for Ralph Mercado Management, or RMM, and when Omer became her assistant, he got to work even more closely with me.

I used to travel with the wonderful Xiomara Fonseca, but her father became ill and she had to attend to him. Omer took her place and began traveling with me. On our first trip to Europe in 1997, we visited nineteen countries in a month and a half! It was very hard work for Omer, but he was so alert and so full of enthusiasm that he proved to me how professional and responsible he was, despite his youth.

In 1986, I toured with Tito Puente in England and Germany. While I was in London, the great Cuban writer Guillermo Cabrera Infante and his wife, actress Miriam Gómez, came to meet me, since they had been living in the British capital as exiles from the time they fled Cuba. I had called to thank him for the lovely preface he wrote for my unauthorized biography, and it was actually the author of that book, my friend Humberto Valverde, who put us in touch. We had an unforgettable time together, and I made sure to let him know how honored I was by his support and for writing such nice things about me. From that moment on, every time Pedro and I were in London, we would visit them.

In March 1987 we were in Europe again, since we were to perform at the Tenerife (Canary Islands) carnival. On March 3, the night of the concert, and just before I was to go on stage, I was told that the crowd was bigger than they could ever have imagined. God blessed us that night with a cool evening, so I felt comfortable as I approached the stage. When I looked out over the crowd, I was amazed. There was an endless sea of people in front of me. Actually, the crowd was estimated at 240,000 people. When I started singing "Bemba Colorá," the whole audience began singing with me. All I could hear were echoes, since there were so many people in that open-air arena. According to *The Guinness Book of World Records,* it was the largest concert in history. I owe a million thank-yous to Javier and Miguel Zerolo, who organized such a life-altering experience. An event like that goes to show the importance of exporting the music of my tiny homeland throughout the world.

Months later, New York mayor Ed Koch honored me with the Pewter Apple. I was very moved by that award, since by that time I no longer felt like an adopted daughter of the city of New York. Not that I needed the imprimatur of City Hall to prove I had become a real New Yorker. Later, in 1988, Mayor Koch also awarded Toni Morrison, the Nobel Prize laureate, and me with the Mayor's Award of Honor for Art and Culture. As Mayor Koch handed me the award at his official residence, Gracie Mansion, all I could feel was my mother's warmth and affection surrounding me. Ollita was with me even then.

Pedro and I were to celebrate our twenty-fifth wedding anniversary in the month of July of that same year. We talked about celebrating by marrying in a church, but we couldn't, since the church required a baptismal certificate and ours were back in Cuba. We hadn't taken those documents with us when we left the island, and the regime would not allow us to have them sent out of the country. Even so, we decided to throw a party and invite our friends and all our relatives. The day of the party was like our wedding day, especially since I hadn't had much of a wedding when Pedro and I officially got married in 1962. Because we were recently exiled, and didn't have much money back then, we really weren't in much of a mood to celebrate at that time. But on this important anniversary, we wanted things to go differently. We had friends fly in from Mexico, Spain, Colombia, and everywhere imaginable.

On the morning of August 1, I woke up very early. Pedro was still sleeping. I just stood there staring at him, thinking about the day we first met in Cuba. I also remembered the day he told me he was in love with me and the day he proposed to me. I remembered my words back to him: "Pedro, you're my friend, my brother, my cousin. You're the only family I have left." I realized that he was still all I had. I laid my head on his chest and began thinking about what a complete woman I had become and what an ideal husband Pedro was. When he finally woke up, I said, "Perucho, when we die, I'll marry you again in heaven," and he said to me, "And if I were to be born again, I would only marry Celia Cruz."

We got up, and we had our normal breakfast of Cuban coffee, cereal, juice, and Cuban toast. After we finished, we had to hurry. We had hundreds of things to attend to, and because we were so nervous, we kept going over the party's final preparations. Fortunately, my friends Zoila, Brujita, Mary, and César had come in a few days earlier from Miami to help me with the final arrangements. When they finally convinced me that everything was going smoothly, I retired to my bathtub to take one of my "royal" baths, since that's the only way I really relax and it was one of the few treats that I ever allowed myself. After bathing, I hurried, since I knew Ruthie was on her way. While I waited for her to arrive, I made sure there wasn't one single wrinkle on Pedro's shirt, and I also made sure that his whole outfit—from his shoes to his tie—was ready and waiting for him when he got out of the shower. Ruthie finally arrived and did my hair with a very romantic-looking wave on one side of my face. She sprinkled my hair with wildflowers. When she was done, Zoila took care of my makeup, while Brujita and Mary completed the party's final errands.

As we were getting ready, flowers kept arriving and the phone kept ringing with calls from friends wanting to congratulate us. Tongolele called and again apologized that she and her husband, Joaquín, couldn't be there. She had been hired to perform and wasn't able to make it. Nevertheless, we had three hundred invited guests who did show up. So many people were there early that the catering hall had no option but to open their doors before they were supposed to. I should admit that the reason people showed up so early was that I had put on the invitation that the event would begin one hour earlier than it was really scheduled for. I know very well how much Hispanic people live at odds with punctuality. I thought that if I put the real time on the invitation, everyone would be late.

Fortunately, everyone arrived on time. I was glad I did what I did because no one missed our lovely ceremony. My sister Gladys and her husband, Orlando; my nieces, Linda and Celia María, and my nephew, Johnpy; Ralphy; Jerry Masucci; my friends from the Fania All-Stars; and my brothers from the Sonora Matancera were all there. I danced and enjoyed myself until my feet began to swell. And since my Perucho doesn't like to dance, I danced with Johnpy and all my other friends. We really did have a wonderful evening, and Pedro and I had a beautiful picture taken that has since become our official wedding portrait.

Two months later, Pedro and I arrived in Los Angeles for the dedication of my star on the Hollywood Walk of Fame. Of all the awards I received, that one is probably my favorite. I'm not saying that all the other awards God has blessed me with aren't important, but what makes my star on the Hollywood Walk of Fame special is the way it came to be.

I have several radio DJ and journalist friends in Los Angeles who are the best in their fields. Since there are so many of them, I call them "El Grupo de Apoyo" ("the Support Group", and they played an important role in getting my star on the Walk of Fame.

In 1986, one of these friends of mine, the Mexican DJ Pepe Reyes, decided to dedicate one of his talk shows to the topic of why Hollywood ignores Latin American entertainers. He was swamped by calls, and one of the callers said, "Look at the example of Celia Cruz. That lady is the greatest of all Hispanic entertainers. Don't you think she deserves a star in Hollywood?" One of the listeners that day was journalist Winnie Sánchez. She decided to speak with Pepe and initiate a campaign so that I'd be given my place on the Walk of Fame. Of course, all this was going on without my being told a thing.

Winnie didn't know whom to go to about getting me a star, but she researched it and learned that the Hollywood Chamber of Commerce is in charge of the Walk of Fame; so she went to their office, asked for an application for a star, and took it home.

Although my friend Winnie doesn't know how to drive, nor does she speak English, she is such a determined and energetic woman that she always accomplishes what she sets out to do.

Winnie started filling out the application with the help of a dictionary. The only question that confused her was the column that read "Category." One of the acceptable categories was "Live Theater," and since Winnie knew what "live" and "theater" meant in English, as *separate* words, and she knew I was alive and performed in theaters, she checked off that option and brought the application back to the Chamber of Commerce. Needless to say, that wasn't my category.

Some time went by, and she didn't hear anything from the Chamber of Commerce. Her colleagues at the radio station began asking her what was happening with her quest, and she told them that it wasn't going very well and that she would initiate a letter-writing campaign to move the process along. Her friends on the radio soon began asking their listeners to mail letters to the Hollywood Chamber of Commerce on my behalf, and the letters began arriving in droves. As a matter of fact, the Chamber of Commerce didn't know what to do with so many letters.

The process of getting a star on the Walk of Fame has nothing to do with how many letters of support a candidate receives. According to the rules, once an application for a star is submitted, it goes from committee to committee. The majority of first-time applications are rejected, so whoever supports someone's candidacy has to resubmit the application year after year. The problem was, no one explained this to Winnie. The Chamber of Commerce actually became upset with the volume of letters they were receiving, so they contacted the radio stations to find out who had begun the campaign, and more important, they wanted to know who Celia Cruz was. Unfortunately for the Chamber of

Commerce, there was no way of stopping the letters once they started pouring in. The campaign had spread throughout the Spanish-language radio stations in the United States and even had a name, Celia Se lo Merece (Celia Deserves It).

Suddenly, every place Hispanics congregated became a center for collecting signatures in the campaign for my star on the Hollywood Walk of Fame. The whole movement became a public expression of affection, so finally, after realizing that the letters weren't going to stop, the Chamber of Commerce gave me my star on the Walk of Fame, and the news was soon announced on the same radio stations that helped initiate the whole campaign.

The press immediately contacted me to get my reaction. I had no idea what the first journalist was talking about when he called me to ask me for my reaction. I called Winnie, and she told me through tears that they were going to give me a star. She was so emotional that Pedro had to get on the phone to help calm her down. Being the doubting Thomas that I am, I asked her if she had it in writing. She kept insisting that they were indeed going to give me a star on the Walk of Fame, but I told her to make sure that it wasn't just a rumor. She did as told. I must admit I was truly shocked when she came back to me with the confirmation and I realized that it was all true.

The day for the unveiling was set, and almost everything was ready. The stars are unveiled the same day as the ceremony, but they're set in cement the day before.

Coincidentally, Pope John Paul II was visiting Los Angeles on that very day, September 17, and I saw His Holiness's presence as a blessing. He was due to leave the city at ten in the morning, and the unveiling of my star was set for noon. He left according to schedule, so there was no undue traffic jam that kept us from arriving at Hollywood Boulevard on time. After that thrilling ceremony, we passed by the headquarters of the Hollywood Chamber of Commerce to personally thank Ana Martínez, who at the time was the only Spanish speaker on staff and who had helped campaign in my favor. We then invited both her and Ernesto Martínez, a good friend who at that time worked with the Galavisión television network, to lunch, where we had a wonderful time.

I've heard that all types of people wrote letters on my behalf, from President Ronald Reagan to undocumented workers. What makes that star so special to me is that so many people made an effort on my behalf. On the day my star was unveiled on Hollywood Boulevard, I had the pleasure of meeting Xiomara Fonseca, who as I mentioned earlier would become my road manager and with whom Pedro and I would travel to many countries. In addition to my star on the Hollywood Walk of Fame, seven others now adorn Hollywood Boulevard in tribute to my fellow countrymen and -women, immortalizing Gloria Estefan, Cristina Saralegui, Israel López ("Cachao"), Andy García, Desi Arnaz, Dámaso Pérez Prado, and Xavier Cugat.

At the end of that momentous year in my life, I was invited by the Cuban American Foundation to record a song and video entitled "Yo Vuelvo a Ti" ("I Always Go Back to You"). It was an amazing experience to be reunited professionally with such great Cuban musicians, and friends, as Rolando Laserie and Cachao. It had been years since I performed with them. It was also an emotional experience, since we relived our days of joy and hope in free Cuba, if only for a few hours.

The foundation invited me to perform two years later at the reinauguration of the Freedom Tower on Miami's Biscayne Boulevard. Apart from being a major landmark in Miami's skyline, the Freedom Tower holds a special place in Cuban exile history, since that is where hundreds of thousands of my fellow countrymen were reprocessed as refugees when they fled to the United States. The Freedom Tower is a Cuban exile Ellis Island. It was a great honor for me to play a role in such a historical event, since that building holds a special place in my heart.

I was blessed with my first Grammy Award in 1989. Throughout my career, I have been nominated for that award nineteen times, but I won my first one for my album *Ritmo de Corazón*. Pedro and I were sitting at the ceremony, waiting for the names to be read, and when I heard, "And the winner is, Celia Cruz!" I became so excited that I jumped to my feet, threw my purse at Pedro, and ran off. Poor Pedro, he didn't find me until two hours later. With all the excitement, the pictures, and the interviews, he didn't know where I had gone.

In April of that same year, I had the unbelievable experience of being invited to a Cuban exile event at the White House, where I was asked to sing the Cuban national anthem. In the presence of President George H. W. Bush, Vice President Dan Quayle, Congresswoman Ileana Ross-Lehtinen, and hundreds of other elected officials, Cuban exile leaders, and special guests, I sang the anthem of the country I was forced to leave, in the center of power of the country that had opened its arms to me. When I started to sing, I actually felt a knot in my throat. So many emotions rushed through me that I couldn't decipher one from another. It was thrilling yet sad. Again, I felt my mother by my side, encouraging me and holding my hand. I will always remember that moment, since I was blessed with the opportunity to use my voice, in the presence of the most powerful man in the world, to publicly express my people's undying quest for freedom.

Soon after the White House event, Pedro and I were at home

when my publicist, Blanca Lasalle, called us to say that Yale University was planning to give me an honorary doctorate for my contributions to music during their commencement ceremonies in May. Not only was I left speechless by the news, I didn't even know why Yale had decided to give me such an honor. Nonetheless, I thank God for that beautiful tribute.

The day of the commencement exercises, I was thrilled to find myself surrounded by so many distinguished people and professors on the dais. I kept asking myself, Celia, how did you, a simple *guarachera,* make it all this way? When they called my name, all those young graduates gave me a standing ovation. All I could think of was my father and the dream he had for me to become a respectable teacher. When they handed me the diploma, I realized that my father's dream had come true. God had chosen music— the most beautiful thing I know how to make—to be the vehicle by which I would show the world one of my country's treasures. In other words, the world became the classroom I asked Marta Rainieri to help me find years ago, before I graduated from Havana's Teachers College. After the ceremony ended, I had the pleasure of meeting Judge Carlos Cabranes of New Haven, Connecticut, who told us that it was he who had suggested to Yale that I be given an honorary doctorate and that he had led the campaign on my behalf. I was touched by what he did for me, and I made sure to let him know it.

In 1982, I was blessed with being reunited with my brothers from the Sonora Matancera when we recorded the album entitled *Feliz Encuentro (Happy Reunion).* It was such an unforgettable, happy, and creative experience, not to mention a success, that my friend the Puerto Rican actress and radio host Gilda Mirós came up with the idea that we would have to stage a special celebration for the seventy-fifth anniversary of the Sonora Matancera in 1989.

Gilda worked very hard on that project, and she actually managed to stage three concerts to commemorate the event. I was so excited we were going to be reunited, I was on an emotional roller coaster all week. Finally, on June 1, 1989, I performed in the seventy-fifth anniversary concert of the Sonora Matancera, singing the greatest hits I had recorded with the orchestra, such as "Guantanamera," "Bembá Colorá," and "La Bella Cubana."

After we began to perform, the audience immediately stood up and remained standing throughout the entire performance. Great singers who had performed with the Sonora throughout the years, such as Daniel Santos, Leo Marini, Caíto, Bobby Capó, Carlos Argentino, and Vicentico Valdés, joined us on stage, and when the concert was over, we received a five-minute ovation.

The following day, we had another concert in New Jersey's Meadowlands Arena, and on June 3, we performed together for the last time in New York's Central Park, at a free concert we dedicated to our fans. Although it was a terribly warm day, it was one of the most memorable moments of my life.

Sadly, that day will never be repeated. Since that wonderful reunion, Caíto, Bobby Capó, and Carlos Argentino have all passed away. And as the years pass, and as God wills it, I'm sure there will be many more good-byes.

Cinco

THE QUEEN OF SALSA

*No sé qué tiene tu voz que domina con embrujo de magia mi
pasión. . . .*
I don't know how it does it, but your voice magically takes hold of
my heart. . . .

—Ramón Cabrera Argote. Celia Cruz, "Tu Voz."

Celia Cruz in concert in Miami's Bayfront
Park, in a celebration for the 20th of May,
Cuban Independence Day.

Guantánamo BECAME KNOWN THE WORLD OVER BE-cause of the classical Cuban song "Guantanamera," with its beautiful lyrics taken from the poetry of Cuban national hero and modernist writer José Martí. God only knows how many times I've sung that song accompanied by drums while dreaming of again seeing Cuba's green royal palms. In 1990, and without ever expecting it, I received news I'd been invited to perform at the U.S. naval base at Guantánamo Bay, Cuba. I actually cried for several days before leaving, given that I felt the Lord had blessed me with allowing me to return to the country of my birth and the land where my parents are buried.

When I arrived at the naval base, I took with me in my heart the names of all those Cubans who had been forced to flee their country and who died in exile without ever again being able to see the palm trees swaying on the island's beautiful beaches. It's almost impossible to describe the emotions Pedro and I felt the day we boarded that plane. It was a combination of joy and fear, along with a tremendous amount of sadness. I was returning to Cuba, but not to the Cuba I left. My Cuba is still enslaved, and all I was visiting was a small piece of the country's territory, occupied by an American naval base.

The military plane we flew on strangely resembled the

one I took when I left Cuba for good. In any case, once we finally took off, I stopped thinking about Cuba's present-day tragic circumstances. Instead, I reminisced about the Cuba I remembered from my childhood. I remembered Havana with its hustle and bustle and streets filled with elegantly dressed people. In my mind, I returned to my beloved Santos Suárez neighborhood, and I saw myself running down the street with my friends, making sure we didn't bump into any sidewalk vendors, knocking down their merchandise.

While I was lost in my thoughts, someone asked me a question. I suddenly snapped back to the present and realized that the person asking me the question was Congresswoman Ileana Ross-Lehtinen, who was talking with journalists and other people on board. I apologized for not having heard what she asked me, and I left my memories of the Cuba of yesterday to discuss the situation Cuba is in now. Nonetheless, we were all very happy, since the journalists, such as Leticia Callava of Telemundo and Eduardo González Rubio from WQBA Radio, were free to do their job, while the invited guests like Pedro and me fantasized about what it would feel like to step foot in Cuba after a thirty-year absence.

I asked why the flight was taking so long, and they explained that we had to circumvent the entire island since we weren't allowed to fly directly over it. When we suddenly started our descent, I looked out the window and was actually surprised when I saw how calm the island looked.

I made out the U.S. base only when the airplane finally touched the runway, and it was then we all began to cheer and applaud. They brought the stairs up to the aircraft, and we began to exit. As soon as I passed through the door, the smell of the tropical air filled my nose, and Pedro grabbed my hand. We were so happy that we wanted to jump up and down. I ran down the steps and knelt on my hands and knees, kissing the Cuban soil three times as I thanked God out loud for having allowed me to return to the island. I immediately walked toward the fence that divides the base from the Cuban town of Caimanera. I stuck my hand through it, and I took soil from the other side of the fence. I put the soil in a pouch I had brought for the occasion. I then turned to Pedro and told him that if I died before Cuba regained its freedom to please bury me with the same soil I handed him.

I have no words to describe what I felt as I thought about my family being trapped behind that disgraceful gate. I had nieces and nephews I'd never met, siblings I couldn't share my life with, relatives and friends on the other side. I couldn't even begin to count all the people I hadn't seen since 1960 whom I couldn't reach out to across the barbed wire. Cuba had turned into a prison. It's a heartbreaking reality.

We gave a lovely and emotional concert that afternoon. When I sang "Canto a La Habana," with lyrics that take the listener through a tour of Cuba's natural wonders, and when I looked out from the stage and saw the royal palms growing majestically on the other side of the fence, I was overwhelmed. I felt that choking sensation that overtakes me on rare occasions, such as when I learned that my mother had died. I couldn't continue. I started crying on stage in front of the audience as the band played. I pulled myself together for a moment, finished the song, yelled, "*Azúcar!*" and the concert ended.

During that visit, I also had the chance to relive an experience I'd had in Cuba before I fled. There are still a handful of older workers on the base who actually live on the Cuban side of the fence and are allowed, by the regime, to travel to the base daily for work, since they've been doing so for over forty years. One of the workers approached me and asked me what at first seemed to be a strange question: "Celia, do you still use Shalimar perfume?" I told him that I still did use it, and I asked him why he asked me such a thing, to which he answered: "Once in 1953, I asked you for your autograph, and you gave it to me on a piece of paper, which I still have. It still smells like Shalimar." I was very moved by this encounter, since it reminded me of better days in Cuba and of a personal past I will never relive.

We left the naval base at Guantánamo Bay that same evening, but this time, unlike when I left Cuba in 1960, I did not look out the window. All I could think of was returning to a free Cuba as a free woman and enjoying my life in peace, as is my birthright. Pedro held my hand throughout the flight back to Florida. I could feel by the way he held my hand that he was thinking the same thing I was.

From 1990 until 1994, it seemed that God blessed me with awards everywhere: I received the Smithsonian Institution's Lifetime Achievement Award; President Bill Clinton presented me with the National Endowment for the Arts Medal on the White House lawn; and Miami's Southwest Eighth Street, the legendary "Calle Ocho" and the heart of Little Havana, was christened "Celia Cruz Way." I was also given a star on Calle Ocho's Walk of Fame; my name was engraved on the Wall of Fame in Madison Square Garden; New York governor Mario Cuomo gave me the Hispanic Women Achievers Award; Miami's Florida International University awarded me my second honorary doctorate; and I received my third honorary doctorate from the University of Miami. The Republic of Colombia gave me its Presidential Arts Medal; and I was thrilled when I was immortalized in the Hollywood Wax Museum.

Every time I received another honor, I would ask myself the same thing I'd asked myself the first time I took the stage at Paris's famed Olympia Theater in the late 1980s: How did a little black girl from Santos Suárez come so far? God can make anything possible, since it's all been His work, not mine.

In 1992, Jerry Masucci told me there was a young musician named David Byrne from a band called the Talking Heads who wanted to record a song with me. Since I didn't know who the Talking Heads were, I asked my nephew, Johnpy, and he explained they were the coolest thing in American music, and he even brought me one of their albums. I listened to it, and I liked their style, although I didn't understand a word they were saying. I then told Jerry Masucci that I was willing to record with David, but when he sent me the demo tape of the song, I panicked, since it was completely in English. Granted, I had already worked extensively with American musicians when I recorded the single "Loco de Amor" for the sound track of the film *Something Wild* in the late 1980s, but I had never recorded in my heavily accented English before.

Pedro told me not to record it if I didn't want to, but I just couldn't let myself turn down the offer. I began to study the song until I felt more or less comfortable with it, but when I arrived at the studio to record the single, I was surprised and relieved to learn that I was to record the song with Johnny Pacheco's Lucumí lyrics and arrangements and not in English. I must admit that it turned out to be a wonderful number.

From the early 1970s, young Hispanics who enjoyed our music had begun to express themselves with their own salsa style. Ralphy realized that they had great potential and began to recruit them. Among them was a lovely young New York Puerto Rican woman known by all as La India, who also happened to be one of Johnpy's favorites. And there was also another salsa singer who was very skinny and had a wonderful voice and personality to match, named Marc Anthony. Both La India and Marc Anthony came to me for advice, and soon we became close. La India became like a daughter to me; she was always so affectionate. I felt bad for her when people started saying that she would replace me as the Queen of Salsa, since that was never her intention. Besides, that would be impossible, since no entertainer *replaces* another. Each artist has his or her place and public. If people like a new artist, that doesn't mean they reject the one who came before. La India and I began performing together, and whenever they wanted to hire me for a show and I couldn't make it, I always suggested that they hire her in my place. La India has lived up to my highest professional expectations of her. She is a wonderful woman, and I love her dearly.

In 1992, Miami celebrated the life and contributions of my dear friend and sister Lola Flores to music and art. As I've said many times, Lola and my friend Roberto Cazorla of the Spanish news agency EFE gave me the support I needed to become famous in Spain. I was thrilled about the tribute to La Faraona, and although it took place during the filming of *The Mambo Kings*—which I will discuss in more detail later—I would not have missed it for the world.

All kinds of artists assembled in Miami to celebrate her life, and the night before the tribute concert, Julio Iglesias threw a party for all of us. Lola arrived with her sister Carmen, her son Antonio, her husband Antonio ("El Pescadilla"), and her closest friends. We had a wonderful time, and even the Spanish singer Rocío Jurado and the Venezuelan José Luis Rodríguez ("El

Puma") were there. Lola and I had some time to sit around a table and laugh and reminisce. It was one of the most memorable evenings of my life.

The tribute concert took place in Miami at the James L. Knight Center the following evening. Lola and I sang "Burundanga" with all the strength we had, and both she and I danced according to our own style. The audience went wild, and after we all calmed down, I publicly thanked God for having given me a sister like Lola. When it came Lola's turn to speak, instead of talking about herself, she spoke of how honored she was to have friends such as the Cuban singer Olga Guillot and me. The three of us just stood there shaking from the emotion of it all. I can't describe how grateful I felt for having had that opportunity to publicly tell Lola how much I loved her.

After the tribute, I returned to Los Angeles for the filming of *The Mambo Kings*. Throughout my career I've worked in many movies, but invariably as a singer. I have never been an actress, and just appearing in a film doesn't make me one. As a matter of fact, I've always said that I'm just a humble singer and that I have no interest in being an actress. Nonetheless, my cinematic experiences have been wonderful. For instance, working on *The Mambo Kings,* where I met the Spaniard Antonio Banderas in his Hollywood debut, was fantastic.

The role itself, apart from representing the first time I acted in a film, came to me in an unusual manner. I didn't know there was a movie in the works based on the Pulitzer Prize–winning novel *The Mambo Kings Play Songs of Love*. I had heard about the book, and I knew it had been written by the Cuban American author Oscar Hijuelos, whom I had the pleasure of meeting while we were filming the movie, but that was all I knew about the project. The most interesting thing about my role in the movie is that my character, Evangelina Montoya, does not appear in the novel. Arnold Glimcher, the producer of the movie and a fan of mine, came up with the idea that there should be a black *santera* in the movie who owns a nightspot called Club Babalú where the Mambo Kings, played by Armand Assante and Antonio Banderas, show up looking for work.

When Arnold gave me the script, I made sure to explain how deeply accented my English is, but he told me that was exactly what he was looking for, and he asked me to read a few lines for him. Although I was nervous, Arnold remained calm and put me at ease, and as a result, he liked how I sounded. Since he was aware of how self-conscious I was about my English, he always spoke to me slowly and clearly. He was very kind to me and made sure I understood all of his directions. He would even bring me food. Arnold Glimcher was a total gentleman.

When Arnold set the timetable for the filming of the movie, he made sure it wouldn't conflict with my performance schedule, and he hired a diction coach named Gabriel Sánchez for both Antonio and me. At times, I was so afraid of my English that I would beg him not to leave my side. Gabriel became my companion throughout the filming of the movie.

I had only a small role in the movie. When they first gave me the script, it was even smaller, but since Arnold liked how I worked, he expanded the character. I had great fun and I learned even more, but I was still nervous about the song I was supposed to sing in English. When we first started, there were two versions of the song, one in English and the other in Spanish. I prayed to God they would decide to use the latter, but they decided to have me sing it in English. Nevertheless, I was pleased, and it ended up sounding lovely. I should also note that when we were doing Antonio Banderas's character's wedding scene, I started singing

"Guantanamera," and Banderas joined in. Although it was an unscripted scene, it came out so well that they decided to leave it in the film.

It was an unbelievable experience to work with actors of the caliber of Armand Assante and Antonio Banderas. Both of them are wonderful, and we all worked together so well that if there were an Oscar for most cooperative cast, *The Mambo Kings* would have won it hands down. I enjoyed watching Armand get ready to perform, since he would scream for a while before his scene was to be filmed. I don't know if he did that to clear his throat or to connect with his character, but it fascinated me. The actresses Cathy Moriarty and Talisa Soto were also of great help, since they speak Spanish. By the end of filming, every time I walked into the studio, the cast would applaud. They did all they could to make me feel at home.

After I worked in *The Mambo Kings,* I was invited to perform in a movie entitled *The Pérez Family (La Familia de los Pérez).* I performed in eleven scenes, but when the film was edited, I appeared in only three. They were all small scenes, and all I really did was walk on and off the set. Unfortunately, the movie did not do well at the box office, but I'm grateful that I had the opportunity to work with that beautiful, talented, young Academy Award winner Marisa Tomei. It's an honor when you have the opportunity to work with people of her talent.

I should mention here that 1992 was not perfect, since that was when Hurricane Andrew ravaged south Florida. The destruction the hurricane left in its wake was devastating, and as soon as Miami was ready to receive help, I volunteered my performances to raise funds for the Hurricane Relief Fund telethon. Although it was a sad occasion, it was good to work for such a necessary cause with the best stars of screen, stage, and music.

My album *Azúcar Negra* (*Black Sugar*), with the hit single of the same name, was launched in 1993. What I really enjoyed about that album was its pleasant pop sound, which worked well with my vocal style. I also taped my first video, directed by Emilio Estefan, for the album's single "Sazón," in which Gloria Estefan and Jon Secada did me the favor of lending me their beautiful voices for the chorus.

Soon after the album's release, the Dominican singer José Alberto ("El Canario"), his band, Pedro, and I performed at a concert at the Rex Theater in Buenos Aires in front of an audience of more than three thousand people—which for a salsa performance in Argentina was a major accomplishment. Salsa still wasn't popular in Argentina back then. I remember asking the Argentines to help us spread salsa music throughout their country. I didn't have to wait long, since salsa soon became all the rage throughout the southern cone, which includes Uruguay, Argentina, and Chile. In fact, within a year of our concert at Buenos Aires's Rex, Tito Puente, Marc Anthony, El Canario, Cheo Feliciano, and I performed at the first Argentine salsa festival. From then on, I performed more often throughout the southern cone. The beach resort of Punta del Este in Uruguay has become one of my favorite places to relax during short winter vacations.

In August of that year, I again made the headlines, but this time it was because of Cuba's political situation. I had gone to Colombia to perform and promote my new album at one of Bogotá's major yearly events, El Festival de la Cerveza (the Beer Festival). It just happened that the same time I was there, Colombian president César Gaviria invited the Cuban dictator for a state visit. I say that it was an error because the horrible civil war that has ravaged the wonderful Colombian people had been supported in part by Fidel, so in my opinion he didn't deserve to be treated lavishly by a country he has helped devastate. While I was being interviewed at a press conference, one of the journalists asked me what I thought of "President" Fidel Castro's state visit to Colombia, and instead of answering, I asked him why he insisted on calling that man "President" Fidel Castro, since he is not a president. I told the journalist that as far as I was concerned, he's nothing more than a tin-pot dictator. Then other journalists began asking more questions about Cuba and the political situation there, and I didn't dodge their questions. Unfortunately, the line of questioning did not change, so I interrupted: "Why do you insist on asking me what I think about Fidel? Have you by any chance asked him what he thinks about me?"

As far as I was concerned, we had strayed too far into a topic that I just didn't want to discuss anymore, so I thought it would be best if we stopped the press conference. Before I left, I said the following:

I know you keep asking me these questions in an attempt to irritate me. So let me put an end to this once and for all, and tell you exactly what I think. I don't understand why you didn't ask that man why he had to fly here and waste so much fuel doing so, since people in Cuba have no fuel to get anywhere. You should have asked him why he had to fly here with a second plane stocked with food and water from his private stock, when people in Cuba go hungry and don't even have a decent water supply. You should go ask him why Cuban exiles have to send money back to Cuba to feed people that are starving on the island. It's ironic, if a couple of years ago they caught you with one dollar in Cuba, you were sent to jail for twenty years. Now that man wants the big, bad exiles, who fled with nothing, to send dollars back to feed the people he can't or won't. The only reason he came here to Colombia is that he's running around begging. He needs money desperately, and he'll do anything to get it. But let's stop here. I never met that man, and I don't want to even think about him. I left Cuba many years ago to make enough money to send it back to Cuba so my dying mother could eat lobsters. The same lobsters that used to abound in Cuba, but that for some reason have disappeared from Cuban kitchens. Why don't you go ask him what happened to Cuban lobsters? Where have they gone? For export for hard currency that ends up in his pocket? Sure, he has plenty of lobsters for himself; that's for sure. Just look at the food he had with him when he arrived. I just want to make it clear to all of you that that man did not allow me to return to my country when my mother was dying, and although I try to be a Christian woman, I cannot bring myself to ever forgive him for that.

My speech made headlines.

In the fall of that year, the producer Quincy Jones, with whom I have worked many times and have developed a wonderful rapport, asked me to perform "Guantanamera" at a show he was producing in Miami for the first Summit of the Americas, a meeting of all *democratically* elected leaders of the Western Hemisphere.

While we were rehearsing, all the vocalists—including Liza Minnelli and Vicky Carr—were told not to make any political statements during our performance, but when it came time for me to perform in front of all those leaders, including President Clinton, I just couldn't control myself. During the violin interlude of my traditional "Guantanamera" I turned to all the leaders and said, "Your Excellencies, I implore you, in the name of my fellow Cubans, please stop aiding and abetting Fidel Castro. If you stop helping him, he'll have to give up power, and only then will Cuba be a free country. Please, help my people."

Although they were heartfelt words, I caused another controversy. How could I not say anything when I had the freedom to do so? In my country, people serve very long prison sentences for saying what I did in that moment. God had given me the opportunity to speak for the Cuban people, and I just couldn't let it pass. If I had, I would have felt that I was turning my back on my most basic principles.

From the moment I was exiled from my country, I've always held the same political stance regarding the current Cuban government. I've traveled the world unmasking the truths behind the Castro regime. I travel without bodyguards and only with Pedro by my side. I've never tried to alter my opinions out of fear of offending anyone. I believe what I believe, and that's how I've lived my life.

In 1993, I made my fashion runway debut. The French designer Thierry Mugler invited me to model some of his clothes. As I sang "Químbara," I paraded down the runway wearing a beautiful dress he had designed exclusively for me. After the fashion show, Pedro and I went out with the other models, who made me feel like an old pro. When a friend of mine asked me how it felt to be a high-fashion model, I responded that I just couldn't believe all I was doing, because deep in my heart I was still that little black girl from Santos Suárez who would have never dreamed of all the opportunities that God put in her path.

In 1994, President Bill Clinton personally gave me one of the major awards bestowed upon American civilians: the National

Endowment for the Arts Medal. The moment the president, with the First Lady by his side, placed the medal around my neck, I was so moved that again I felt a knot in my throat. It was thrilling for me to be so greatly honored by the nation that gave me a home after the regime in Cuba forced me to flee. President Clinton, who is a charming man, told me he likes to dance and that he was well acquainted with my music and loved my voice. I was very moved by his gallantry and kind words. I was also thrilled to be honored alongside such American greats as Gene Kelly, Harry Belafonte, Pete Seeger, Julie Harris, Dave Brubeck, and Richard Wilbur. As I looked at my fellow honorees, and at the president and the First Lady, I felt like pinching myself. How blessed I was to represent this magnificent country—my country.

Late that year, the Billboard Magazine Awards honored me by inducting me into their Hall of Fame during their yearly ceremony in Miami. Shortly afterward, the Univisión network and *Billboard* joined forces to award me with their lifetime achievement award. When I accepted, I shared the award with Pedro and Ralph Mercado.

On September 25, 1994, the Lord blessed me with another special award, this one given to me by the University of Panama. With the award, the University of Panama created a scholarship in my name, to be given to an accomplished student in the Arts. Just knowing that future generations of Panamanians would have the opportunity to get a college education made that award precious to me.

Shortly thereafter, I was off touring when I received a call from Mexico inquiring as to whether or not I was interested in performing in a *telenovela,* or soap opera, entitled *Valentina.* I liked the idea, because it would be an opportunity to act in my native language and with Mexican actors I admire greatly, such as

Juan Ferrara and Verónica Castro. We reworked my schedule, and Pedro and I went off to film in both Cancún and Mexico City.

I played the role of Lucumé, an *espiritista,* or Caribbean clair-voyant. It wasn't a difficult role for me to do since it was a typical Cuban folk character. *Valentina* was a hit, and while filming, I made many new friends in the acting field and was also able to spend more time with old friends such as Los Misukos, Roberto González, and Mitsuko Miguel.

Los Misukos were very generous to us, and again they offered us their home in Mexico City. I was grateful for the offer, as Pedro is a diabetic and I have to cook meals that are appropriate to his diet. I needed a comfortable kitchen to work in. I'm serious about protecting my husband's health. I consistently monitor his blood sugar levels, and I'm always telling him he can have only one type of sugar: Celia's *azúcar!*

Roberto actually helped me immensely with what was then a grave problem. I had lost a piece of luggage on a trip to Mexico from New York. I panicked when I realized that all my shoes had been packed in that suitcase. All of them! When I realized that my favorite pair of high heels were missing, I was distraught, as they were one of a kind. Made especially for me in Mexico by a man named Mr. Nieto, the shoes were unique because the heel began at the ball of the foot rather than down by the actual heel itself. At first glance they looked like platform shoes, yet they held the form of a high heel, giving them a wildly stylish look. Roberto did his best, but unfortunately those shoes were lost forever.

After we finished filming *Valentina,* which was first broadcast throughout Mexico and Latin America and then became a world-wide hit, I started doing the promotional tour and found out that it had already been dubbed in Russian! I had a lot of fun thinking about how I sounded in Russian. Actually, my "Russian" became the butt of jokes on a famous television appearance of mine with my dear friend Mario Kreutzberger ("Don Francisco") on his Univisión network show, *Sábado Gigante*.

In the mid-1990s, I was involved in an unpleasant controversy. That was the period when "psychic" hot lines became popular. Several stars had lent their names commercially to some of these phone lines, so my agent, Ralph Mercado, suggested I record a tape saying, "Hello. You have called the Celia Cruz Psychic Hot Line. In a few moments, I will transfer you to one of my psychics." I don't really know why people were so critical of my involvement in that, since don't we all have the right to believe or think any way we please in this country? In any case, I never claimed to be a psychic. That was never my intention.

I apologized publicly if I had offended anyone with my recording. I have always tried to do the best I could, and never do I go out and hurt anyone intentionally. My dear friend Cristina Saralegui invited me on her show to allow me to apologize publicly. I felt relieved to be able to explain what had happened, and when we finished taping the show, we were given a standing ovation. Needless to say, when my contract with the hot line expired, I didn't renew it.

In that same year, I had the chance to return to *Sesame Street*. In 1989, I first appeared on that show at the invitation of my friend Luis Santeiro, one of the program's creators, when he encouraged me to do a scene in which I sang "Sun Sun Ba Baé" with Big Bird. In 1994, I was asked to perform "Burundanga," but the real fun came when the Muppets and I sang "Químbara." Imagine, the Muppets singing "Químbara"! That was the ultimate "crossover" moment.

In November 1994, I was performing in Europe when I was

asked to interrupt my tour and go to Panama to perform for a group of Cuban *balseros* (refugees who had fled in makeshift rafts) who were being held on a U.S. military base on the isthmus. Earlier that year, antigovernment riots had broken out across Cuba, so to relieve the pressure, the regime allowed anyone who wanted to leave the country to do so. The Cuban government opened its pressure valve, and another mass exodus, like the Mariel boat lift of 1980, was under way.

It didn't take long for the U.S. Navy to start picking up the rafters in the high seas before they reached American soil. The U.S. government wanted to discourage more refugees, so they wanted to return them to Cuba and have them process their immigration to the United States in an orderly and legal manner. I was appalled by that policy, since experience has taught me that you can never trust the word of the Cuban regime. God only knows what would have been done to them if they had been repatriated, so the U.S. government decided to send them to American military bases throughout the Caribbean basin and fence them in behind barbed wire while they decided what to do. As far as I was concerned, fencing people in is something only the Cuban regime does, since it doesn't respect any civil or human rights. And although I understand that the U.S. government needed to process them in an orderly fashion, I was appalled by the way the Cuban refugees were being treated. There were thousands of *balseros* in the Panama bases, including women, children, and even newborns. They had been held for so long that they became desperate. Some actually went on hunger strikes to protest how they were being treated.

I attempted to help get the attention, and hopefully the intervention, of U.S. president Bill Clinton through a press conference held before the concert. I wanted to do all I could to help grant the *balseros* entry into the United States. I told the *balseros* that I was sure President Clinton was doing all he could to ensure a quick resolution to the situation and that with God's help they would soon be set free.

Right before I performed, the *balseros* actually performed for me. With the little they had, they tried to do all they could to make me feel welcome and entertained. Not only did they make a commemorative plaque for me, they gave me a special gift I will always treasure. One of them made a model of the typical raft used to flee Cuba, and as I was singing, they passed it around until all of them had touched it, and then the last *balsero* handed it to me, since they wanted me to have a collective souvenir of what they had gone through.

In any case, and regardless of the terrible conditions, we enjoyed ourselves tremendously. It was fascinating to discover that all those *balseros,* most of whom had been born after I left Cuba, knew who I was and even knew the lyrics to many of my most famous songs. Although the regime they were escaping from had erased me from the country's official history, my people never forgot how much I always loved them, and they responded in kind. I should also mention that in the middle of the concert I told the audience that I had spoken to the president about their plight and that their situation would soon be corrected. Fortunately, virtually all the *balseros* were eventually processed and given refuge in the United States. I was grateful to them for having allowed me to help lift their spirits when they found themselves alone and without a country to return to.

When I returned to Europe to continue with the tour I had interrupted, all I could think about was how I never imagined that my country would have such a terribly sad destiny, in which the best thing people could aspire to was to flee. When I was a child and a young adult growing up in Cuba, never did I dream that my people would one day literally be dying to leave. As a matter of fact, Cuba was a place where other people immigrated *to*. And now look what's happened to us. I pray to God to see the day when all of it will be something of the past.

Shortly thereafter, the Proposition 187 referendum issue was sweeping California. "Prop 187" stipulated that all government services were to be denied to all undocumented immigrants, including children. I was against children being denied basic human rights, like the right to an education, since the situation they're in is not of their making—and furthermore, their parents have come to the United States to do the jobs most Americans would never dream of doing. Why should they be treated as if they aren't God's children because they lack a bureaucratic piece of paper? I myself experienced life as an undocumented immigrant, since my own country stripped me of my citizenship and left me stateless. Therefore, I made my position on this issue very public. Unfortunately, the struggle for the fair rights of immigrants is far from won.

In January 1995, I performed in Cali, Colombia, in a huge concert before sixty thousand people with the Venezuelan musician Oscar D'León and the Puerto Rican Pete "El Conde" Rodríguez. After the performance I was filled with energy, since those types of concerts always thrill me. So imagine my surprise when we returned to the Cali Intercontinental Hotel and I was told that I was dead. Apparently, several Venezuelan newspapers ran headlines saying I had died, in New York, of a massive heart attack.

The press began calling to inquire what happened to me. Needless to say, the Cali journalists knew I was fine, but when my friends and relatives heard the news, they became very worried. I received calls from many people who were crying because they thought I was dead and who cried even more, out of relief, when they found out I was still alive. The story spread so quickly that I had to hold a press conference to prove I was alive. Although it was an unpleasant situation, I was very moved to see how so many people worried about me.

In February, my friend Willie Chirino and I toured Mexico to promote our album *Irrepetible*. Willie is a wonderful and creative young man, and I had a great time working with him. We included singles that I liked very much, such as "Que le Den Candela" and "Limón y Menta" and old Cuban classics like "Duerme Negrita." I think that album did so well because Willie is a consummate professional. He is the perfect person to work with.

During a press conference to promote that album in Mexico City, I was again asked for my opinion about Cuba. Yet again I explained to the journalists that I did not want to talk about politics, and as I had said earlier in Colombia, I told them to ask Fidel what he thought about me, although I really don't care what he thinks. We were supposed to talk about my future plans to record with the Mexican singer Juan Gabriel, but once more, we were sidetracked by politics.

The year 1995 was filled with travel and tributes. I toured extensively and received several lovely tributes, including a star on Caracas's Walk of Fame on their Paseo Amador Bendayan Boulevard. I would like to note that wherever I travel, I take my collection of religious image cards, my rosary, and pictures of my nieces and nephew. I am devoted to my saints because I was taught in catechism classes back in Santos Suárez's Miraculous Medal Parish that saints are holy human examples to follow, and with their intercession, the Lord helps us. Thus I always take them with me. As a matter of fact, as soon as I set myself up in my room, I call my sister Gladys to tell her I have arrived, and then I arrange my images of the saints, my rosary, and my pictures on a night table. That way, when I leave the room, the last thing I see are the people I love the most, surrounded by holy articles, and when I return, they're the first thing I see. Right before I fall asleep and as soon as I awaken, I ask God to help all my family, and especially my nieces, Linda and Celia María, and my nephew, John Paul.

That same year, Pedro and I were in Puerto Rico when we heard that John Paul had been hospitalized. We immediately left for Miami. As soon as we landed, we went straight to the hospital, where all our family, Zoila, and Brujita were waiting for us. I went straight to the chapel, said a few prayers, and then went up to my nephew's room. From the moment he was born, John Paul had been the son I never had, but my poor sister suffered tremendously all his life because he was born a hemophiliac. Ever since he was an infant, we had to be very careful with Johnpy. He didn't have a normal childhood, since he couldn't play with other kids. As a matter of fact, he spent more time in the hospital than on the playground.

Even so, Johnpy always made sure to have a smile on his face. In fact, no one ever heard him complain. He accepted the reality he had been dealt and carried his head high. He was such a gentleman and so kind that it was hard not to love him. He underwent many painful procedures. All the same, he was very brave and positive.

Johnpy was always thrilled when he heard the stories of our tours, and invariably, when Pedro and I returned home, he was the first one to come see us. He was always attentive to others.

John Paul never forgot a birthday or an anniversary. He thought more of others than of himself.

I remember once, when he had turned twenty, Johnpy got a job and decided to treat his whole family to dinner. So one evening off we went—Johnpy, his mother, his father, his sister Linda and her boyfriend, his sister Celia María, Pedro, and me. Pedro was worried that Johnpy was going to spend his whole paycheck on the dinner, so he offered to pay for half, but Johnpy insisted on paying the whole check on his own. It was not cheap. But that's the generous soul he was, always trying to make everyone happy.

We were at his bedside when God took John Paul from us, leaving an enormous gap in our lives. He was only twenty-three years old. His death was devastating for his parents, and until today there's no earthly power that can ease their pain. But I try not to dwell too much on his death. John Paul Bécquer was a perfect young gentleman, so I would rather think about how he lived than how he died. I really do miss him, and I think about him every day.

Pedro and I keep Johnpy's picture in the foyer entrance to our home, so every time I go in and out, I see him smiling at me. When I leave I say to his picture, "Johnpy, watch the house for me. I'll be right back," and when I return I say, "I'm back, Johnpy. Thanks for watching the house." I repeat his name constantly, since I want to keep his spirit alive. I will never fill the void his death left in my soul, but I do look forward to seeing him again when God calls me home.

After Johnpy's death, I appeared in several taped public service ads to raise awareness of diabetes-related blindness. In view of the fact that Pedro suffers from diabetes, and that it also afflicts many Hispanics, the fight against that disease is very important to me, so I was happy to work on the project. After the ads aired, I was surprised by how many people came up to me to talk about how diabetes has impacted their lives. More often than not, their stories were tragic. Still, I was glad to do a small part in raising awareness of such an important health issue.

In that same year, God blessed Pedro and me with some free time to rest and recuperate in the company of good friends. I remember spending time with a wonderful Cuban family, the Fanjuls, at their Casa de Campo resort in the Dominican Republic, and I remember sharing a wonderful time at the Coca-Cola party in Caracas with my friends Roberto Goizueta, the former president of the Coca-Cola Corporation and a fellow Cuban exile, may he rest in peace, and Patty and Gustavo Cisneros. Pedro and I were happy to relax and unwind, in the beautiful Venezuelan capital. After losing Johnpy, we both needed some time to heal.

In 1997, my relationship with La India became even closer. As I said earlier, I had enjoyed her company from the moment I met her. One day she told me that her mother had never had her baptized, and she asked if Pedro and I would be her godparents. We were both moved that she thought of us so highly, so we enthusiastically accepted her invitation. On Valentine's Day 1997, we met La India in a New Jersey parish. I had come dressed all in white to symbolize the washing away of original sin through the sacrament of baptism. After the priest christened our new goddaughter, we hugged her and gave her our blessing. Afterward, Pedro and I invited our new goddaughter to lunch at a Cuban restaurant, where we drank wine and dined on superb paella. While we were eating, La India confessed to me that she had felt a calming spirit enter her when I gave her my blessing. I told her she was feeling the love I have for her and that from that moment on, she would be my daughter.

At around that time, Juan Osorio, the Mexican television director and producer, offered me a role in another soap opera. I was excited by the idea, but I told Juan that I would do it only if the filming schedule could be worked into my performance schedule, as was the case when I worked in *Valentina*. Juan did all he could to accommodate me, and soon thereafter we started filming *El Alma no Tiene Color* (*Souls Don't Have a Race*), starring Laura Flores and Arturo Peniche.

My character was the black mother of Laura's character, a white woman. That's what attracted me to the soap opera when I read the script, that it dealt with the issue of race, and I was happy to finally work on a project that openly discussed the pain and ignorance of racism. Both Pedro and I were satisfied with the whole project when it was finished, and we really enjoyed the opportunity of befriending many young and rising stars. We were pleased to see what consummate professionals they were.

I spent most of 1997 traveling and touring, as I usually do, but I always make time to return home to New York. In that year, I was awarded a very special and unexpected honor. The beautiful city of San Francisco named October 25, 1997, Celia Cruz Day. Pedro and I were thrilled that San Francisco thought so highly of me to give me such a tribute. Unfortunately, it was the same year in which I had an unpleasant experience during a concert in Madison Square Garden. For weeks before the concert, it was widely reported throughout the media, and during the promotion, that a surprise guest singer would be performing with me. I thought that the invited guest was Gilberto Santa Rosa, the Puerto Rican salsa singer and a dear friend of mine, so I went out on stage and performed. When I was finished, I heard the name of the surprise guest, Isaac Delgado, and since I had never heard the name before, I began asking everyone who he was. That's when I was informed that Ralphy had called a press conference for after the concert, at which time he would formally introduce Mr. Delgado to the public.

I don't remember who told me, but right before the press conference was to take place, I learned that Isaac Delgado was a performer officially sanctioned by the Castro regime and still living in Cuba and that Ralphy was promoting him in the United States and trying to get his records distributed. I found out who Mr. Delgado really was when everyone else did. I had to quickly call my own press conference to make sure everyone understood that I had not known Mr. Delgado was a regime-sponsored performer and that if I had, I would never have shared the same stage with him. At the time, I was very hurt with Ralphy, since he should have known better than to do that to me. I understand that Ralphy is half Puerto Rican and half Dominican, and therefore he may not be as sensitive to Cuban feelings when it comes to these issues. But I was saddened that he didn't tell me the truth before putting me on stage with someone who, because of his political affiliation, is offensive to me and my Cuban brothers and sisters in exile. Why should I have to perform with officially sanctioned Cuban musicians and singers, since all they are really doing is making money that keeps a horrible regime afloat? In any case, although this misunderstanding caused a momentary rift between Ralphy and me, it was soon resolved, and in the press conference I called, I made it clear that Mr. Delgado's appearance had nothing whatsoever to do with me.

I should note that I hold no ill feeling toward Ralphy because of this well-publicized incident. On the contrary, I'm grateful to him for helping me to get where I am today. No one can make it completely alone, and during the twenty-five years I worked with Ralphy, I reached heights I never dreamed. He was always and will always be my friend.

Nevertheless, everything has its time and place, and my time with Ralphy had come to an end. His company, RMM, had grown tremendously, and he was also representing newer artists with promising talent. It just became too difficult to speak calmly with Ralphy since he was too busy running all over the place. Apart from that, I didn't feel that my records were being distributed as they should have been; so, as I had previously done with Sydney Siegel and Morris Levy, I decided to terminate my contract with Ralphy.

I had just been honored with the Hispanic Lifetime Achievement Award and the 1998 Grammy Awards were about to take place when I started thinking of how to actualize my decision with Ralphy. Pedro, Ralphy, Omer, and I went to Los Angeles, and while we were at the Grammys, I decided I would tell him of my decision on the flight back to New York.

Wycliff Jean, Jeni Fujita, and I had been nominated for our recording of "Guantanamera." We didn't win the award, and I think it was a shame, since it was a beautiful rendition of the song. In fact, many young people began to know me from my work with Wycliff and Jeni. I'm happy that our recording did so well for them.

The day before we were set to return to New York, I bumped into Ralphy in the hotel lobby and he told me that he'd had to change his flight, so he wouldn't be returning with us. That's when I decided to tell him of my decision.

Ralphy was shocked when I told him, and he asked me if something was wrong. I told him that it had nothing to do with something being wrong, and that if he had already booked me for anything, not to worry, since I had every intention of keeping my obligations. I also told him that I had decided not to record anymore, since my records weren't selling. As a matter of fact, I convinced myself that I would never record with anyone again. First of all, I had to film a video with every song, and I don't like dubbing my voice. Second, the recording industry wasn't what it used to be, and I really was tired of all the hassle. What I did want to do was keep performing before live audiences, since that's always been my first love. I have never been a studio singer; I'm a live performer. I never want to retire, unless, of course, I lose my voice or no one cares for my music anymore. I would like to die as my friend and brother "Mr. Babalú," Miguelito Valdés, did: on stage. My poor Miguelito, may he rest in peace, died while performing on stage at the Tequendama Hotel in Bogotá, Colombia.

Ralphy was disappointed with my decision, but he still wished me the very best, and since then, we have remained friends. Omer then decided also to leave RMM and become my manager. Apart from Pedro, he has been my greatest ally. Omer assured me that when the record labels found out that I no longer had a recording contract, they would be knocking at the door, since according to him I was a great artist. I thought he was just flattering me, but he insisted that it would happen. Since he had worked with us for eight years, and we knew how professional he was and how well he knew the business, Pedro and I thought that perhaps Omer knew something we didn't.

Our change in management didn't affect our performance schedule. As I had planned, and before I decided to go on my own, at the end of 1998 we performed at the Feria de Cali, the annual main event in Cali. What thrilled me was that the year's theme song was my single "La Vida es un Carnaval." I was awarded the Sebastian de Belalcázar Medal, the city's top distinction, and they treated me like royalty. I must add that I suffer tremendously for all the tragedies that have befallen the warm and generous Colombian people and their beautiful country. I pray to the Lord every day that they may achieve the peace and prosperity they so deserve, and whenever I've been fortunate enough to visit Colombia, I've made it a point to express my strong feelings for the country and its hopes for the future.

As my career in Spain evolved in the 1990s, I recorded many year-end specials of José Luis Moreno's *Noche de Fiesta* on the Spanish television network TVE, along with the Spanish singers Julio Iglesias, Rocío Jurado, Rafael, and Miguel Bosé. I should also note that Miguel and I did a show together entitled *Séptimo de Caballería*.

By the end of the decade, I recorded a song entitled "A lo Loco" with the Catalonian Pau Donés, from the group Jarabe de Palo, for the sound track of the Spanish film *El Milagro de Padre Tinto*. Pau and I became friends, and we later performed together at the *Pavarotti and Friends* concert in Modena, Italy.

In 1999, my friends the Cuban exile singers Albita and Lucrecia, the saxophonist Paquito D'Rivera, and I went on an extensive tour of the whole Iberian Peninsula entitled Pasión Cubana (Cuban Passion). Albita, who lives in Miami, is an outstanding musician and has a wonderful gift for improvising lyrics. Lucrecia, who lives in Spain, is a beautiful and intelligent young woman with a lovely voice; she is all the rage in Spain, and I'm proud of her for all her achievements. And of course, Paquito, my dear Paquito, is a gentleman and magician of music. I love him dearly. We were a hit in every city we performed in Spain and Portugal. Pasión Cubana was a truly unforgettable experience.

It was unfortunate that my dear friend and sister Lola Flores, La Faraona, did not live to see it. I'm sure she would have loved it. Even so, I was able to spend quality time with my friends Rolando and Gilda Columbie, who had moved to Madrid from the Canary Islands. In fact, Gilda turned her kitchen over to me, and this black girl—yes, yours truly—quickly became a gourmet chef.

We then went on to Mexico, where we promoted my album *Mi Vida es Cantar,* produced by the Mexican Isidro Infante. It was my seventy-sixth album, without counting singles. This album includes some lovely songs and my heartfelt tribute to Lola. The Cuban director Ernesto Fundora filmed the video in the historic heart of Mexico City, and for other shots they re-created a block party in the city's Chinatown. Although I had to dub my voice, the filming was such a pleasant experience that I actually began to enjoy the experience.

Just as Omer had promised, with his work in New York and with the help of Emilio Estefan in Miami and Oscar Gómez in Spain, offers started pouring in from an array of labels. We chose to go with Sony Music International, and Pedro, Omer, and I met with Angel Carrasco and Frank Welzer of Sony to sign the contract. Once that was done, we immediately started working on our first Sony recording, "Siempre Viviré" ("I Will Survive").

The millennium may have been coming to a close, but my career was entering an entirely new phase, and the future seemed as brilliant as ever.

Seis

SIEMPRE VIVIRÉ
I WILL SURVIVE

En el alma de mi gente, en el cuero de un tambor, en las manos del conguero, en los pies del bailador, yo viviré
In the soul of my people, in the sound of drum, in the hands of a conga player, and in the dancer's feet, I will survive.

—Frederick Perren, Dino Fekaris, and Oscar Gómez. Celia Cruz, "Siempre Viviré" ("I Will Survive").

Celia at her house in Edgewater,
New Jersey, after her surgery
December 2002.

The NEW MILLENNIUM WAS APPROACHING, AND I WAS excited by what it would bring. I didn't know whom to believe, though, as some thought the world would end. There were even mass suicides in California. All I kept hearing on the news was that the Y2K virus would make computers crash throughout the world and cause all the lights to go out and bring all transportation to a standstill. It sounded like a nightmare, or Havana after the revolution.

I was excited about the turn of the millennium, since one does not often get to celebrate such an event. I wanted to greet the new century performing on stage, as I always like to do, so I left it to Pedro to get everything ready. I always say, Pedro's so good at what he does that it seems as if he's doing the work of two people.

We decided to ignore all the millennium naysayers and left for the resort city of Punta del Este, Uruguay. Pedro, Omer, and I had a wonderful time, and when January 1, 2000, rolled around, I was relieved to read in the newspapers that the turn of the millennium had gone off without a hitch. No catastrophes, and all the lights stayed on. As a matter of fact, I could feel optimism in the air.

I didn't want to start the new century with a hectic performance schedule, so I asked Omer to plan a less frantic tour for me. From Uruguay, we toured Argentina and Chile, where I was honored with the Viña del Mar Festival's Gaviota de Plata (Silver Seagull Award). I was thrilled to receive that award, since it's Chile's highest honor for performance artists.

While I was touring, I heard I had been nominated for a Grammy Award for my album *Celia Cruz and Friends: A Night of Salsa*. We were elated when we received the news since that was the last album I recorded with my "three Cotton Heads," Pedro, Johnny Pacheco, and the legendary Tito Puente.

I was terribly affected by Tito's death. Years ago, he had a heart attack when we were performing in Puerto Rico, so I knew he had to take care of himself. I never thought God would take him from us so quickly.

When Tito passed away, we were performing in Buenos Aires's Rex Theater. It was June 1, 2000, and Pedro and I were resting in our room in the Albear Palace Hotel a few hours before I was to go on stage. I suddenly heard the secret knock on the door—the one we had made up years ago to serve as a measure of security in case someone wanted to enter my room uninvited—and I immediately knew it was Omer. I opened the door and saw that Omer had a very sad expression on his face. He immediately told me that Ruthie Sánchez had called to tell him that Tito Puente had died. I didn't want to believe it. I began to scream in shock. I immediately ran to the TV, and the news channel was indeed running a bulletin confirming that Tito Puente, El Rey de los Timbales, had died at New York University Medical Center. The news anchor said that with his passing, the world had lost a musical genius. I agreed completely.

I couldn't think straight. I had lost a dear friend. It was the only thing that mattered at the moment. I asked Omer to make the arrangements to return to New York as soon as possible, but he reminded me that we were under contract and could not simply leave. Granted, there was a clause in the contract that excused me from my obligations in case of death, but only if the person who passed away was a blood relative. Tito, my dear brother, had died and I wasn't able to be at his side during his funeral, just as I had not been allowed to return to Cuba to bury my mother. All Pedro and I could do was send flowers in our name. Both Pedro and I prayed the rosary for the repose of his soul. While we prayed for him, I kept thinking of what it will be like the day God brings us back together again, with Tito playing his drums and me singing, both of us surrounded by dancing angels. From the day he passed away until this very day, and solely in his honor, I have included his world-famous cha-cha, "Oye Cómo Va," in all my performances.

Fifteen days later, we returned to New York. As I was checking my answering machine, I was shocked to hear a message from Tito. Tito was not the type of person to leave messages, so I found it even more odd. When I listened to it, his clearest words were, "See you later, *negra.*" When I looked at the date of the call, I realized he had called to say good-bye on the eve of his death. Those were his last words to me. I immediately removed the tape from the answering machine and put it in my safe. Those words were his last gift to me, and I will cherish them until my last day on earth.

It took a while for Pedro and me to recover from Tito's death. We had to keep living and performing, though, since I felt that was the best way to honor his memory and his contributions to music.

Shortly thereafter, Cristina Saralegui called to tell us that she bumped into Whoopi Goldberg at some event and that Whoopi had told her that she always wanted to make a movie based on the story of my life. I was surprised, since I didn't know how Whoopi even knew who I was. Cristina reprimanded me. She asked me how it was possible that I didn't know how well-known I was among many Americans and that Whoopi told her that when she was a kid, she would stand in front of a mirror with a Coke bottle in hand and imitate me singing. I didn't know what to say, so I told Cristina that Pedro and I would have to discuss the idea, but that I was excited about the prospect.

A few months later, at an event where I performed in Washington's Kennedy Center for the Performing Arts, and after Pedro and I decided that we should go ahead with the movie project, Whoopi and I finally had the opportunity to meet. She told me how much she admired and respected me. She told me that she began studying Spanish in order to be able to portray me more accurately. I was happy to have met Whoopi and I am sure she will do a wonderful job with the film, since she is known for being a model of professionalism and a great actress. I am also comfortable with the project since both Cristina and her husband, Marcos Ávila, are going to produce the film, with Marcos writing the script. Whoopi later told me that there would be two scripts and that I would get to choose the one I liked best. I don't know when the film will finally go into production, but I am sure that it will be a great success, since it's in the hands of three extremely talented individuals.

I hadn't planned on going to the Grammy Awards at the Los Angeles Staples Center that year for two reasons. First of all, I had already been nominated nine times, but I won only once; and second—and most important—I was recovering from knee surgery. But the moment Emilio Estefan called to inform me that he was producing a tribute to Tito at the Grammys and that he wanted Ricky Martin and Gloria Estefan and me to perform, how could I not be there? I wasn't able to attend his funeral, so there was no way I could miss a tribute to him that would be broadcast worldwide. I forgot about the pain in my left knee, and Pedro and I left for California.

I usually pack our luggage. The reason I don't let others pack for Pedro and me is that when they do, I can't find anything. But with my recent surgery, I had no choice but to ask my sister Gladys and Omer to pack for us for our trip to Los Angeles. I was in such pain that for the first time in my life, I had to walk with the use of a cane. Omer didn't want me to move more than I had to, so when we arrived at Newark Airport, he requested that I be taken to the gate in a motorized cart. Unfortunately, the airline had no carts available, and the only thing they had that could help me was a wheelchair. I wasn't that bothered by the wheelchair, but what did bother me was that the airline employee who was pushing me began saying, "Look who I have here," to everyone she saw. Needless to say, my trip to the gate turned into a circus.

When we arrived in Los Angeles, I refused to get into another wheelchair. Omer insisted that I couldn't walk, and that I needed a wheelchair, but that he would not leave the terminal unless he was allowed to push me. The airline officials explained to us that they were the only ones allowed to handle airline wheelchairs, but Omer insisted that neither Pedro nor I wanted to be unduly bothered, and he explained what had happened to me in Newark. They finally relented, and we left Los Angeles International Airport the way Omer and I had requested. All the same, I vowed never to use another wheelchair again, even if it meant having to take baby steps to get anywhere.

While we rehearsed for the Grammys the following day, Gloria Estefan and Ricky Martin seemed to be more concerned about me than even Omer and Pedro were. They didn't allow me to move. I was very careful, but once I step on a stage, I forget about everything else. To make matters worse, the doctor said I had to use a cane if I intended to perform.

I had a simple blue dress made for the occasion, but I couldn't wear the shoes I normally do because of my knee surgery. I tried the dress on the morning of the awards ceremony, and when I saw myself in the mirror, I told my stylist, Marcos, that I felt something was missing. I told him that although I was walking with a limp, I needed something that would call attention away from my injury. We decided to go to the store on Sunset Boulevard where I buy all my wigs, and I bought ten of them. One of them was blue, and I bought it impulsively. After he finished my makeup, Marcos told me that although I had many nice wigs, I should try on the blue one. I complied, but when I looked at myself in the mirror, I took it off immediately. I told Marcos that I was just too old to wear such a wild wig. But Marcos insisted, and when he was done with me, I reluctantly agreed to wear the wig. Off I went with the blue wig on my head. And since I didn't want to be seen walking with the help of a cane, I left it with Marcos.

As soon as I arrived at the Staples Center, I heard a man say with a Spanish accent, "*Negra,* everything *does* look good on you." It was Antonio Banderas, whom I hadn't seen in almost five years. I was thrilled to be reunited with him, since by coincidence he was given a seat right next to mine. I had very handsome men on either side of me: Pedro and Antonio.

That wig made such a splash that I even appeared wearing it on the cover of the following week's edition of *¡Hola!* magazine, Spain's largest weekly. As a matter of fact, until that moment, that specific magazine never paid any attention to me. I think the blue wig had more of an impact than the Grammy Award I won that night.

Eleven years had passed since I'd last won a Grammy, so I really thought I wouldn't win that year. But when I heard Robi Rosa and Jon Secada say "And the Grammy goes to Celia Cruz, *A Night of Salsa,*" I forgot about my knee operation. I jumped out of my chair and ran up the stairs with surprising speed. My poor surgeon, who was watching the show live in New York, later told me that when he saw me run on stage, he immediately thought I would need surgery again. But thank God, nothing happened to my knee. As a matter of fact, it didn't even swell up.

Pedro and Omer were waiting for me backstage after I won the Grammy, and the three of us together took the traditional Grammy winners' photo. I was having a wonderful time talking with the international press when Pedro asked me if my knee was all right, which was the first time I had thought about my injury since I heard Robi Rosa call my name. I wasn't going to let my knee bother me, and I made that clear to Pedro.

My husband thought we would be returning to the hotel immediately after the ceremony, given that we were leaving the next morning for Portugal. I turned to him and told him I wanted to celebrate. Tommy Motola was giving a party for a small group, and I wanted to go. Pedro kept insisting that we were leaving the next morning, and I kept insisting that I wanted to go to the party. Pedro always does his best to please me, so off we went to the restaurant, where Tommy Motola had managed to bring my whole artistic family together. Gloria Estefan, the Mexican singer Thalía, Jennifer López, Jose Feliciano, Ángel Carrasco, and a Sony representative, María Elena Guerreiro, among others, were there having a great time. We partied until daybreak. We didn't sleep a wink that night, even though we had to be at the airport at seven o'clock in the morning for our flight to

Lisbon. When we arrived at Los Angeles International Airport, I saw a picture of myself wearing the blue wig on the front pages of every newspaper. I had really done it this time!

I lost another important figure in my life in that year. Tía Ana, my godmother, confidante, and second mother, passed away in Havana. Unlike what happened when my mother was near death, this time I was able to see Tía Ana again. Starting in the late 1980s, the Castro regime began allowing older Cubans to visit their exiled relatives. Of course, those of us abroad had to pay a hefty sum for the privilege, but when it came to my second mother, money was no barrier. Tía Ana was allowed to leave Cuba and visit me several times in New York and Cancún. We shared wonderful moments together, and I thanked God for the opportunity to be able to give something back to her, since she was instrumental in my development as a woman and an entertainer. My dear brother, Bárbaro, was also allowed to leave Cuba to visit me, and we also tried the best we could to relive all the years we were forced to spend apart. Both Bárbaro and Tía Ana always chose to return to our family in Cuba every time they were allowed to travel abroad. Finally, in the year 2000, God took my *tía*. Of course, I was not given permission by the regime to attend her funeral, although I am comforted by the knowledge that she was laid to rest in Havana's Colón Cemetery, where my mother rests. These two sisters who shared a wonderful bond are now together forever. I just pray to God that one day I be allowed to visit their tombs.

The year 2000 came to a close as happily as it started. In October, *Billboard* magazine honored me by dedicating an issue to my fiftieth anniversary on stage. In December, Pedro and I were invited by the Basilica of Our Lady of Guadalupe to sing "Las Mañanitas," a traditional Mexican greeting song. To be invited to sing "Las Mañanitas" in the presence of the image of Our Lady of Guadalupe on the eve of her feast day, December 12, is one of the highest honors that the Mexican people can bestow on an artist. That evening, with the Basilica filled with pilgrims, and as it was broadcast live throughout the Spanish-speaking world, I sang "Las Mañanitas." Pedro and I prayed and thanked Our Lady of Guadalupe for the wonderful life she had given us, which began in her country the very same day we had to flee ours.

We greeted 2001 in Spain's Santiago de Compostela, which followed with a year full of very moving professional events. First I was listed on the Walk of Fame of the Jackie Gleason Theater for the Performing Arts in Miami Beach, and then I had the wonderful opportunity to sing "Guantanamera" alongside Luciano Pavarotti in the yearly concert he always gives in Modena, Italy, to help needy causes. That year, the concert was dedicated to all the children living under the Taliban regime in Afghanistan. I was humbled when someone of Pavarotti's caliber and fame invited me to perform with him. Pavarotti was a perfect gentleman, and his kind sister invited us to dine with her family. Those concerts were unforgettable, and I am grateful to Pavarotti for having given me the opportunity to perform with him and to become known throughout Italy.

By September, we had returned to the United States from our foreign tour. I was invited to perform on the special *VH-1 Divas Live: With the One and Only Aretha Franklin,* and I later sang "Quím-bara" with Marc Anthony at a concert in Radio City Music Hall. Life was good, and I couldn't have been happier. Unfortunately, the world would take a horrible turn.

Omer was at home with Pedro and me when we received the call informing us that I had been nominated for a Latin Grammy. The awards ceremony was scheduled to take place in Miami on September 11, 2001. Regrettably, a controversy arose around the issue concerning musicians still living in Cuba and sanctioned by the Castro regime and their appearance in a ceremony in a city so central to all Cuban exiles. Again, Fidel's evil grasp had complicated our lives. In any case, and at the last moment, the ceremony was moved to Los Angeles. Pedro, Omer, and I left for California and arrived at the Beverly Hilton on September 9, 2001. Upon landing, we went immediately to rehearse. The following evening, the Latin Academy of Recording Arts and Sciences, or LARAS, was going to honor Julio Iglesias with its Lifetime Achievement Award. On the eve of the ceremony, the Italian singer Laura Paussini, the Colombian Juanes, the Mexican Thalía, the Cuban Jon Secada, and I performed in his honor. After the performance, Pedro and I decided to return to the hotel and rest up for the next day.

It was very early in the morning when Omer knocked on our door. I am usually an early riser, but that day I slept a bit later than I normally would. When I opened the door, I saw Omer looking very nervous as he told us that an airplane had crashed into one of the Twin Towers in New York. We ran to the television and turned on the news, and less than thirty minutes later, we saw a second plane crash into the second tower. We were horrified.

Up until that moment, we thought the first crash was an accident, but the second crash made it clear that this was a planned terrorist attack. I became so nervous that Pedro and Omer began to worry about my state of mind. We then heard that a passenger airplane had crashed in Pennsylvania and that another one had crashed into the Pentagon in Washington. I didn't know what to think. I began to panic when I tried calling my sister Gladys, my cousin Cachita, and Omer's mother, Magaly Cid, in New York. We couldn't get through to anyone.

I refused to leave my hotel room. That's when a wonderful Puerto Rican woman named Marlene Martínez, who works for LARAS, came to our room to keep us company. I felt sheer anguish, since as far as I am concerned, any attack on the United States is an attack on me. I will always be grateful to the United States for having given me security and freedom. This is my country, too, and I have lived here longer than I did in my native land. How can I not be devastated when the United States is attacked?

We were glued to the television set. The staff of the Beverly Hilton was very accommodating, and they actually brought another television to the room so we could watch the news in English on one channel while we watched the Univisión network coverage, reported by anchorman Jorge Ramos, on the other. I couldn't stop crying at all the suffering and the deaths of so many innocent people playing out on live television. Later that afternoon, I finally heard from all my loved ones in New York, and I calmed down a bit when I found out everyone was fine. All the same, it was a day filled with anguish.

The Grammy Awards were canceled that night. In its place, LARAS put together a low-key awards ceremony in Los Angeles's trendy Conga Room. I won an award that night, which I dedicated to the rescuers who were risking their lives in their heroic attempt to save others at ground zero. It was a very sad event, since understandably we were all overcome by grief.

Three days after the attacks of September 11, I was desperate to get back home to New York City, but since all the nation's airports were closed, we had no option but to rent a car and drive cross-country. Omer went out to find a comfortable car that he was willing to drive all by himself, and Pedro, practical man that he is, wanted to buy food, water, and other provisions for our trip.

Although he looked everywhere, Omer wasn't able to find a suitable car. Just as it began to look as though we would be trapped in California, Sony's María Elena Guerreiro informed us that the company was chartering a plane to take the entertainers back to New York City and Miami and that we would probably be leaving the following day.

We were actually supposed to perform in Mexico after the Grammy Awards, but we had planned to return to New York and then leave for Mexico from there instead. We didn't have our passports with us. I felt terribly stressed that we would have to cancel our performance in Mexico, but the situation was out of our hands.

Sony was able to hire an airplane once the airports finally re-opened. The limousines picked us up at the hotels we were staying in and took us to the airport. We were all nervous at having to fly, but we had no other option. We flew back with Sony executives and other performers. Coincidentally, Colombian singer Shakira was on our flight, but she didn't even bother looking at me. I guess I'm not her cup of tea. In any case, we flew in silence. What would normally have been a fun flight was as quiet as a tomb. I'm sure we were all pondering the same question: How can anyone take a plane full of people and turn it into a missile?

We landed in suburban New York's White Plains Airport in the afternoon of September 16, 2001. Harley, our chauffeur, was waiting for us, and he took us straight home. God only knows how relieved I felt when I saw Johnpy's picture greeting me with a smile back home. I started crying and thanking the Lord for having brought us home safe and sound, although I couldn't erase those horrible images from my mind.

Since I never like to disappoint anyone who hires me, we somehow managed to make it to Mexico to perform on September 25. While I was there, several journalists asked me why I didn't cancel after what had just happened in New York, and I told them that the show must go on. That's what I did when my mother died in Cuba and when Tito Puente died in New York. The stage, my performances, and my audience have always been my refuge. I was actually looking forward to performing in Mexico after 9/11, if only to keep me sane.

I don't think I'm exaggerating when I say that we were all looking forward to the arrival of 2002, which in my family's case brought with it both good and difficult moments. For instance, our album *Siempre Viviré* was a sensation. The title, *I Will Survive,* is my reality, since although no one lives forever in the physical sense, I believe that God has blessed me with immortality through my music. My music has been my passport to the world, since music is the one truly universal language. When I arrive in countries whose language I don't understand, all I need to do is sing and I am received with opened arms. As I said earlier, I love all types of music, and as a matter of fact, in Cuba I even used to enjoy the music of the Chinese immigrants who lived on the island. That's why when the salsa rap piece "La Negra Tiene Tumbao" was brought to me, I thought it would be wonderful to record.

Although the video was a bit risqué, the song became a hit. When we started filming it with the director Ernesto Fundora, who also did my video, "Mi Vida es Cantar," I knew it would be wonderful, since I really do enjoy his work. Once we arrived in Mexico to start filming, Ernesto explained the whole process to Omer, and when Omer explained it to me, it sounded perfect. The casting began for the main role, and a stunning young Guatemalan woman named Deborah David was chosen. We were introduced, but Omer and Ernesto never told me that Deborah would appear nude, with only body paint covering her. Since I had only one day to film, because I was on my way to perform in Venezuela, we had to work a long, full day, so I was too concerned with my own role to ask what other people in the video were doing. Pupi Fernández, my hairdresser in Mexico, prepared my whole wardrobe for the shoot. The dress I was to wear was decorated with peacock feathers, so Pupi did my hair beautifully, complete with peacock feathers throughout my coif.

After we recorded my part in the video, so much time seemed to pass before I saw it that I forgot all about it. We went to Miami to record Cristina's show as part of the promotional tour for the album, and before leaving for the studio, Omer pulled Pedro and me aside and said, "Celia, you know that times have changed, and we are in a new millennium. We've just received a copy of the video, and it's very modern. You look very good, but the model is wearing very few clothes. I think it would be best if you record Cristina's show tonight first, and then we'll ask her and Marcos if we can watch it in their office."

When I heard Omer's words, I knew immediately that something strange was going on, but I tried to ignore it. Later, when Cristina, Marcos, Pedro, Omer, and I were watching the video in the office, I almost fainted. I said that it couldn't be shown to the public that way. I was afraid that people would start saying that I had lost my mind. But Cristina convinced me that it was fine and acceptable the way it was and that people would love it. And she was right. The video was a great help for the single and the album in general, and it became especially popular among men. But the best thing about it is what it did for Deborah's career. She became so popular that she's now a famous fashion model in Mexico. I am very happy for her, and most important, I am very proud of her.

The whole production for that album was a new experience for me, since I was able to work with many young performers. The popularity of the video was something else I didn't expect. The frosting on the cake was when the album was nominated for a Grammy. I was amazed that the song had such an impact, since it was something new, a combination of music styles that more often than not are mutually exclusive: salsa and rap. This time I had a feeling that the song would indeed win the award.

May came, and so did my favorite yearly event, the Anti-Cancer League telethon. Although the economy had taken a nosedive, we were able to break the $3 million mark. As always, the telethon was a magnificent experience, and again I was grateful to all involved for giving me the opportunity to do something so wonderful in my mother's name.

About a week later, Telemundo invited me to the meeting where they would present their programming schedule for the following season, and that's where I heard of the network's plans to broadcast a tribute in my honor in March 2003. I was very moved by this, since I knew that all involved were going to work on the event out of the affection they felt for me.

I also had the marvelous experience of co-hosting a lovely documentary entitled *La Cuba Mía* (*My Cuba*) with the beloved Miliki. Miliki, a Spaniard whose real name is Emilio Aragón, was one of a three-man act of brothers known as Miliki, Gaby, y Fofó, which had a long and distinguished career in both Cuba and

Spain. In *La Cuba Mía,* Miliki and I covered the history of popular Cuban music in the twentieth century with the help of such great Cuban musicians such as Willie Chirino, Albita, Lucrecia, Arturo Sandoval, and Donato Poveda. The film turned out wonderfully, and I couldn't be prouder to have participated in it.

Pedro and I decided to take a few days off to relax. We took this time to see the doctor for our yearly checkups. We went together; Pedro had his tests, and I had mine, which included a mammogram. Initially we received good news, so we decided to go to Los Angeles and spend some quality time with Luisito, his wife, Letty, and their children.

A few days after we arrived at Letty and Luisito's house, Pedro and I received a call from a doctor's assistant, who told us that the doctor had been trying to locate us for several days. Apparently, my mammogram had revealed a minor abnormality, so the doctor wanted to run a few more tests. He wanted me to return to New York as soon as possible, so Pedro and I did. Needless to say, we left Luisito and his family terribly worried.

From one day to the next, my life changed radically. I left a life of touring and performing in order to devote myself totally to my health. As soon as Pedro and I arrived in New York, I underwent a battery of tests, and we were given another appointment with the doctor to hear the results.

The doctor told me I had to undergo a surgical procedure. I did two performances that I had already scheduled, and then I immediately went into the hospital for surgery.

Pedro, Gladys, and Omer were in the recovery room with me when the doctor told me that the procedure went perfectly. I went home to recover, but within a few days I received another call informing me that on top of that first surgical procedure, I had to undergo radiation treatment. Since I hadn't been told about that before, I was surprised when I heard the news. Actually, I was very upset.

I must admit that I felt a bit desperate, since I have never had medical problems. I had never even caught colds. I contacted my friend María García, who was close to Dr. Manuel Álvarez. I guess since I've never intentionally harmed anyone, the Lord always sends me His angels in my times of need. Pedro and I went to see Dr. Álvarez, who held my hand and was more than understanding with us. He took me to see several specialists who could tell me what my options were. After speaking to several of them, I decided that a mastectomy, and not radiation treatment, would be my best option. It was hard to accept the fact that I had breast cancer, but the doctor assured me that I would be cured after undergoing the mastectomy. My mind raced back to 1959 Cuba, when I took my mother to the doctor and I first heard the word *cancer*. I started crying like a baby. I don't know why I cried so hard. Maybe I was crying for myself, maybe I was crying for my Ollita, or maybe I was crying for all those other people I saw having cancer treatments that day. I started thinking about the twenty years I volunteered at the Anti-Cancer League's telethons. Although we had gone far in the fight against cancer, we still had such a long way to go. I even cried when I began to think of my friend Lourdes Águila. I no longer remember what else I cried about, but poor Pedro couldn't stand seeing me that way, so he got up and walked out of the office. Omer stayed with me, held my hand, and cried along with me. After a short while, I calmed down and returned home. I decided that it would be best if I went through my mail and attended to things I hadn't paid attention to for a while. I spent a few days organizing my desk and papers so I wouldn't think so much about what was going on.

I always say that when God closes one door, He opens another. Shortly after receiving the awful news of my cancer, I heard that for the first time in my career, I had been nominated for four Latin Grammy Awards: Best Song of the Year, Best Album of the Year, Best Video of the Year, and Best Salsa Album of the Year. The news was a blessing, since it allowed me to think about more positive things. I asked the doctor if I could attend the awards ceremony in Los Angeles, and he told me he saw no problem with that. I was so thrilled that I could go that I immediately began daydreaming about what I was going to wear. I called Sully Bonnelly, my designer, and we set an appointment to meet the following week.

Once I arrived at his studio, Sully showed me several fabrics and designs he had in mind for me. We decided he would make me two dresses, a red one for the red carpet and a blue one I would wear during my performance and to receive the award, should I win one. Later that same day, I heard from Omer, who told me that Emilio Estefan had told him that morning that they wanted me to open the show singing "La Negra Tiene Tumbao," and this really raised my spirits. The greatest pleasure I derive in life comes from my music and work, so the news that they wanted me to open the awards ceremony was just what I needed to hear. As I said in one of my recordings, *"Mi vida es cantar,"* or "Singing is the main purpose of my life."

Annie González of Sony Records, Pedro, Omer, Zoila, and Raymond García accompanied me to Los Angeles. When we arrived, we went to a dinner party in honor of the great Mexican singer Vicente Fernández, who had just been given the Personality of the Year award by LARAS. The night before the awards ceremony, I was given a nomination medal. When I saw they gave me only one, I asked Omer if he was sure I was nominated for four Grammys. He started laughing and assured me that indeed I had been nominated for four awards. I was a little skeptical, but even so, I was content with my little medal.

With so much running around, I didn't have time to buy a new wig, so I asked Luisito's wife, Letty (who is also the mother of my godchildren), to buy me a wig that went well with a blue dress. Letty brought me a few to pick from, and I chose a white-and-blue one that was so loud that when I walked on stage, the audience was more amazed than they were the previous year, when I wore the blue one that caused such a stir.

I closed the show, which was broadcast live on the CBS network. My wig and Deborah, the same model who appeared in the video, were a sensation. I really don't know if it was my wig or that beautiful black woman, but the audience immediately jumped to their feet once the music began. It was a wonderful show, and I actually won in the first category I was nominated for, Best Song of the Year. The Spanish singer Alejandro Sanz won the Grammy for Best Album of the Year, and he was kind enough to dedicate it to me when he went to receive it on stage. It was such a joyous night that I was able to forget about my health for a while. Gloria and Emilio Estefan threw us a party at the trendy Asia de Cuba restaurant. It really was an unforgettable evening.

The following day, I had to record a commercial with the Mexican singer Paulina Rubio for Dr Pepper. We worked all day until midnight. It was a grueling but fun experience, and after we were done, we rested in our hotel rooms until we returned to New York the following day.

Soon thereafter in September, I had an appointment to be interviewed by Ana Cristina Reymundo for the American Airlines in-flight magazine, *Nexos*. The morning of the interview, I went to the hospital for my preoperative tests. Everyone around me kept asking me to cancel the interview, but I refused. First of all, I don't like disappointing anyone. Second, Ana Cristina had already arrived in New York with her crew. How could I cancel on her just like that? If I was planning to cancel, I should have done so before I left for Los Angeles, not on the day the interview was to take place. And third, that interview would include my last photo shoot with my bust intact. Nothing was going to stop me from taking that picture.

I called Ruthie and told her to meet us in a lovely restaurant and club called La Belle Époque on Broadway. I was to come straight from the hospital, and that's where they were going to take the pictures. I thought it would be best to get ready at the restaurant. Ruthie arrived earlier than we did, since they took longer than expected with my tests. In any case, we were late, but that didn't keep Pedro and me from immediately commenting on what a nice place La Belle Époque is.

After greeting everyone, Ruthie and I went into the tiny bathroom to do my makeup and get dressed. While she was working on me, I told her, "Ruthie, they're going to remove my breast early tomorrow morning." She couldn't believe what I was saying, but I told her not to worry since I had thought it all out and was sure I had made the right decision. I asked her to make me look as nice as possible, since these would be the last pictures of my complete body.

The interview and photo session went on until ten p.m., and we didn't get to bed until past midnight. The next morning, Pedro and I awoke as if it were any other day. We spoke for a while as we waited for Omer and Harley to arrive and take us to the hospital. But poor Pedro, he didn't have his usual morning cup of strong Cuban coffee—since I couldn't have anything to eat or drink, he wouldn't have anything, either. Pedro looked worried, but I kept telling him that everything would be fine and that we were in this together.

We left for the hospital with Omer, his mother, Magaly, and María García. Unfortunately, my sister Gladys couldn't be there because she had to attend to her daughter, my niece Celia María, who was in Atlanta at the time. I'll be eternally grateful to all those who were there with me that day, in body and in spirit.

When I awoke from the operation, I felt fine. I don't know why, but things usually go well for me. I don't know if it's because I have special angels protecting me or because of the faith I carry in my heart, but everything usually works out. Even the nurses were amazed by how quickly I recuperated.

While I was still recovering in the hospital, Pedro also had to undergo colon surgery. His procedure also went well, but it was quite a sight to see both of us in separate beds, sharing the same hospital room. I was released about five days after my operation, but Pedro had to stay behind. It was awful to have to leave him, and it was even worse when I was instructed not to visit him so that we could both get our rest. All I was allowed to do was speak to him a few times a day on the telephone. I was heartbroken that Pedro was in the hospital and I wasn't allowed to see him.

More than a week passed, and Pedro was still in the hospital. No one wanted to let me know he was getting weaker, until one day Gladys, Omer, and Luisito came home to tell me that I needed to see him because his health had taken a turn for the worse. Imagine my surprise when I found him unconscious in the intensive care unit. I was scared and in slight shock. Although I know I am a strong woman, I can't imagine living without my husband. I said hello to him, and then I just stood there next to his hospital bed, staring. I told him how much I loved him, and I begged him not to give up. Then, and I just couldn't help it, I blurted out, "Pedro! I need you, *mi negro*. Don't even think of leaving me here alone. Please, Pedro, I beg you, wake up!" He moved his eyelids. I thought that was his way of letting me know he could hear me.

It was a short visit, and I was soon asked to leave. I went home and started praying for Pedro. For a few minutes I actually felt defeated, and I begged God for guidance, since I did not understand what was suddenly happening to my life. The next day, the Lord answered my prayers and allowed Pedro to regain consciousness. He may have been weak, but his general condition had improved dramatically.

I had to go to Miami without Pedro. I had a scheduled event to go to, and I was afraid that if I canceled, the public might find out about my surgery. Up until that moment, only my closest relatives and friends knew I had cancer. I still wasn't ready to let the world know. Omer accompanied me on that trip, and when we arrived in Miami, Tony Almeida, who worked for Emilio Estefan and had been instructed to keep people from touching me and unintentionally injuring me, met us in the airport. That same evening, the Hispanic Heritage Council gave me the Don Quixote Award at the Hotel Intercontinental Miami. Since Pedro was not with me, two dear friends, Jenny and Gilberto de Cárdenas, never left my side. I will always be grateful to them. Brujita also stayed with me while I was in Miami, and both she and Zoila helped me in every way they could. When we went out, Brujita and Zoila would stand on either side of me, since my arm still hurt too much and I was afraid that a fan might touch it. Both of them showed me what good friends they were during those difficult moments.

When I returned to New York, I received the best news any-one could've given me: Pedro was to be released from the hospital that same day. Since I saw he was better, we went forward with our plans to go to the concert, billed as a tribute to my first fifty years on stage. Even though Pedro was getting better by the day, he still wasn't his usual self. It's very hard for us to be apart, and I didn't want him to miss such an important event, the first of its kind in such an important theater as the National Auditorium in Mexico City. Pedro tried to regain his energy as fast as he could, and under a nurse's supervision, we traveled to Mexico together.

The tribute, entitled *The Fiftieth Anniversary of Celia Cruz's Musical Career* started at eight-thirty p.m. on November 1, 2002. More than ten thousand people came to the show, including Gabriel García Márquez and his wife, Mercedes.

I must say that I looked wonderful that night, in a light pink dress designed by Willie especially for me. I sang with my Mexican friends Marco Antonio Muñiz, Daniela Romo, Pedro Fernández, and an orchestra of forty-five musicians. My Perucho looked very handsome that night in his tuxedo as he sat off stage with a nurse by his side, although he really didn't need her to watch him, since he always feels good when he sees me having fun on stage.

Without my knowing what he was planning to do, Pedro walked onto the stage. The audience saw him before I did, and they erupted into applause. I turned to see what was happening, and I was shocked when I saw him walk to me with his handsome, masculine posture. I love him so much that I feel as if I'm being tickled every time I see him come toward me. When he reached me, we both sang "Usted Abusó." But suddenly I felt tired. I thought it was due to all the emotions that were simulta-

neously running through my mind, but I knew something was really wrong when I suddenly forgot some of the lyrics to the song.
At that moment, all the entertainers who had participated in the
show came out on stage to give me a standing ovation.

By the time Pedro and I returned to New York, I wasn't feeling right. I was never sick, and suddenly it seemed as if I were
being invaded by a spirit bent on turning my happy life into a
medical tragedy. A cancerous tumor had appeared in my brain,
and I had to have it surgically removed. The doctors said I had no
other option.

I entered New York–Presbyterian Hospital on the morning of
December 5, 2002, with Pedro, my cousin Cachita, my sister
Gladys, Ruthie, Omer and Luisito by my side. I underwent five
hours of surgery with the most professional team imaginable. I
knew that with the help of my family and friends, and the faith I
have in God, everything would turn out for the best. And so it
did. I think God also lends me His angels during my hospital
stays, since while I was recovering from my second operation, I
bumped into two of Mary's nieces, Mercedes Perry and Felicia
León. During that stay at New York–Presbyterian, they became
my guardian angels.

Although I had undergone three surgeries in four months, I
was able to keep the matter very private. Only my closest relatives and friends knew of the two operations I had in September.
In those moments, it's important to have peace and quiet, and
able to escape from the public, if only for a few days or weeks, is
very helpful. Unfortunately, many people don't seem to understand that. After my brain tumor was removed, I wasn't able to
keep it from the public any longer.

While I was still in the recovery room, one of the hospital

employees called the press and told them I was recovering after having had plastic surgery. When Omer told me what that hospital employee had done, I said, "Plastic surgery? Who? Me? I would never get plastic surgery. This face, this smile, and these big fat black lips are part and parcel of my personality. I'm fine just the way I am."

Omer told me he spoke with Pedro about how to handle the press, and he thought it would be best if I wrote a letter asking my fans for their support during this difficult time, and that the press would most certainly treat me with the same respect and affection they always have. On December 7, 2002, I wrote the following letter to the media:

Dear friends:

I just wanted to write a few words to thank you for your concern about the recent challenges to my health.

I am currently in recovery from surgery and having to deal with a test of will that we human beings sometimes have to face.

Although my life has always been a happy one and an open book, I humbly ask you to please respect my privacy and that of those closest to me.

Your prayers and messages of solidarity have shown me how deep your affection for me is, and they serve as an inspiration that on a daily basis gives me more strength to confront this new challenge in this period of my life. I thank you for your unconditional support throughout these years, for always greeting me with opened arms, and for having given me the opportunity to brighten your hearts with my music.

During my recovery phase I pray you understand that I wish

to keep this situation private, as it deals directly with my per-
sonal life.

I wish all of you a Merry Christmas, and a New Year full of
good health, peace, and prosperity.

Until next time, your friend always,
Celia Cruz

The press respected my request, and so did the public. Still, my letter was read in all the Spanish-language media. I even heard that when my friend Rafael Pineda, the Cuban anchor at New York's Univisión affiliate, gave the news of my letter to the public, he did so with tears in his eyes. I was very moved when I heard his reaction, since I knew that it was heartfelt.

I began receiving thousands of cards and letters from all over the world. It was overwhelming to receive so much support. Still, the paparazzi did not give up. Omer later told me that during the night after my operation, a paparazzo dressed as a nurse tried to sneak into my room, and that when Omer saw him, he reported him to the hospital authorities. From that moment on, the hospital posted a guard at my door to protect my privacy.

Pedro and I spent a quiet Christmas, just the way I like them, at the home of Johnny Pacheco and his wife, Cuqui, and we later greeted 2003 at home with Omer, his mother, Magaly, my niece Linda, and my cousin Cachita. As a matter of fact, Magaly and Cachita cooked a wonderful meal, and many of my friends called us to wish us a Happy New Year. It was obvious to me that those who cared for us the most were very worried about me and were trying their best to lift my spirits. My friend Mario Kreutzberger sent me an orchid arrangement so large that it covered my whole bedroom window. I was surprised that I enjoyed that New Year so much at home, since I always considered it good luck to be working at New Year's Eve events. When the holidays were over, Pedro, Omer, and I met with Oscar Gómez and Sergio George to set up the recording schedule for my album *Regalo del Alma (A Gift from the Soul)*. We soon decided that we would record during the first two weeks of February in New York and New Jersey.

Pedro and I decided to sell our house and move to a penthouse apartment in a building not far from where we lived. I liked my house, but with my bad knee, I was tired of going up and down stairs, and although the house did have an elevator, it always seemed to break. One day, as I was trying to get down to the main floor, I got stuck in the elevator. I started screaming for Pedro to help me, and the poor man ran to help me while Omer called the technicians to ask them to come and repair that monster. All I could hear was Pedro cursing the elevator as he tried in vain to get me out. Since I had to wait for the technician, I decided to kill time, so I sat down and started to sing.

Several weeks passed, and the press started calling Omer to ask about my condition. Over time, the volume of calls increased. There were all sorts of speculations about my condition, and I did not want to go through the experience I had in Colombia when the Venezuelan press declared me dead. That's when Omer came to me and suggested that I take several pictures with three recently published magazines to prove to the public that I was alive and well. I agreed with the idea, and we called Ruthie to come over and do my makeup and hair for the pictures. Omer took a picture of me holding a copy of the American Airlines *Nexos* magazine published on January 1, 2003, another one with *Cristina* magazine that was published shortly thereafter, and a third one of me reading the daily newspaper. After he developed them, Omer distributed them to the press. We also thought it necessary that I do an interview, so we decided to do it with *People en Español,* since it has the highest circulation of any magazine published in Spanish in the United States. The interview took place at the end of January, and with that done, I decided to focus my energies on our new album, *Regalo del Alma.*

We recorded mainly at the studios in Englewood, New Jersey, where we also rehearsed. We recorded all ten tracks of the album during ten days of heavy snowfall. I love snow, so I think it inspired me. We had fun during those ten days, since when I'm surrounded by music, I come alive. Sergio George, Oscar Gómez, the production crew, and I picked the songs I was going to record. I liked all of them, and I especially enjoyed the great range of musical styles we were working with.

After we finished recording, we had to start getting ready for the tribute that Telemundo was preparing in my honor for March 13. I still had to pick a dress and a wig and address several last minute details. Since Pedro was almost fully recovered, I was looking forward to the Telemundo special with great enthusiasm.

We flew to Miami on March 12. That night we dined with friends, and the next morning I slept in. After I awoke, we had breakfast and we talked for a while until it was time for me to get ready. I took one of my "royal" baths, and after I was finished, Zoila came in to do my makeup. When she was finished, Ruthie came in to help me with my dress and put on a superb silver wig. I should note that my dress, which was also silver, was a Narciso Rodríguez design. We had met only recently, but he and I immediately hit it off. I know God has blessed that child. It's a real joy to work with him.

When we arrived at Miami Beach's Jackie Gleason Theater for the Performing Arts, the enthusiastic crowds were waiting for us. It was the first time I appeared in public since my last surgery, but it was the moment when I finally realized how deeply so many people felt for me. That Telemundo tribute, entitled *Celia Cruz: Azúcar!* was one of the most memorable moments of my career. I had the unbelievable privilege of being honored by almost all the giants of the Spanish-language music industry. When I arrived, Gloria and Emilio Estefan, Patti LaBelle, Marc Anthony, Gilberto Santa Rosa, Víctor Manuelle, Gloria Gaynor, Ana Gabriel, Rosario Flores, La India, Milly Quezada, Los Tríos, José Alberto, Johnny Pacheco, Tito Nieves, Alicia Villarreal, Alfredo de la Fe, Arturo Sandoval, Luis Enrique, and Paulina Rubio were waiting for Pedro and me. Once the show began, Gloria Estefan and Marc Anthony had the difficult task of emceeing the event, and that's when I realized how much Marc Anthony really loves me.

The tribute was beautifully done. Rosario sang "Burundanga" in the same style her mother, La Faraona, and I used to do it. Gilberto Santa Rosa serenaded me with "Bemba Colorá," which was great fun, since the whole audience joined in the chorus. Gloria Estefan and Patti LaBelle sang "Químbara," while Arturo Sandoval accompanied them on the trumpet, and Víctor Manuelle improvised the lyrics beautifully during the last thirty seconds of his performance. The great musician Cucco Peña conducted the orchestra, made up mostly of the best of Puerto Rico's musicians. I was truly impressed with so much young talent, and when I heard them perform so many of my hits, I felt assured that my music would outlast me for several generations. Finally, my Pedro came out to serenade me with the song "Quizás." I have no words to describe what I felt when I saw him descend from the stage to where I was sitting.

Once on stage, I had the opportunity to thank all involved for dedicating such a beautiful show in my honor. I also asked them to pray for me so I could finally be freed of my illness. When the tribute finished, hundreds of people came to me to wish me the best and congratulate me, but it was I who should thank and congratulate four remarkable individuals who made that unique night a reality: Emilce Elgarresta, Tony Mojena, Johnny Rojas (my friend from our early days at CMQTV Studios in Havana), and Christian Riehl. Thanks to all of them, I enjoyed a night like no other in my life.

After the Telemundo tribute, we immediately returned to New York and completed the formalities necessary for buying our penthouse. Omer took care of the moving, and Javier Fernández was put in charge of the interior design as I underwent another battery of medical tests.

Finally, on April 1, I was taken to my new home like a queen. When I walked in, the first thing I said to Pedro was how beautiful my house looked. I ambled around and studied every nook and cranny. In the other house, I had all my trophies, awards, proclamations, gold records, and memorabilia all on one floor. I don't know how they managed, but Pedro and Omer were able to make room for it all in the new penthouse. It really did look beautiful.

In the new penthouse that God blessed us with, Pedro and I have a stunning living room with floor-to-ceiling windows that face a spacious terrace. I enjoy having lunch out there with the sun overhead and Pedro right next to me, and at night, we have a breathtaking view of the New York skyline. In a corner of the living room we have a white grand piano, where we placed pictures of famous and important people we have had the honor of meeting. In front of the living room windows, we placed a couch where we sit to watch the sun set. And on one or two occasions, Pedro and I have seen the sunrise from our bedroom windows, which also faces toward the terrace and the Hudson River. I consider it a blessing to be able to watch the colors of the sky change from dark blue to pink and from pink to daylight white. I never get tired of seeing that kaleidoscope of colors unfurl before me. That's an image I would like to have engraved in my mind for eternity.

Soon after we moved in, Johnny Rojas came to visit, and since he hadn't seen the penthouse before, I gave him a detailed tour. Afterward, we sat down to eat and reminisce about how we used to dream about the future on "the bench of dreams" but never thought we would live out the rest of our lives in exile.

Another person who has been a consistent and loyal friend is Mario Kreutzberger, "Don Francisco." As soon as I became ill, he started calling me on a daily basis to inquire as to how I was doing. You know who your friends are when things are not going well, and Don Francisco has proven that he is a true friend.

Gloria and Emilio Estefan also came to visit our new penthouse apartment. Our friendship goes back almost thirty years, but in the last ten, we have become family. I get along very well with Gloria's mother, Gloria Fajardo, and I really enjoy Gloria and Emilio's son Nayib's personality. I should mention that in the world of Cuban exile entertainment, Emilio and Gloria, Marcos and Cristina, and Pedro and I have become a bit like royalty, since our marriages have lasted. We have known how to live successfully as married couples under the watch of the media and with all the demands of the industry. This is not an easy task, and many people in the business never manage to do it, no matter how hard they try. I guess that's why so many people admire how we have conducted ourselves in our marriages.

Mary, Zoila, and Brujita also stayed with us for three days in the penthouse during a surprise visit. As soon as they arrived, I gave them all a task to do. Mary massaged my feet, Zoila did my makeup, as she always does, and Brujita cooked a wonderful *harina,* a typical Cuban flour dish. It was wonderful to christen my new home with such a great visit from my three sisters.

Luisito, Letty, and their youngest son, Benjamin—whom I have yet to christen, although we're planning the event—left their homes and lives in California to spend over a month with Pedro and me. Meanwhile, Omer spends every day keeping me company. He and Luisito take care of all our needs, and if we didn't have them, it would be just too hard for Pedro to handle everything alone. That's why I will always say that Omer and Luisito are forever our sons.

Ruthie comes by almost every day to do my hair and makeup so I can look pretty. And as she works on me, she's always telling me how much she loves me—something she doesn't have to tell me, since I know. I just hope she knows how much I love her back.

I've enjoyed my life in the penthouse. I feel very comfortable and relaxed here. I am able to enjoy the company of relatives and friends, which I couldn't do in the old house since it seemed I was invariably on tour. And in this new home, Pedro still brings me coffee in bed, just as he has done for years. Pedro likes to put a little yellow flower on the tray he uses to bring my coffee. I must admit that at the beginning I wasn't thrilled with the flow-ers, but as time went on, and with the love he showed me through them, I grew to like them. In any case, our forty-first wedding anniversary was fast approaching, and we had to get ready to celebrate, as we always had.

In the late spring, I was very happy when the single "Ríe y Llora" ("Laugh and Cry"), from the album, *Regalo del Alma,* be-came a hit on radio stations, especially in Miami. I played it over and over again and clapped with the beat. I'm very satisfied with the way it sounds, and I was looking forward to seeing the CD cover, since all I had was a demo tape with all the songs I recorded for the album.

I was also blessed with the support and understanding of Zeida Arias, whom I befriended in my early years as a refugee in New York. Zeida came to see me almost every day, bringing me Spanish-language newspapers and magazines. I really enjoy gazing with her at the picture postcard view of Babylon on the Hudson from the peace and tranquillity of my terrace.

Throughout my career, I recorded many public service announcements to raise awareness about diabetes and cancer. Now that the latter has affected me personally, I hope that my struggle will serve to help others understand how lethal it is and how anyone can become its victim. What I have learned most about this disease is that one has to confront it head-on and with faith in the Lord. We must come to grips with the fact that we're here only until God wills it otherwise.

Pedro also promised to take me on a cruise as soon as I regained my strength, since he knows how much I enjoy them. I also like the sea, but I avoid it because it weakens my vocal cords; also, I have never been one to sunbathe, and although I think most beaches are beautiful in their own way, I find them too noisy. The sound of the waves crashing against the sand and rocks is too much for my ears. I prefer the soothing effect of looking at the horizon across an endless sea.

Johnny Pacheco and his wife often come to visit. I spend some wonderful moments talking and reminiscing with them. One day, Johnny and I were alone in the living room, and we suddenly stopped talking. We both remained quiet for a while.

I started thinking about what a great man he is and what a

Siempre Viviré / I Will Survive

loyal friend he has been to both Pedro and me. Johnny is a great musician, a gifted composer, and most important, the man who rescued Cuban music when it was on the verge of disappearing forever. I admire him and love him like a brother.

I turned my head and stared at Pacheco, and I suddenly felt very grateful to him. I wanted to fix my hair and makeup a bit, so I asked him to help get me on my feet. He helped me to the foyer that faces my bedroom and a bathroom. Before he let go of my hand, I squeezed his arm with all the strength I had left and said: "I love you with all my heart." I noticed that a few tears streamed down his face. I then turned and entered my room.

I have no regrets in life. In my old age, I truly realize how lucky I am. With Pedro, my family and friends, and the everlasting love I have with the music that God granted me the opportunity of recording, I can heal feeling blessed that if I had it all to do over again, I would change nothing.

With the exception of my beloved Cuba, my life has thus far been stroked by God. Hopefully, when my health returns, I'll find myself back on tour, doing what I do best: giving my fans a good show, making them want to dance until dawn.

Epílogo

THE WEEK OF JULY 9, 2003, BROUGHT WITH IT SOME OF
the most difficult moments I've ever faced. There was no way
of hiding from the facts as they were explained to Cuqui
Pacheco and me by the doctors at New York–Presbyterian
Hospital after Celia's last battery of tests. Despite all the ther-
apies she received, the tumor in her brain kept expanding. We
knew the inevitable was fast approaching, so I had to speak
to Pedro and tell him that no matter how heartbreaking it
was, we had to confront reality and prepare for the funeral of
someone as beloved as Celia Cruz.

On July 11, Pedro, Luisito, and I went to Manhattan's
Frank E. Campbell funeral home, since they are well-known
for handling funerals for dignitaries, and we left everything in
order for the unavoidable days that lay ahead. We then went
to Woodlawn Cemetery in the Bronx to pick the plot of land
where a mausoleum would be built after her death, although
we never imagined it would happen in less than a week. As a
matter of fact, Luisito returned to his family in California,
since we all thought Celia would remain with us a while
longer.

The weekend before she passed away, we received a FedEx
package containing the first five cuts of her last album, *Regalo
del Alma (A Gift from the Soul)*. On Sunday, July 13, Pedro, the
nurse, and I saw how much Celia enjoyed the recording, tap-

ping her fingers and listening to it several times in one day. All the same, her health was deteriorating rapidly, and that same night, Luisito and his wife, Leticia Rodríguez, flew back to New York from Los Angeles.

The next day, July 14, was Celia and Pedro's forty-first wedding anniversary. When he asked her if she knew what day it was, a tear streamed from her eye, thus letting him know she was indeed aware it was their anniversary. Sadly, her condition had deteriorated so quickly that she did not have the energy to express anything else.

We knew the time was near, so we decided to make concrete plans that would adequately address any predictable situation. At around ten that evening, Emilio Estefan's assistant, Janet de Armas helped me contact Emilio in Machu Picchu, Peru, where he was with his wife, Gloria, recording the video for her album *Unwrapped*. When I finally reached him, I said, "Emilio, I think the moment we dreaded is almost here, and I need your help. We have to plan a funeral worthy of Celia. She once told me that if she didn't die in Cuba, she wanted her wake to be held in Miami, since not only is it the American city that's closest to Cuba, but it's also the capital of all Cuban exiles. I think the Freedom Tower would be the best place for the wake, since every time she saw it she talked about the thousands of Cubans who passed through it during their flight to freedom." Without delay, Emilio called Jorge Mas Santos, the owner of the Freedom Tower, who immediately offered it to us for as long as we needed it.

Those were crucial and very difficult moments, and we didn't have a second to lose. That's why I called a very close friend of Celia's who made sure that all our needs would be attended to: Jorge Plasencia, vice president of the Hispanic Broadcasting Corporation. Twenty minutes later, I was on a conference call with

Miami mayor Manny Díaz, and Miami-Dade County mayor Alex Penelas. Both of them assured me that they would do everything necessary so that all who wanted to pay their respects to Celia could do so. They made sure that all necessary municipal agencies, such as the police and fire departments, the parks department, and the transit authority, would be at our disposal.

Pedro, Luisito, Cuqui, two nurses, Ruth Sánchez, and Celia's niece Linda, who had driven up that day from Virginia, were in the penthouse apartment with Celia, but none of us slept that night. By daybreak, the press had congregated two blocks away from the building, wondering what was going on, since the whole country already knew that Celia's condition had taken a turn for the worse. Since we were so concerned with the impending death of a person we loved so dearly, the last thing we wanted was to get drawn into a press frenzy.

At six in the morning, I awoke Celia's publicist, Blanca Lasalle, when I called her to tell her we needed a priest to give Celia extreme unction. At around noon of that same day, Father Carlos Mullins arrived and met with Pedro, Linda, Gladys, Leticia, Luisito, two nurses, Pacheco and Cuqui, Celia's cousin Cachita, and Blanca before giving Celia her last rites. Johnny Pacheco couldn't stand being there with us, so he left for the living room to sit alone.

Immediately after receiving the sacrament, Celia took a deep breath and sighed, letting us know she was at peace and calm. A few hours later, at four forty-five p.m., Celia abandoned her fight against the cancer that had invaded her brain, and her spirit quietly left her body. God was merciful to Celia, since he allowed her to leave the world as if she were Sleeping Beauty. We all stood around looking at her for a few minutes, and we hugged and consoled one another.

That was a terrible moment for me, since I had never seen anyone die before, nor had I any experience with wakes or burials. Yet what I thought would be a terrifying moment was actually very spiritual. I felt a warm light invade my whole body, and then I began to cry and asked Celia to give me strength and courage to face what for her would be a dignified adieu.

Luisito and I were worried about Pedro, so we turned our attention to him. After a few minutes, I left him with Luisito and went to talk with Blanca on the penthouse balcony, and I told her we needed to contact the press immediately. We both proceeded to contact the two major Spanish-language networks, Univisión and Telemundo, and we were taken totally by surprise when we saw that both networks immediately suspended normal programming to report the news of Celia's passing. As a matter of fact, most of their programming for the next week was dedicated to Celia's life and funeral, and I should also mention that many broadcasters were teary eyed as they spoke about her.

Within an hour of Celia's death, the nurses called Dr. Manuel Álvarez to inform him of what had just transpired and asked him to come to the penthouse, while the rest of us began calling relatives and close friends. Pedro called relatives in Cuba, and I spoke to Gilda and Rolando Columbie, to Cristina Saralegui and Marcos Ávila, to Gloria and Emilio Estefan, who were on a layover in Panama on their way back to Miami from Peru, and to Mario Kreutzberger, while Cuqui contacted Mary, Brujita, and Zoila. Within minutes, Dr. Álvarez arrived and declared Celia dead.

As news of Celia's death spread, the worldwide press began to report the event and recall her life and contributions. The following morning, the news appeared on the front pages of major newspapers everywhere, and even the American newspaper of record, *The New York Times,* wrote an eloquent obituary of the queen. Sadly, though, the government of Cuba, the country she loved with all her heart and whose good name and struggle she so eloquently defended, basically ignored her. Yet although Celia had been erased from Cuban history decades ago by the Castro regime, the Cuban people could not ignore her death. Just hours after it happened, *Azúcar!* graffiti appeared throughout the island. The regime's response to this was a backhanded "obituary" in the official Communist Party newspaper, *Granma,* in which the regime stated in just a few lines that "Celia Cruz, a counterrevolutionary icon," had died in New York. Since Cuba does not have anything resembling a free press, no other mention of her appeared in the state-controlled media. Still, the news of her death had such an impact inside the island that even imprisoned dissidents commented on what had happened and offered their condolences. The more the regime ordered the *Azúcar!* graffiti to be covered up, the more it appeared, and that went on for several weeks. Celia's family in Cuba held "wakes" for her, and requiem masses were given in her honor throughout the island's besieged churches, including at her beloved Miraculous Medal Parish in her Santos Suárez neighborhood. Unfortunately, Celia never realized her dream of returning to a free Cuba, and the regime that took her country from her never desisted in its unprovoked disdain of her. Nevertheless, her people celebrated her life and her role as a national hero, which no doubt one day will be duly recorded in its history.

Everything was happening so fast that I couldn't grasp the reality of it all. Luisito and I accompanied Celia in the hearse that took her from her Fort Lee, New Jersey, penthouse to the Frank E. Campbell funeral home in Manhattan with a New York City police escort. The motorcade moved slowly across the George Washington Bridge, and when we crossed and arrived in Washington Heights, a predominantly Dominican neighborhood, I looked up and saw a multitude of people holding flowers and lining the streets, crying and trying to touch the hearse as it passed. There were so many people that the hearse had to move very slowly, but that only made it easier for the crowd to approach their beloved queen and kiss the automobile carrying her body. That's when I really realized what Celia Cruz's death meant to her fans. Up until that moment, I was numb and functioning reflexively, but when I saw the adoring crowds waiting for her, I was finally able to grasp the enormity of what had just transpired.

All that affection expressed so openly by the crowds that lined Broadway was a beautiful beginning to a heartbreaking few days. I should mention that the people of Harlem also came out to greet Celia as we passed through their neighborhoods. I was very moved when I saw so many African Americans paying spontaneous homage to the Cuban diva.

When we arrived at the funeral home, Ruth Sánchez was there waiting for us. A few days earlier, I had asked her if she would have the courage to do her dear friend's hair and makeup for the last time. Ruthie told me that she would do it for Celia, although I knew how difficult it would be for her. And as could be expected of her, Ruthie did a wonderful job for what would be Celia's last tour. We had already bought two white dresses, as symbols of the purity of the soul, and two wigs. One dress and wig would be used for the wake in Miami, and the other ones would be for the events in New York. As we were getting Celia ready for the trip to Miami, we heard the news that their queen would soon be there for the last time had swept the city, and the anticipation of her arrival was already being marked by public expressions of grief.

At around eight p.m. on Friday, July 18, an American Airlines plane with Celia's body landed at Miami International Airport. Twenty-five of her relatives and closest friends accompanied her on the flight, and as we exited the plane, Emilio Estefan and Miami mayor Manny Díaz were waiting for us on the tarmac. We immediately noticed that the airport was eerily quiet and that hundreds of employees from several airlines had surrounded our aircraft. When the door of the cargo bin opened and the casket was removed, the employees couldn't contain themselves and started crying in unison. The coffin was then placed on the tarmac, and all who were there solemnly filed past. Some of them touched it as a sign of respect, while others knelt in front of it, waiting for their turn to approach. Needless to say, Celia's friends and relatives were very moved by this unexpected display of affection. Those closest to her always knew that our beautiful black Celia was an amazing human being, but we never realized how central she was in the lives of so many people. After that welcoming ceremony concluded, we were then led through a private exit ramp to the cars that were waiting to drive us to our next destination.

On her last trip to the capital of Cuban exiles, Celia did what she vowed years ago to do when she first arrived in Miami: we took her to visit her beloved Cachita, the Virgin of Charity. At Our Lady's Shrine, Celia's earthly remains were blessed by Monsignor Agustín Román, a leading Cuban religious figure, and from there, we proceeded to the Freedom Tower on Biscayne Boulevard, where the staff of Frank E. Campbell were waiting for us to make all the preparations necessary for the next day, when tens of thousands of mourners were expected to file past her casket.

The Miami and Miami-Dade County authorities worked

closely with us and were extremely generous with their time and energy. They even set up special bus routes to take the mourners to the Freedom Tower from different points of the county free of charge. As a matter of fact, even the MetroRail system did not charge the mourners who went by train to the Freedom Tower.

Although the doors were opened to the public at ten a.m., the line of mourners had actually taken shape four hours earlier. Consequently, by the time the public was allowed into the building, the line ran for several blocks, and by three p.m., 250,000 people were waiting in the Miami summer heat for their turn to enter the Freedom Tower.

At seven p.m., the Freedom Tower was closed to the public, since we had to leave for downtown Miami's Gesù Church, where Father Alberto Cutié was scheduled to celebrate a mass for the repose of Celia's soul. Unfortunately, tens of thousands of mourners did not have the opportunity to personally say good-bye to her inside the building, but they still accompanied us as we marched behind her casket down Biscayne Boulevard, through downtown Miami, and all the way to Gesù Church. So many people joined the motorcade that all traffic was paralyzed throughout downtown Miami and its environs, while the roar of the television and radio news helicopters overhead deafened all of us. As a matter of fact, there were so many of them that they looked like a swarm of dragonflies over a pond.

When we finally arrived at Gesù, Father Alberto was waiting on the steps of the church while thousands congregated on the sidewalks. To accommodate the overflow, Gesù placed loudspeakers on its facade to broadcast the beautiful mass celebrated with the participation of the Miami Cuban Chorale. When the mass concluded, the motorcade returned to the Freedom Tower to make the final arrangements for Celia's last return home to

New York. Over 150,000 people lined the sidewalks around the Freedom Tower throughout that night in their desire to say good-bye to the "Cuban Nightingale," as the *New York Times*'s celebrated journalist Walter Winchell used to call Celia.

In the early morning of July 20, we departed from Miami International Airport for New York's JFK, and we arrived at Frank E. Campbell shortly after noon, where we were greeted by the crowds that had begun to gather in the vicinity. Late that evening, and under torrential rains, the funeral home opened its doors to receive dignitaries such as Governor George Pataki, Mayor Michael Bloomberg, and Senator Hillary Rodham Clinton, and the next day, it opened its doors to the general public.

The morning of July 22 was warm and rainy, yet a seemingly endless line of fans blocked off East Seventieth Street from Fifth to Madison avenues from six in the morning until eleven p.m. The crowd cried, sang her songs, and danced to the music that seemed to come from all directions. I should note that Frank E. Campbell had planned to close its doors at eight p.m., but owing to the enormous number of mourners, Governor Pataki asked them to extend their hours until eleven. In the end, Frank E. Campbell estimated that 150,000 mourners filed past her casket in New York City alone. Still, thousands remained in the street without having had the opportunity to personally say good-bye to their diva.

The following day, Celia's closest relatives and friends arrived at the funeral home early in the morning, and there's where we said our adieus. As per her final request, we placed in her casket the bag of Cuban soil she had brought back with her when she visited the U.S. naval base in Guantánamo Bay. Meanwhile, a white horse-drawn carriage waited outside to take her body for a mass of resurrection at Saint Patrick's Cathedral. Immediately behind the carriage was a convertible driven by a close friend of Celia's known to all as Manito, on which a beautiful image of Our Lady of Charity from the House of Our Lady in Union City, New Jersey, was carried to the cathedral. The nineteen-car motorcade then followed the horse-drawn carriage down Fifth Avenue from Eighty-second Street to Saint Patrick's on Fiftieth, while thousands of people stood on the sidewalks under the rain in silent tribute to their queen—a silence interrupted only by thunder, lightning, and screams of *"Azúcar!"*

When we arrived at the cathedral steps, His Excellency the Reverend Josú Iriondo, auxiliary bishop of New York, was waiting for us. The funeral mass was co-celebrated by Father Carlos Mullins, Father Carlos Rodríguez, Father Tomás del Valle, Father Michael Melendez, Father Alberto Cutié, Father Roberto Pérez, Father Hugo Martínez, and Father Manuel Rojas; and during his moving homily, the bishop reminded the overflow crowd at the cathedral that Celia forever left her *azúcar,* her "sweetness," in the "coffee," or "essence," of her people. The Spanish actor Antonio Banderas, the Cuban musicians Paquito D'Rivera and Jon Secada, and the Panamanian singer Rubén Blades then brought the offerings to the altar. After holy communion, Patti LaBelle sang her beautiful rendition of "Ave Maria," and the mass concluded with the Puerto Rican singer Víctor Manuelle's a cappella interpretation of Celia's hit single "La Vida es un Carnaval" ("Life Is a Carnival").

When Celia's casket was brought out of the cathedral, the sun suddenly pierced through the rainclouds. Thousands of those assembled along Fifth Avenue and the surrounding streets began to yell, *"Azúcar!"* and, "Celia!" It was a momentous final ovation for the Guarachera de Cuba, a simple black woman from humble origins who never imagined that her death would bring hundreds of thousands out to mourn her or that her earthly remains would be carried in a white horse-drawn carriage and bring the noontime traffic to a standstill in the capital of the world.

When we arrived at Woodlawn Cemetery, we were greeted by thousands of people who weren't deterred by the pouring rain. In fact, more and more of them kept coming as we proceeded to the grave site. That's when I realized that wakes and funerals are really for the living, and in Celia's case, that was more than evident, since both her wakes and her burial were the last embrace she gave her fans.

Celia always allowed her fans to show her their affections, so in death, she allowed them to mourn her. She was always aware that the expressions of love she received from the public were genuine, and she responded in kind. In life, she gave everyone her all, so it was natural that she did the same in death. Her adieu was just a mere reflection of the deep and affectionate rapport she had with all those who loved her for the multifaceted, unique, and truly gifted woman she was.

Celia's Legacy

Apart from the hundreds of audio and video recordings that were the product of such a long career, Celia left us another means by which to celebrate her extraordinary life. Before her death, Celia established the Celia Cruz Foundation with the mission to aid underprivileged youngsters who dream of having a musical career and to help in the fight against the disease that took her life and that of her mother. Knowing she would not be with us forever, Celia wanted to be sure of helping her fellow man from beyond the grave just as she had when she was alive.

Apart from the Celia Cruz Foundation, Celia left us the example of how an entertainer or celebrity should behave. She loved to give advice when she was asked, and she did so with the same generosity and sincerity that she gave her love. Given that her career spanned over half a century, many young entertainers can trace their success to the influence she had on their careers. For instance, she would always give them the following words of advice:

Don't ever forget that promoters don't pay your salaries; the fans do. Record labels don't pay you either. It's all thanks to the fans, because if they don't buy our records or come to our shows, we as entertainers have no one else to turn to. Promoters and record labels live off of the entertainer's talent, and the entertainer depends on his fans. So the most important thing entertainers have to do is show their fans affection and respect. If you don't, you're not letting them know how grateful you feel toward them. And if they feel taken advantage of, they will abandon you. And how do you show respect and affection for your fans? You treat them the way you wish to be treated. It sounds easy, but it isn't, since when you become a celebrity it's very easy to start believing that you deserve it because you're talented, or because you're beautiful, or something along those lines. But that just isn't so.

Fans *lend* fame and fortune to the entertainer. I say "lend," because when the day comes that they decide not to "lend" it to you, you'll be left asking yourself, Where did all my fans go? Just look at the thousands of entertainers who one day were on top of the world and now no one even remembers who they were. The secret doesn't lie in being fashionable or in prancing around half-naked. Although I have always been very cutting-edge and I have used many styles of music in my repertoire, I don't adapt myself to a specific style of music just because it's in vogue. The secret lies in the way you treat your audience. You have to promise to give them the best of your God-given talent. And that's why I always say that if you can't conduct yourself that way, you should look for another career path, since the career of an entertainer is not for you.

Bodyguards who mistreated and even hurt fans who try to get close to approach stars incensed Celia. She believed that entertainers had to offer the best they had to their fans, whether it was by the way they dressed or the way they behaved on stage and in public. Celia never used bodyguards, since she had no need for them. People respected her, and she was naturally a loving person. Where there is real love, there is no room for fear; therefore, Celia did not fear anyone.

Although she was a flamboyant and colorful performer, Celia avoided vulgarity and crudeness at all costs. She never needed to go beyond her natural talent to reach her fans. She was very aware of how uncomfortable it can be at times for an entertainer when he or she wants to go shopping or do something else that other people take for granted. Whenever she went out on her own, her fans would surround her and talk to her, or when she was dining in a restaurant, she usually couldn't finish her meal because of the long line of autograph seekers that invariably materialized. Still, she never complained about it, since she understood that her fans wanted to express their affection for her. Granted, Celia created her own inner circle of relatives and friends among whom she could be herself, but she never did so with the intention of hiding or running away from those who consistently demonstrated their fondness for her.

For over half a century, Celia enjoyed a wonderful and productive relationship with the media. In general, the media were her fans, too. And on those rare occasions when specific individuals resorted to yellow journalism, she never held the whole media responsible for the actions of the few. The press cherished her, and she appreciated them, and that was manifested in the way they supported and encouraged her throughout her career and, finally, during her illness.

Celia's philosophy of life could be found in every word she uttered and in every step she took. Although she considered herself just a simple, humble woman, she received an adoring farewell worthy of her greatness, which in fact was just a public display of the joy and affection that she inspired in all who were blessed with knowing her or hearing her song.

Omer Pardillo-Cid

Gracias

SINCE WE BEGAN WORKING ON MY WIFE'S MEMOIR, I'VE been amazed to see how so many people have been so generous with their time in order to make it a reality. But when I think of it, maybe I shouldn't be so surprised. Life has taught me that you get back what you give, and in view of the fact that my late wife was a constant source of affection and warmth, her wonderful ability to love is still at work in all the friends who have worked on her memoirs.

In the final months of her life, our "son," Omer Pardillo, convinced a hesitant Celia how important it was that she leave a record of her life—in her own words—for posterity, and the more involved she became in the project, the more excited she became. As the teacher at heart she always was, she realized the significance of giving her "classroom" (as she called the world) one last lesson with this memoir, which in reality is a closing song.

My wife was looking forward to seeing her memoirs published, but God chose otherwise. And when He did so, Celia entrusted her final project to us, so we have treated it with the respect it deserves. I must admit that reliving the story of our lives together was not a painless task, but whenever I felt overwhelmed, I felt Celia giving me the strength to go on.

Apart from this memoir, Celia entrusted me with the Celia Cruz Foundation and the movie project based on her life and starring Whoopi Goldberg. All the same, it would be impossible for me to do all of this alone, so when it comes to the book, I must thank the following individuals who made it possible. First of all, I thank Omer Pardillo, who has been like a son to us, and because he helped Celia realize how important this book would be. Raymond García has also worked very hard on seeing this project through. Ana Cristina Reymundo, who put her entire heart into it, must also be commended. I'd also like to thank: Blanca Lasalle, Alfredo Santana, Luisito Falcón, Michelle Zubi-Zarreta, Mary García, César Campa, Elia Pérezdealejo, Zoila Valdés, Ruth Sánchez, Gilda and Rolando Columbie, Roberto and Mitsuko, Tongolele, Beatriz Hernández, Miguel Cubiles, Carlos Pérez, María García, Narcisco Rodríguez, Johnny Rojas, Johnny Pacheco and Cuqui Pacheco, India, Omar Cruz, Carlos Rodríguez, Michelle Garcia, the late Ernesto Montaner and Lourdes Montaner, Leonela González, Amalia Gómez, Ángel Carrasco, Luciana Evangelina García, Manuel Álvarez, Iván Restrepo, Roberto Cazorla, Gladys Rodríguez-Dod, José Lucas Badué. Everyone at Rayo: René Alegría, Andrea Montejo, Jeff McGraw, Justin Loeber, Jean Marie Kelly, Carie Freimuth, and Cathy Hemming. Thank you also to Dr. Maya Angelou, whose beautiful words graced the foreword of this very special book.

I'd especially like to thank Gloria and Emilio Estefan, Cristina Saralegui, Marcos Ávila, Jorge Plasencia, and Mario Kreutzberger whose love and support have helped make life without Celia more bearable. Each of you began as friends and colleagues, and over the years have become a member of our family.

Finally, I wish to thank my beautiful wife, *mi negra*, Celia Cruz. Of all her fans, I'm surely the luckiest.

Pedro Knight

Discography

Secco

CELP 432—Cuba's Foremost Rhythm Singer with Sonora Matancera

SSS 3001—*Mi Diario Musical, Celia Cruz*

SCLP 5197—*Con Amor: Celia Cruz con la Sonora Matancera*

SCLP 9067—*Canta . . . Celia Cruz*

SCLP 9101—*La Reina del Ritmo Cubano, Celia Cruz*

SCLP 9124—*Grandes Exitos de Celia Cruz*

SCLP 9136—*La Incomparable Celia y Sonora Matancera*

SCLP 9171—*Su Favorita Celia Cruz*

SCLP 9192—*La Dinámica Celia Cruz*

SCLP 9200—*Reflexiones de Celia Cruz*

SCLP 9215—*Canciones Premiadas de Celia Cruz*

SCLP 9227—*México Que Grande Eres con Celia Cruz*

SCLP 9246—*La Tierna, Conmovedora, Bamboleadora, Celia Cruz con La Sonora Matancera*

SCLP 9263—*Celia Cruz Con Orquesta: Canciones Que Yo Quería Haber Grabado Primero*

SCLP 9267—*Canciones Inolvidables, Celia Cruz*

SCLP 9269—*Homenaje a Los Santos con Celia Cruz*

SCLP 9271—*Sabor y Rítmo de Pueblos, Celia Cruz*

SCLP 9281—*Homenaje a Los Santos con Celia Cruz*, Vol. II

SCLP 9286—*El Nuevo Estilo de Celia Cruz*

SCLP 9312—*Homenaje a Yemayá de Celia Cruz*

SCLP 9317—*Festejando Natividad con Celia Cruz*

SCLP 9325—*Celia Cruz Interpreta elYerbero y la Sopa en Botella*

Tico

SLP 1136—*Celia Cruz y Tito Puente, Cuba y Puerto Rico Son*

SLP 1143—*Son con Guaguancó*

SLP 1157—*Bravo Celia Cruz*

SLP 1164—*A Ti México, Celia Cruz*

SLP 1180—*Serenata Güajira*

SLP 1186—*La Excitante Celia Cruz*

SLP 1193—*El Quimbo Quimbumbia, Celia y Tito Puente*

SLP 1207—*Etc., Etc., Etc., Celia Cruz*

SLP 1221—*Alma con Alma, Celia Cruz y Tito Puente*

SLP 1232—*Nuevos Exitos de Celia Cruz*

SLP 1304—*Algo Especial Para Recordar, Celia y Tito Puente*

SLP 1316—*The Best of Celia Cruz*

SLP 1423—*A Todos Mis Amigos*

Vaya

VAYA 31—*Celia y Johnny*

VAYA 37—*Tremendo Cache*

VAYA 52—*Recordando el Ayer, Celia, Johnny, Justo y Papo*

VAYA 77—*The Brilliante Best of Celia Cruz*

VAYA 80—*Eternos*

VAYA 84—*La Ceiba, Celia Cruz with La Sonora Ponceña*

VAYA 90—*Celia, Johnny, with Pete "El Conde" Rodríguez*

VAYA 93—*Celia yWillie Colón*

BARBARO 212—*Felíz Encuentro, Celia with La Sonora Matancera*

FANIA 623—*Tremendo Trio, Celia, Baretto, y Adalberto*

FANIA 651—*Ritmo en el Corazón, Celia con Baretto*

VAYA 105—*Homenaje a Beny Moré, Celia con Tito Puente*

VAYA 106—*De Nuevo, Celia with Johnny Pacheco*

VAYA 109—*The Winners, Celia Cruz*

VAYA 110—*Tributo a Ismael Rivera, Celia Cruz*

RMM

RMM 80985—*Azúcar Negra*

RMM 81452—*Irrepetible*

RMM 82201—*Celia's Duets*

RMM—*Celia and Friends*

Sony Music

SONY—*Siempre Viviré*

SONY—*La Negra Tiene Tumbao*

SONY—*Regalo del Alma*

Awards and Honors

Billboard Awards, "Top Latin Album Artist" and "Top Female
Tropical Album" for *Regalo del Alma,* and "Top Artist of the
Year."
APRIL, 2004

Lo Nuestro Award from Univisión.
FEBRUARY 26, 2004

The week of February 16 is dedicated to Celia Cruz at the Santa
Cruz de Tenerife Carnival. A street is also named after her.
FEBRUARY, 2004.

Grammy Award, "Best Salsa/Merengue Album," for *Regalo del
Alma,* Los Angeles, California.
FEBRUARY 8, 2004

Congressional Gold Medal.
JULY 28, 2003

Michael R. Bloomberg, mayor of the city of New York, names a
high school in the Bronx after Celia Cruz and dedicates the
Latino Festival to her.
AUGUST 20, 2003

The Miami Dolphins dedicate the game and half-time to Celia Cruz. Pedro Knight receives a Miami Dolphins jersey with Celia's name on it.

SEPTEMBER 21, 2003

The Congressional Hispanic Caucus Institute honors Celia Cruz at their annual gala. Ricky Martin presented Pedro Knight with a special recognition.

SEPTEMBER 24, 2003

The People's Choice Award is dedicated to Celia in Las Vegas, Nevada.

OCTOBER 16, 2003

The state of New Jersey names a street in her honor, Celia Cruz Way, in the town in which she spent her last years.

OCTOBER 22, 2003

Grammy Award nomination for her last album, *Regalo del Alma,* Los Angeles, California.

DECEMBER 4, 2003

Four Lo Nuestro Awards from Univisión.

FEBRUARY 5, 2003

Grammy Award, "Best Salsa Album," Los Angeles, California.

FEBRUARY 23, 2003

Telemundo dedicates a tribute to Celia, *Celia Cruz: Azúcar!,* with the participation of many of her friends and colleagues.

MARCH 2003

Celia is named International Godmother of the Puerto Rican Day Parade.

JUNE 2003

Condecoración Nacional de la Orden "Vasco Nuñez de Balboa," Panama.
FEBRUARY 1, 2002

Honors and the keys to the city of Orlando, Florida.
JANUARY 22, 2002.

Honors and the keys to the city of Merida, Mexico.
"Celia Cruz Day" in Merida.
JANUARY 6, 2002.

Grammy Award: Second Latin Grammy Awards, "Best Traditional Tropical Album," Los Angeles, California.
2001

Smithsonian Institution, James Smithson Bicentennial Medal, Washington, D.C.
OCTOBER 2001

Proclamation from the city of Miami Beach, "Celia Cruz Day" in Miami Beach, Florida.
MAY 19, 2001

Induction to the Jackie Gleason Theater of the Performing Arts "Walk of Stars" and the keys to the city, Miami Beach, Florida.
2001

Grammy Award: First Latin Grammy Awards, "Best Salsa Performance," Los Angeles, California.
2000

Gaviota de Plata award, Viña del Mar Festival, Chile.
2000

Award, "Artist of the Millennium," Telemundo Network, Miami, Florida.

1999

Recording Academy Heroes Lifetime Achievement Award, New York City, New York.

1999

University of Miami doctorate, Honoris Causa in Music, Coral Gables, Florida.

1999

Grammy Award nomination, "Best Tropical Album," *Mi Vida es Cantar,* Los Angeles, California.

1999

ASCAP Lifetime Achievement Award, New York City, New York.

1999

Cruz Sebastián de Belalcázar Medal, Cali, Colombia.

1999

Hispanic Heritage Lifetime Achievement Award, Washington, D.C.

1998

Acapulco Festival Medal, Acapulco, Mexico.

1998

ACE Award, "Best Tropical Performance," New York City, New York.

1998

Grammy Award nomination, "Best Rap Performance by a Duo or Group," "Guantanamera" with Wycliff Jean and Jeni Fujita, New York City, New York.

1998

Proclamation from the city of San Francisco, "Celia Cruz Day," San Francisco, California.

OCTOBER 25, 1997

Smithsonian Institution Lifetime Achievement Award, Washington, D.C.

1997

ACE Award, "Best Tropical Music Concert," New York City, New York.

1997

Costa Rica's Walk of Fame, San José, Costa Rica.

1997

Mexico's Galeria Walk of Fame, Mexico City, Mexico.

1997

Special Recognition from the state of New York for her concert *The Lady and Her Music,* New York.

1996

Andalucia Award, "Universal Artist," Coral Gables, Florida.

1996

ACE Award, "Extraordinary Artist of the Year," New York City, New York.

1996

Venezuela's Walk of Fame, "Amador Bendayan," Caracas, Venezuela.

1995

Casandra Award, Dominican Republic.
1995

Desi Lifetime Achievement Award, Hollywood, California.
1995

ACE Award, "Best Musical Video," New York City, New York.
1995

Angel Award, "Ole La Vida," Hollywood, California.
1995

ACCA Award, "Pan Art," Miami, Florida.
1983–1995

Recipient of the President's Award for the National Endowment
    for the Arts, Washington, D.C.
1994

Premio Lo Nuestro/Univisión (nominations), Miami, Florida.
1992–1995

Billboard Music Hall of Fame Award, Miami, Florida.
1994

University of Panama Lifetime Achievement Award, Panama.
1994

La Musa de Oro Lifetime Achievement Award, Caracas, Ven-
    ezuela.
1994

Movieland Star Hall of Fame, Buena Park, California.
1993

Aplauso 92 Award, "Best Latin Female Vocalist," Miami, Florida.
1989, 1991, 1992

Encuentro Lifetime Achievement Award, Washington, D.C.
1992

Florida International University doctorate, Honoris Causa, Miami, Florida.
1992

Desi Awards, "Favorite Film Actress," Hollywood, California.
1992

Sculpture in Hollywood Wax Museum, Hollywood, California.
1992

Hispanic Women Achievers Award, New York City, New York.
1992

Miami's Calle Ocho Walk of Fame star, Miami, Florida.
1991

Golden Eagle Lifetime Achievement Award in Music, Hollywood, California.
1991

Madison Square Garden, "Garden Greats Wall," New York City, New York.
1991

Premio Lo Nuestro, Univisión/Billboard, Miami, Florida.
1990–1991

Miami's Calle Ocho renamed "Celia Cruz Way," Miami, Florida.
1990

Grammy Award, "Best Tropical Latin Album," Los Angeles, California.

1989

Yale University honorary doctorate in music, New Haven, Connecticut.

1989

Otto Lifetime Achievement Award, Miami, Florida.

1989

Hollywood Walk of Fame star, Hollywood, California.

1987

ACE Lifetime Achievement Award, New York City, New York.

1987

Liberty Medal Award, New York City, New York.

1986

Grammy Award nominations, Los Angeles, California.

1979, 1983, 1985–1988, 1992–1993

Daily News Front Page Award, "Best Latin Female Artist," New York City, New York. 1975–1982, 1985

Guinness Book of World Records, "Most People Ever Recorded at a Concert," Carnaval Tenerife, Islas Canarias, Spain.

1987

Bravo Award, "Best Tropical Female Vocalist," Los Angeles, California.

1986

Monarch Merit Award, New York City, New York.

1986

Tu Musica Award, "Best Female Vocalist."
1984

Tribute at Madison Square Garden (sold-out concert), New York City, New York.
1982

ACE Award, "Best Female Vocalist," New York City, New York.
1978–1980

Latin New York Music Award, New York City, New York.
1975, 1976, 1978

Billboard Award, "Best Tropical Album," New York City, New York.
1977

Rita Montaner Medal, Miami, Florida

El Heraldo Award, "Best Tropical Vocalist," Mexico City, Mexico.
1967, 1968, 1970